REVISED EDITION

Writing for Children
and Teen-agers

BY LEE WYNDHAM

Writer's Digest Books
9933 Alliance Road
Cincinnati, Ohio 45242

Second printing 1969
Revised edition 1972
Second printing of revised edition 1974
Third printing of revised edition 1976
Fourth printing of revised edition 1977
Fifth printing of revised edition 1978
Sixth printing of revised edition 1979

Library of Congress Catalog Card Number 72-80826

ISBN 0-911654-23-2

Acknowledgments

Material from *Chip Nelson and the Contrary Indians*, by Lee Wyndham, Copyright © 1960 by Franklin Watts, Inc., used by permission of the publisher. Material from *The Family at Seven Chimneys House*, by Lee Wyndham, Copyright © 1963 by Franklin Watts, Inc., used by permission of the publisher. Excerpts from *Writing for Young Children*, by Claudia Lewis, Copyright 1954 by the Bank Street College of Education (Simon & Schuster), used by permission of the Bank Street College of Education and the author. Excerpts from *Wee Joseph*, by William MacKeller, Copyright © 1957 by the author (Whittlesey House), used by permission of the author and publisher. Excerpts from *Showboat Holiday*, by Lee Wyndham, Copyright © 1954 by the John C. Winston Company, used by permission of the author and publisher. Extracts from *Beth Hilton, Model*, by Lee Wyndham, Copyright © 1961 by the author (Julian Messner, Inc.), used by permission of the author and publisher. Excerpt from *The Timid Dragon*, by Lee Wyndham, Copyright © 1960 by the author (Lothrop, Lee & Shepard), used by permission. Extract from the article, *"They Call It Kid Stuff,"* by Adelaide Field, Copyright © 1963 by The Writer, Inc., used by permission of the publisher. Material from the article, *Writing the Juvenile Mystery,"* by Phyllis A. Whitney, Copyright © by The Writer, Inc. 1963, used by permission of the author and publisher. Excerpt from *Are You There God? It's Me, Margaret*, by Judy Blume, Copyright © 1970 by the author (Bradbury Press), used by permission of the author and the publisher. Chapter 28, *"Writing for the Look 'n' Listen Age,"* first appeared in somewhat different form in the April 1960 issue of The Writer magazine. Chapter 26, *"Bringing Them Back—Alive,"* is based on a lecture delivered at the Drexel Institute, and on material supplied by Gertrude Blumenthal, publisher and editor of Julian Messner.

Other Books by Lee Wyndham

Candy Stripers (Messner)
Beth Hilton, Model (Messner)
The Timid Dragon (Lothrop)
Mourka, the Mighty Cat (Parents')
The Winter Child (Parents')
Russian Tales of Fabulous Beasts and Marvels (Parents')
Tales the People Tell in Russia (Messner)
Sizzling Pan Ranch (Crowell)
Silver Yankee (Winston-Holt)
Slipper Under Glass (Longmans-McKay)
Golden Slippers (Longmans-McKay)
Showboat Holiday (Winston-Holt)
A Dance for Suzie (Dodd)
Susie and the Dancing Cat (Dodd)
Susie and the Ballet Family (Dodd)
On Your Toes Susie (Dodd)
Susie and the Ballet Horse (Dodd)
Camel Bird Ranch (Dodd)
Binkie's Billions (Knopf)
Ballet Teacher (Messner)
Lady Architect (Messner)
Dance To My Measure (Messner)
The Lost Birthday Present (Dodd)
Ballet for You (Grosset)
Bonnie (Doubleday)
Chip Nelson and the Contrary Indians (Watts)
The How and Why Wonder Book of Ballet (Grosset)
Family at Seven Chimneys House (Watts)
Thanksgiving (Garrard)
Florence Nightingale, Nurse to the World (World Pub. Co.)
The Lady with the Lamp (Scholastic)
The Little Wise Man—with Robert Wyndham (Bobbs)
First Steps in Ballet—with Thalia Mara (Doubleday)
Buttons and Beaux—with Louise Barnes Gallagher (Dodd)
Anthology—*Dancers, Dancers, Dancers* (Watts)
Anthology—*Acting, Acting, Acting* (Watts)
Adaptation—*Folk Tales of India* (Bobbs)
Adaptation—*Folk Tales of China* (Bobbs)
Adaptation—*Tales from the Arabian Nights* (Whitman)
Adaptation—*Mark Twain's The Prince and the Pauper, from Walt Disney's screenplay* (Whitman)

To Phyllis Whitney
Whose torch has helped to light so many candles.

Table of Contents

Actual people—composites—types of caricatures . . . How to "collect" characters . . . Characterization for different age levels . . . What to avoid . . . Selecting and individualizing your story people . . . The *flat* and *rounded* characters . . . Traits—variety and value . . . Secondary characters—delight and danger . . . Tagging your story people . . . Naming them.

You and your main character . . . Considering the function of your story people . . . Choosing the good traits and the bad—and why . . . To *show* or *tell?* . . . The villain—what must he *do?* . . . Parents and other relatives . . . Naming the villains . . . The *why* of villains . . . Viewpoints considered . . . The most serviceable viewpoint . . . Describing your viewpoint character . . . First aid for an ailing viewpoint . . . Instead of mirrors—the "camera view" . . . Character growth.

Signs of dialogue and what they mean to the reader . . . What dialogue means to you . . . Cultivating an ear for dialogue . . . Tone quality and how to use it . . . Your story actor's vocabulary . . . A touch of flavor—foreign and domestic . . . Characterizing the speech of foreigners . . . Regional talk, dialect, idiom . . . Beware of slang . . . Written dialogue and the talk around you . . . How dialogue can move your story forward . . . Some don'ts and do's . . . Tag lines to conversations . . . The good old "said" and variations.

The urgent problem . . . What *must* he have that he *cannot* easily get? . . . Three types of problems . . . Motivation—the *why* behind the *what* . . . Three powerful urges . . . Human psychology—and helpful books about it . . . Significance—having something to say . . . Themes and variations—how to use universal themes for story purposes . . . The basic needs.

To be moved—to "get a feeling" . . . Escape through fiction . . . Basic emotions—major and minor . . . The right words . . . Emotion from experience . . . Training yourself to observe emotion—in yourself and others . . . Facts and feelings . . . If the story has a vital problem . . . The author in control . . . An emotional chart for story people . . . Show and feel . . . Visible and audible signs of emotion . . . Mood.

track of it . . . And one to grow on! . . . The value of the section at the back.

and why . . . Common faults of first drafts . . . Sentence length and readability . . . Your attitude—and preparation . . .Four-step plan for revision . . . Reading aloud—why and how . . . Time limit for revision sessions . . . You and your *style*—what it is—What it depends on . . . The indispensable word finders . . . The fine-tooth comb—the right word in the right place . . . The "banana peels" of language . . . Verbs and their value . . . Some do's and don'ts for the invisible story teller . . . Injecting your opinions . . . Redundancy . . . Silly actions and impossible feats . . . Eye maneuvers . . . Word weeding . . . The hesitant and non-committal, and the "What else?" category . . . The grace notes—and what they can do . . . Making the image fit the picture . . . A word of caution.

Importance of professional appearance . . . Typewriter ribbons . . . The paper to use . . . Value of carbon copies . . . Pen names . . . The format . . . Do's and don'ts on page 1 . . . How to type letters, telegrams, etc., in body of text . . . Extra first and last pages—and why . . . Margins, pagination, estimating wordage . . . Consistency and your own style sheet . . . Punctuation and grammar . . . Proofreading the manuscript . . . How to send it . . . The do's and don'ts . . . Common-law copyright . . . Letters to the editor—when it's not needed and when it is . . . The stamped-self-addressed postal—and what it can do for your peace of mind . . . The waiting game—when to inquire about your manuscript—and how . . . You and the post office . . . Special rates and special safeguards . . . Cons and pros for delivering in person.

Your need to study markets . . . Invaluable market aids . . . How to make up your own lists . . . Guideposts for books—review sections . . . Your manuscript itinerary . . . a permanent record . . . Don'ts and do's on submissions . . . To query or not? . . . Stacking a choice against yourself . . . Seasonal material . . . A kind word for the "slow reading" editors . . . Magazine payment methods . . . Your check and your "rights"—Beware! . . . Vanity publishers . . . The business side of writing . . . What's tax deductible . . . Looking ahead—you and posterity.

your audience . . . A clip-trick . . . Know thy product . . . How to get the *feel* of a book . . . Testing your script for *different pictures* . . . How to type a picture story for submission . . . Speaking of illustrations . . . Have a story to tell . . . The simple plots . . . Value of the refrain . . . Plot material—where to look for it . . . Fantasy . . . Stories in verse . . . First aid for unsuccessful stories in verse . . . Magazine markets . . . Personified inanimates, hackneyed plots—what to avoid . . . What the writer needs . . . What the editors look for . . . What the reader wants . . . Stories to study . . . The five senses—in the child's words . . . And the finished product.

Illustrations

PART I

A PRACTICAL GUIDE TO PUBLICATION

Chapter 1

Readers, Readers Everywhere . . .

A writer must have readers—for reading is the other half of writing. A writer whose work is not read might as well be keeping a diary. Fortunately, there is a clamor for books and magazines all over the world. Never have so many been published, imported, exported, reprinted, re-issued, translated, and put in paperbacks. In the United States, between two and three thousand children's books are brought out annually by some 160 publishers; our children's magazines have a combined circulation of more than thirty-five million copies.

Library circulation of books for children has increased phenomenally in many areas. There is no dearth of readers. From the age of three and up, we have at least sixty million boys and girls—and *each one is a potential reader of what you write!*

Government activities and subsidies for book purchases, the efforts of teachers and librarians, and high-powered private promotions have made people increasingly aware of the fact that reading is the primary tool of learning. Today publishing is Big Business. Its chief product is books, its major need, authors.

Hundreds of editors are constantly on the lookout for authors. At the same time, hundreds of authors are in search of markets for their work. Editorial safes, filing cabinets, and window sills groan under the weight of manuscripts. However, most unsolicited manuscripts submitted to juvenile departments return to their authors, often because the writers did not realize they were competing in a highly *specialized* field.

The primary purpose of this book is to help you achieve publication. The chapters are arranged in the order which I have found most effective in class teaching. The headings outline the course; the "run-in" table of contents for each chapter outlines the topics covered. A comprehensive index at the back of the book is designed to simplify your search for specific items.

Emphasis throughout is on practical guidance to professional competence, which will not only help make you a better writer but will also furnish much professional know-how that might otherwise take you years to acquire. Even if you have achieved publication on your own, you will find valuable pointers, drawn from a wide writing, publishing, and lecturing experience.

What It Takes to Be a Writer for Children

You already have the first requisite—you want to be a successful writer—or you would not be reading this book.

The second requisite is that you must *know* and *like* children. If in your secret heart you think they are little monsters and potential juvenile delinquents, then writing for juniors is not for you. You must respect your audience, whether it be three-year-olds or fifteen-year-olds.

If you do not have children in your own family circle, make friends with the progeny of your neighbors—especially in the age range for which you'd like to write.

Books *about* children and teen-agers will help you to understand the younger generation. These will be discussed more fully in other chapters (and listed in the bibliography).

In preparing to write, study material already published for the specific age group you have in mind. Such reading will put you into the proper mood for your own effort, and also indicate how to handle subject matter, sentence structure, vocabulary, and length of story. A good book list will help you find what you need in the library. *Best Books for Children,* published annually by R. R. Bowker, covers over four thousand titles, broken down by age and subject.

For you, too, reading is the other half of writing—not *merely* for entertainment, now that you're studying the craft of writing, but for research, general knowledge, and object lessons in how professional writers deal with their material.

Writing for young people is a great responsibility because their minds are impressionable and what they read can affect not only their current lives but even their futures. Writing for them should be approached with a serious regard for the possible influence of your words. Do not plan to write for children because you think it is easy, or the writing does not need to be as good as that in books for grownups. Requirements for good juvenile writing are far more strict than they are for adult fiction, and there are many dedicated people on guard to see that they are observed, for the very reasons mentioned above.

There is much to learn about this special field. But if you have the qualifications, really love to write, and have the necessary spark of God-given talent, learn you can.

And the rewards—the very special heart-lifting ones will emerge as you turn these pages and learn the how's and why's of writing for young people. As for financial returns, few authors write only for the money. There are much easier and more dependable ways of earning a living. And yet—well, you may not ever make $20,000 a year—but on the other hand, with new market possibilities for children's books opening up, you just might! If you become a prolific and popular writer, after a few years a backlog of books can provide sufficient royalties for a comfortable living—or at the very least, a nice supplementary income.

Life Spans of Junior Books

A number of children's books have achieved such popularity that they continue to sell years after their first publication. *Mike Mulligan and His Steam Shovel* has been selling merrily since 1939; *Dr. Doolittle* and his adventures, since 1922; *Johnny Tremain*, since 1943; *Mary Poppins*, since 1939—and look what's happened to her! *Understood Betsy* charmed today's grandmothers in 1917 —and their granddaughters love her, too.

Many favorites outlast the life spans of their authors. Glance over the classic titles available in multiple editions in the bookstores: *Black Beauty* has been selling steadily since 1877; *Heidi* was published in 1880; *Treasure Island* in 1883; and the beloved

Little Women—forever new to girls who first discover it—was published in 1868! From a child's point of view, a "new" book is one he has not read before—even though the author may be long dead. Enthusiastic fan letters are still penned to Daniel Defoe, Robert Louis Stevenson and Louisa May Alcott.

Who's to say that *you* won't write a best-selling classic that will live forever! But even if you don't write deathless prose, there is a place for you if your work catches the popular fancy. Look at the *Bobbsey Twins*—1904 (continued in an up-dated version today); and *Tarzan*—who's been swinging through the trees since 1914. *There are all kinds of readers in the world, with all kinds of tastes; it takes all kinds of writers to please them.*

There is also such a thing as the "serviceable" book, written with professional competence and grace, if not with resounding literary style. It, too, can enjoy an extraordinary long life as a children's favorite in our ever-expanding world of readers. And there are many niches where a capable writer can fit. Let's look them over in the next chapter.

Chapter 2

A General Survey of the Junior Magazine and Book Fields

According to the most recent lists in *Writer's Market*, a Writer's Digest publication, there are over one hundred juvenile and teen magazines and story papers buying fiction and freelance articles. Most of these are church affiliated, published once a week for Sunday school distribution. Because of their frequency of publication, they use a great deal of material. With a few notable exceptions, the rates paid are generally low. However, to the beginner, *publication* means more than money at this stage. The writer whose work is published gets a definite psychological lift. He begins to feel, act and write like a professional.

The Juvenile Short Story Field

In the church magazines, material should be helpful and practical, designed to aid young people to meet and solve the problems they face daily. The stories must encourage, inspire, build honest, loyal, clear-thinking, moral young people.

Although "lesson stories," they still must serve the primary function of fiction; *they must entertain the reader*. The valuable lesson—kindness, understanding, brotherhood, honesty—must be slipped into the plot through the actions and reactions of the story characters. The reader, however young, must not suspect that he is being taught anything through a fictionized sermon. If he does, he'll stop reading.

So denominational magazines look first of all for *entertaining* stories which do not flout the rules of ethical conduct. In a sense, the stories are bait to catch the reader's attention with something that's fun to read; and as he turns the pages, the hope is that he will also read and absorb the specially prepared spiritual messages usually written by the staff.

Taboos

The "don'ts" are getting fewer, but they still exist, and you'll save postage, wear and tear on your manuscripts and your nerves, if you become aware of what these taboos are and where they apply, both in denominational and secular markets.

In books you'll have a much broader scope in which to work. Magazines, however, depend on subscriptions, and so controversial material, such as religious bias, politics, situations involving unethical conduct (without retribution), or the casting of aspersions on a particular geographic area or cultural or ethnic group, which might offend a substantial number of subscribers and/or advertisers, is generally avoided. For example: "no reference to drinking or smoking" — *The Beehive* (Graded Press); "no hunting, fishing" — *Wee Wisdom* (Unity publication); "war, crime and violence are taboo" — *Highlights,* one of the best paying junior magazine markets. Racial problems used to be taboo and still are in some magazines. When used in story, they must have skillful handling. Slang, swearing, and bad taste are not wanted, even as horrible examples. Rampant crime and youngsters chasing adult bandits are usually frowned upon in most — but not all — quality publications Some magazines do not want any adolescent love themes; others welcome light romance.

Taboos, like everything else in publishing, change, and the only way to keep up with what they are is to study market reports and lists—and these will be discussed later on. A study of sample issues of the various magazines will indicate the position taken on all such matters. In addition, many publishers supply writers with "Editorial Requirements" leaflets on request. Be sure to enclose a stamped, self-addressed envelope to get yours.

The Age Brackets

Except in rare instances, an author cannot write for the three-year-old and the ten-year-old in the same story, or reach the six-year-old as well as the sophisticated teenager. Although age groups do not bind the reader hard and fast in his reading, there have to be arbitrary divisions in a publishing program. To send your winged horses to the right stables you must be aware of the age ranges into which reading matter for juniors is divided. There are small but important differences between the groupings used by the magazines and by book publishers. Magazines separate into three groups.

Primary. Material for six-, seven-, and eight-year-olds must be simply presented, in easy-to-understand language. Stories should have a single idea, and everything that happens in the story should contribute to this idea. A simple plot is required to hold the reader's interest. Lengths are from 300 to 500 words, sometimes 700, but seldom over 900. Some of these magazines include material that will interest even the youngest members of the family —the two- to five-year-olds. For samples of the different publications you can write to denominational houses. For non-denominational magazines, check your local newsstands for *Humpty Dumpty's Magazine, Jack and Jill, Child Life,* and *Highlights for Children.* There is always a need for publishable material for this age.

Elementary and Junior High. The nine- to thirteen-year-olds want lots of action set in the framework of an exciting, unified plot. The stories should be centered around their own interests, contemporary problems and experiences. Since the appeal should be to both boys and girls, it is wise to use boy and girl characters in your stories.

The writing must be subjective—narrated from the viewpoint of the main character. Everything should be presented through his eyes, senses, and emotions. Get in drama and suspense, and good brisk pace. Lengths are 700 to 2,000 words, with 1,500 to 1,800 considered most desirable. Serials may have from four to ten parts, each with the same word lengths as above.

Write for denominational and educational samples (names, addresses, requirements, and rates are printed at intervals in writers' magazines, and in detailed lists in *Writer's Market*). On the magazine stands, look for *Young World, Young Miss, Jack and Jill*, and *Children's Playmate*. You will probably find *Child Life* and *Highlights* in your community library or your doctor's waiting room. The *Instructor* and *Junior Scholastic* may be found in a school library. Check with the librarian there.

High School. Stories for thirteen- to seventeen-year-olds must become more complex. Teenagers demand all the elements of good fiction technique: plot, characterization, conflict, complications, suspense, drama—and the satisfying solution.

Story backgrounds should be of interest to high school youth: school life, part-time jobs, sports, camp life, adventure, foreign backgrounds. Problems might involve getting along with others, tolerance of other people and other ways, finding a job, personal and business ethics, sportsmanship. Some of the magazines for this age are designed for girls or for boys only, but most have to please both. So again, you have a better chance of making a sale if you use boy and girl characters in your stories, although one or the other plays the leading role.

Generally stories for the high school group range from 1,800 to 3,500 words, with 2,400 preferred. Serials run in the same lengths for each installment. For samples of this kind of writing, look for *Seventeen, In Touch, 'Teen,* and other magazines for teens on the stands. Write for samples in the denominational and educational fields.

Scholastic Scope, one of the newer Scholastic publications, always needs a special kind of material, written for the fifteen to eighteen age level, but with a fourth to sixth grade reading vocabulary. This is for problem and reluctant readers, or young people with reading difficulties because they do not yet know English fluently. They need high interest subjects with a vocabulary they can handle. Wanted are problems of contemporary teenagers (drugs, dating, prejudice, runaways, failures in school, family relations, etc.). Stories should show relationships among people (interracial, adult-teen, employer-employee, etc.) in family, job, school situations.

The writing must be direct, realistic, there must be lots of action, carried through dialogue rather than exposition. It's not a market for crime fiction, however. What the editors hope to get is material from American Indians, Chicanos (Mexican-Americans), Puerto Ricans, and black authors, among others, so that authenticity will be unmistakable. *Scope's* kind of reader can sense any false note instantly, and will be turned off by it. Lengths range from 400 to 1,200 words; plays run 3,000 words.

For additional guidance, see the chapters on markets and marketing.

The Junior Book Field

Here the publishers' age divisions are so varied that for practical purposes in my book reviews and lectures, I have found it more useful to divide the books into five main groups.

1. *Picture Books*—ages two to five. Very little text and pictures on every page. The pictures are supposed to carry fully half of the story, supplying descriptions and character details. If your story is accepted, your editor will arrange for all the art work necessary. That is *her* business. (Most juvenile editors are women.) Unless you are a professional artist, *do not send art work*. It might kill her interest in your story. The number of words in the text might be 50 or 150 or 1,000—but I once received a book for review which had a text of exactly seven words! (The artist was also the author.*)

In Part II of this text I shall deal more fully with the particular requirements of the picture book field.

––––––

* *Snail, Where Are You?* by Tomi Ungerer. When I thought I'd seen everything, a book with *no* words came in, and on its heels still another gem—with just *one* word, "Oh"—Gertrude Espenscheid's *The OH Ball.*

2. *Picture Story*—ages six to nine. More text, fewer pictures, lots of action in the story. A definite plot line, which leads the main character to a desired goal, is usually developed and makes of this "a real story." The book is still a "two-lap" affair, with an adult reading to the child, so the vocabulary need not be over-simplified. However, the story should be easily understood by the child, so erudite words have no place here.

Keep out adult whimsey, too—plays on words or situations that will be over the head of the child-listener.

The text of the picture story may run from 2,000 to 5,000 or 6,000 words. My *Timid Dragon* is an example in this category.

3. *Easy-to-Read*—ages six to nine (grades one to three). These stories are designed for children to read on their own with their newly acquired reading skills. Don't let the idea of the "simple" vocabulary frighten you. Plan your story, write it. *Then* check the vocabulary, sentence length and structure, and simplify as needed. Manuscript length should be 1,500 to 10,000 words.

Stories with controlled vocabularies are usually assigned to experienced writers, and the editors either provide the word lists or make general recommendations. Some houses favor a partic-ular list, since word lists seldom agree. Common sense and familiarity with the basal reading texts for the specific grade must also be used as guides by the writer.

The most important thing to remember is *never* to start with a word list limitation on your imagination. Many educators now urge writers not to hesitate to use some words outside the stan-dard list if they are needed to tell a story. How else can children enrich their vocabularies!

To be publishable, a story with even the most severely con-trolled vocabulary must be told in rhythmic, natural style—as in the Random House Beginner Books, designed for the first grade. This is difficult and many an author has grown gray in the process —or given up altogether.

In non-fiction, my book, *Thanksgiving*, written on assignment, is an example of this type of writing: blood, sweat, and tears—in 5,300 words for grades two to three! But it has proved well worth the agony. I did not use a word list, but several which may prove helpful, should you wish to undertake this kind of work, are given in the note below.*

4. *The 'Tween-Age*—children aged eight to twelve compose the biggest reading group, the "Golden Age" of reading. The interests of the boys and girls are limitless. Stories of today, yesterday, tomorrow, all are read avidly. Funny situations—and grim ones, too, mysteries, stories about families, sports, adventure, animals. Stories about conservation, ecology, air pollution, our fantastic space explorations—fact and fiction about people and places, all are popular. Books definitely for girls and definitely for boys appear now, but mixed groups of characters are very welcome. Best lengths for manuscripts are 20,000 to 40,000 words.

5. *The Teens.* Although theoretically "teens" means readers of twelve to sixteen, actually they can be from ten to fifteen, seldom older. Yet these young people of today are reading more serious books, often dealing with themes and experiences unheard of in junior fiction a few years ago. Heroes and heroines strive to understand themselves and others, and the new concepts of morality, and the pill with all its implications. They're concerned with war and the draft and politics and civil disturbances—and with idealistic new worlds, the lifting up of the underprivileged in an egalitarian society, new freedoms and rights for women. These

------

*Buckingham & Dolch, *A Combined Word List* (Ginn).

Chall, Jeanne, *Readability, an Appraisal of Research and Application* (Ohio State University).

Dale, Edgar, and Barbara Seels, *Readability and Reading: An Annotated Bibliography* (International Reading Association).

Flesch, Rudolf, *How to Test Readability* (Harper).

Gates, Arthur, *Reading Vocabulary for Primary Grades* (Teachers College, Columbia University).

Hunnicutt & Iverson, editors, *Research in the Three R's,* pages 194-213 (Harper).

Klare, Roger George, *The Measurement of Readability* (State University Press, Ames, Iowa).

Lorge, Irving, *Lorge Formula for Estimating Difficulty of Reading Materials* (Teachers College, Columbia University).

Thorndike & Lorge, *The Teacher's Word Book of 30,000 Words* (Teachers College, Columbia University).

book and story characters explore, experiment, come to grief with the shattering realism of their real life counterparts.

The "boy-meets-girl" romance gets the cold shoulder from most editors, unless it is garnished with some contemporary concern of the young, and set against a background that lifts the story above the ordinary, as in Betty Cavanna's *A Time of Tenderness.* Jobs and careers may also form relevant backdrops for action. The liberated Ms-heroines can tackle what were formerly considered strictly male occupations. And story mothers can lead fuller lives away from home, managing careers—if they so desire—and their homes and families, too. Adventure yarns, mysteries, suspense and spy tales, and mini-gothics (like *Mystery at Saint-Hilaire,* by Priscilla Hagon, or Joan Aiken's *Black Hearts in Battersea* and *Died on a Rainy Sunday,* with its bizarre and horrific conclusion) are ever popular. And so are sports stories and biographies. All these will be dealt with more fully in the following chapters and in Part II.

Scope/Action Books—fiction 8,000 to 12,000 words, are aimed at secondary school students who read at levels from the second to fourth grade. No writing down! Settings and characters should be easily identifiable to average teen boys and girls, though science fiction that starts from a contemporary setting would be welcome. Plot must move rapidly into action that "hooks" the very poor and reluctant readers. This kind of writing is not easy but it is much needed, not only by the Scholastic Book Services but by a growing list of educationally oriented publishers who'd like to provide this type of reading for children of all ages, not teens only. Consult *Writer's Market* and periodic lists and tips in the writers' magazines for news on this field.

In each age group children like to read about youngsters in the leading roles who are as old or older than themselves—almost never younger. In your writing avoid diminutives for the heroes ("little Dick," "tiny Sally"). The usual aim of these readers is to be "bigger," "older," "stronger," than they are at the moment, so they do not take kindly to "littleness" in the characters with whom they are to identify.

Adults in the stories should be kept to an absolute minimum.

Introduced upon a scene they have an annoying way of taking over—just as in real life. Keep your stories for children *about* children, working out problems suitable to their years, with as little grownup help as possible.

Don't go orphaning them, however, to make their problems more difficult. Editors take a dim view of wholesale elimination of parents through auto and plane crashes. This kind of mayhem became so prevalent among authors a few years ago, that several editors took a militant stand and declared that all the stories *they* published must come equipped with a full set of live parents. It is permissible, however, to send pater and mater off to far, far lands on archeological, bridge-building, or diplomatic missions—until that, too, becomes too popular a solution!

What Do Editors Want?

Very often they don't know *exactly*. But an editor is like a roving reporter: neither knows precisely what he is looking for, yet he recognizes it at once when he finds it.

Primarily editors want stories which are fun to read. The chief business of fiction is to entertain the reader, whether the writing be for children or grownups. In addition, your story should have some plus values, such as an interesting background, information, a message perhaps—something that will make the editor feel your story or book is worth publishing.

Most wanted are stories about today's children in American settings, working out contemporary problems suitable to their years. Urban settings are especially welcome. With today's emphasis on getting along with people of different races, cultures and beliefs, stories with foreign backgrounds are welcome both in the magazines and in the book field—but the backgrounds must be authentic, whether you get them from personal experience or research. The chapter on contemporary research deals with this special phase of writing.

In historical background stories, the young people must figure as main characters. Stories of courage, daring, or exploration are always popular.

Trends in Subjects and Problems

In subject matter, trends reflect whatever currently concerns large numbers of people. That which makes headlines and thoughtful articles in the magazines, and leads to discussions in the PTA's, civic groups and lecture halls is a guide to those concerns—and can suggest what *you* might write about, if you too feel strongly on the given subject(s). Just hope this "concern" won't fizzle out before your book is published. A sense of timing is a valuable asset for the author—and I've sometimes wondered if a dependable crystal ball might not be a good investment.

Editors (for all ages) are always on the lookout for current themes, with authentic, realistic treatment. When they were made acutely aware of the lack of books and stories about black children—in the middle class and among the disadvantaged and deprived—editors eagerly sought to correct the situation. In their initial enthusiasm to fill a void, almost anything went. Now there is no lack for such books and the editors have become stringently selective both in subject and quality of what they accept for publication. It is no longer a catch-penny get-on-the-bandwagon market, and the examples cited in the note below should make clear the quality that will be expected in current submissions.* (Incidentally, many of the titles mentioned here and elsewhere in the text are available in paperback editions. Check a bookstore or library copy of *Paperbound Books in Print*.)

Other ethnic groups are pressing for recognition, and there has been a healthy spate of stories of Spanish-Americans (sometimes in dual-language, so if you speak and write in Spanish, you might check what has been published and see what you can add to it). The American-Orientals want recognition also, for

---

*Read: *Stevie*, by John Steptoe; June Jordan's, *Who Look at Me*, and *His Own Where; Call Me Charley*, by Jesse Jackson, also, *The Sickest Don't Always Die the Quickest*. There's room for humor, too, and there should be more of it: see *Boss Cat*, by Kristin Hunter. Note the appeal in Eleanor Clymer's *The Big Pile of Dirt*; and in Joan Lexau's *Benjie* stories. Virginia Hamilton's *The House of Dies Drear* is a real thriller, and her *Zeely* is poignant and beautiful. Read *Evan's Corner*, by Elizabeth Starr Hill; and Louisa Shotwell's *Roosevelt Grady; Citizen Pablo*, by Banella Robinson; *Our Cup Is Broken*, by Florence Means; and *The Lucky Ghost Shirt*, by Teri Martini.

their contribution to our society, so books of the past and present, if well done, would be welcome.

Experience has shown that it is difficult for the middle class, white writer to portray authentically, realistically, the life style, thought and viewpoint of the black person—the black child—especially in the ghetto or otherwise disadvantaged situation. Unless you can *think black,* or for that matter, Puerto-Rican, Chicano, Indian, or whatever, do not attempt such writing. The errors, the false notes in your presentation will be pointed out to you in short order by groups who stand ready to spot and pounce upon misrepresentations, real or imagined "racism" and what not.

Characters in all these stories must be presented as *individuals,* not stereotypes—the Negro with the great sense of rhythm, the "lazy" Mexican, the stoic Indian, the gesticulating Italian, the bowing Chinese. Neither satires nor caricatures are wanted in literature for the young.

My own *Chip Nelson and the Contrary Indians* grew out of an interest in Cub Scouts and the YMCA Indian Guides program, in which youngsters delve into American Indian lore. In a scholarly Yale tome I found an item on Indian Medicine Men of the Cheyenne whose magic lay in doing everything backward. The item caused the plot seed in my head to sprout into a book based on historical facts, mixed with a set of lively modern children.

Stories of adolescence, the physical and emotional changes that come with it, and the anchors young people need to keep from drifting aimlessly, are certainly of interest to the older 'tweens and teens. Judy Blume wrote with perception and humor —and today's total frankness—about a girl affected not only by the problems stemming from her parents' mixed marriage (Jewish-Catholic), but also the ordeal of "becoming a woman." *Are You Listening God, It's Me, Margaret* has shocked some ladies, but brought much more praise than censure from others, plus an assignment to do an up-to-date booklet on maturing girls for the educational department of a major drug company.

Boldly Judy took the next step, and gave the same treatment to the boy's side of the story: *Then Again, Maybe I Won't,* in which Tony Miglione is swamped not only with the sudden changes in the economic status of his family, but also with his own disturbing physical changes and the embarrassment these heap upon him. Neither book is glum or heavy reading. The author's bright, effortless humor sparkles through the novels and makes especially palatable reading of "controversial" material. But controversy is acceptable today.

I asked Judy Blume why she wrote these books. "It was something I felt needed to be said," she told me. So, if you feel strongly about some topic, wrap it around a set of interesting characters, place them in a human situation, and write about their actions and reactions, out of your own convictions and sense of need. If a bit of controversy does result, it will only boost the sales!

Modern Fantasy

For any age, fantasy is the hardest material to write, and even harder to sell. So much of it that is simply dreadful has been submitted to hapless editors that many of them have declared flatly in the market guides: *No fantasy.* Yet recent publishers' lists reveal that more fantasy is published today than has been in years. Pressed for an explanation, the editors admit that what they really mean is, they don't want to see rehashed old classics, like latter-day Alices, and tales modeled on the bones of easily recognizable fairy tales told so well by Andersen and the Brothers Grimm.

Fantasy for today must be sparkling fresh and original and clearly recognizable as such. What is more, the excellence of the writing required can be achieved only when the author is thoroughly familiar with his craft and all the techniques that enable him to tell a gripping story.

My heartfelt advice to all my students has been to learn their craft first, through the writing of here-and-now stories, and then zoom off into fantasy or science-fiction or whatever their hearts desire. By then they will be able to make the fantastic come off with the necessary special logic and skill which will give the imaginary and bizarre the illusion of reality, the conviction and believability, which is a must for this genre.

Alas, the fantasy-prone seldom heed this advice and put their flat-wheeled apprentice carts before their wingless, plodding horses. If you plan to do likewise, at least study examples of some of the best *modern* fantasies before you dash off your own.*

Picture book fantasy will be dealt with in Part II of this text.

Now let us talk about you and your work habits, and how you can make the most of *your* potential.

---

*Read: the works of Lloyd Alexander—*The Book of Three, The Black Cauldron, The High King, The King's Fountain* (for younger children); George Selden's *The Cricket in Times Square;* the *Danny Dunn* series of hilarious adventures, by Jay Williams and Raymond Abrashkin; Oliver Butterworth's *The Enormous Egg;* the *Miss Pickerell* stories of Ellen MacGregor; Beverly Cleary's *The Mouse on a Motorcycle; The Shy Stegosaurus of Cricket Creek,* by Evelyn Lampman; Jane Little's *Sneaker Hill*—with a correspondence course in witchcraft thrown in. There's Eleanor Cameron's *Wonderful Flight to the Mushroom Planet;* and Madeleine L'Engle's *A Wrinkle in Time,* which has been gaining in significance and stature ever since publication in 1962. This book won the Newbery medal "for the most distinguished contribution to American Literature for that year," and yet the manuscript of that book had something like twenty submissions before it made a hit with the perceptive editor at Farrar. So you see, even the best writers have problems with fantasy.

In the science-fiction category, Madeleine L'Engle also has *The Young Unicorns,* with a micro-laser and fast-paced psychedelic action; read also André Norton's *The Time Traders,* and *The Zero Stone;* anything by Robert Heinlein, Ray Bradbury, or the versatile Isaac Asimov, will give you goals to strive for—and some idea of how much you must know in order to write in this field.

Chapter 3

You and Your Work Habits

Having read the previous chapters, you now know something of what's involved in writing for young people. It is a specialty, it demands the best you have to offer, and it can be a rewarding vocation.

You may be one of the fortunate few with all the time in the world to write, but what is more likely is that you have a job, are the family breadwinner, or the keeper of the hearth. There's just no time to write! Remember, however, that we can always make time for the things we really want to do.

How to MAKE Time to Write

You have a job? Some writers get up two hours earlier and go straight to their typewriters. Then there's time after supper, on weekends, and holidays.

Everything has its own price, even *time*. To get time to write, you may have to give up something, perhaps social life. While you don't need to become a recluse, you'll have to strike a balance that will favor your writing time.

You're a homemaker with young children and a husband? Then you must organize yourself and your work. Your routine *can* be changed. No one is going to die if you become a less perfect housekeeper—and let a bit of ironing slide till next week. A fifty-cent paperback of housekeeping hints can give you hundreds of time-saving ideas. Moreover, somewhere in your day there must be times when the children go to school or nap or amuse themselves in the playpen.

During one semester, after I had expounded on this subject at NYU, a student who had previously bewailed her lack of time suddenly began to turn in a story a week for criticism. Before the end of that fifteen-week session she had begun to write a book, which was accepted for publication upon completion. Betty learned how to *make* time to write. And so can you.

You are also "writing" when you are thinking out a story or turning over ideas that might be developed into one. And "think-writing" you can do anywhere, at any time. Routine jobs—dusting, vacuuming, mowing the lawn—can be productive "think-times," while the hours you spend waiting for buses and riding on commuter trains can provide you with note-making time, and even writing time.

Disciplining Yourself to Write—Regularly

Self-discipline is something else again, and not easy, for there are always siren voices calling: attractive social engagements, inviting books to read—and even self-deluding reasons as to why you can't write now. Writers become past-masters at inventing alibis for procrastination. The reluctance to write is a peculiar phenomenon of the professional author as well as the beginner. What causes it? Perhaps it is the overwhelming knowledge that there are so many ways in which to tell your story—and the disquieting thought that you may start (or continue) on the wrong tack. But we revise to correct our mistakes. You are not working in marble, but on paper—and the words can be easily changed. So get busy!

The one thing a writer must be is a self-starter. In the final analysis there is no one who can make you write but *you*. *Writers are self-made.*

Make it a rule to spend at least two consecutive hours in actual writing *every day*. It is difficult to be productive in less time because it usually takes about half an hour to warm up to your subject each time you come back to it. Try to establish regular working hours in your daily schedule, but if this is not possible, don't despair. You can train yourself to write even in the snippets of time available—and under almost any circumstances. I know.

You don't *need* a book-lined, air-conditioned study, either. I have one now, but my first eight books were written in an all-purpose room filled with two children, a big black and white collie, two cats, and a TV set. I wrote right through the most gripping episodes of the Lone Ranger and Captain Video. My "desk" was a rickety typing table and my typewriter an aged portable. My husband was a recording engineer then, and many of his sessions were run at night. So I wrote at night, too, and lullabyed the children with the sound of my tapping keys.

Women are the interruptible, the adaptable sex, and must be able to adjust to circumstances. I had to adapt myself to my husband's odd hours until we were both able to work at home; to the children's needs (with one foot on the gas pedal); to what seemed to be overwhelming problems at times. And I know many other writers who managed to work in spite of unfavorable conditions. Successful books and stories have been written laboriously in bed by ailing men and women; and in attics and jails, concentration camps and at the bottom of the sea in submarines. They have been written at kitchen tables on brown paper sacks. There's no such thing as "no place to write" just as there is no such thing as "no time to write."

What You Have to Give

What can you bring to this particular field of writing? Can you remember what it was like to be a teen-ager, a "'tweener," a small child? I hope you can, because it will give you greater kinship with your readers, a deeper understanding of the lights and shadows of childhood. Take yourself back a few years at a time. What happened in your life five years ago? . . . ten? . . . and before that? When you get to the teen years, remember more carefully—and don't shut out the emotions, the triumphs, the disappointments and the tears. Slip down the years to the earliest things you remember.

When you have *felt* yourself a child again, you will have a deeper insight into what it's like to be young and vulnerable, with no mature philosophies with which to cushion the bumps of life. I say "you" because in writing a story, *you* become the character you're writing about, just as an actor becomes the person he portrays.

There is the lighter side, too. Everyone likes to laugh. Humor is a great leavener, so cultivate your own sense of fun and inject it into your stories when you can.

Develop enthusiasm and a sense of wonder; to a child the whole world is *new*. Nothing about it is tired, or worn, or hopeless (for very long). And children are seldom nostalgic. They do not look back, nor do they spend much time peering into the future. Anything promised for "tomorrow" seems forever away. Because they live in the present, stories written for them should have the urgent quality of "something happening—*now*."

Apprenticeship

Everyone knows that in order to become a doctor, a nurse, a carpenter, a musician, or a magician, one must serve a period of apprenticeship, of intensive study. But people often expect their very first efforts at writing to be masterpieces worthy of instant publication. This is seldom the case.

Although I now prefer to write books, I broke into the juvenile writing field as a short-story writer—and I'm glad I did. In writing short fiction you can learn all the basic fundamentals of the writing craft and at the same time sharpen your ability to tell a story in relatively few words. The brisk pace becomes such a habit that when you graduate to booklengths, you will have overcome the tendency to ramble and will instead leap right into your plot and carry it along with lively action.

Grownups, more patient than children, will bear with a slow-paced author who does not really begin his tale until page fifty. But a child's story must begin immediately—and never at any point slow down. Once you have learned to tell a story in 2,000 words—or less—you have also learned to free yourself of unnecessary details. Your stories will move ahead in the manner the modern reader has come to expect. In the course of a year you can write a great many short stories—and very possibly start to earn even as you learn how to write for children.

A full-length book, on the other hand, must be from 30,000 to 60,000 words long. It requires much more preparation and time to write, and for a beginner, is just too much to tackle.

In short stories you can also experiment with different age groups and different styles of writing. Where do you fit best? Now is the time to find out—not through 200-page books but through 1,000- to 3,000-word stories. Brief—and expendable.

One of my students suddenly discovered after struggling for weeks with stories for the very young that she could write first-rate teen fiction. You might discover that you are sufficiently versatile to write fiction, or even non-fiction, for several age groups. The change of pace each group requires is refreshing and stimulating for the next effort.

I had fifty shorts and serials published before my first book was accepted. *This first book had ten rejections before it found a buyer on the eleventh submission.* It sold also as a five-part first-rights serial, made a book club, and was re-sold for second serial rights to another magazine.

However, if I had not already had the short-story and three- and four-part serial training—and a baptism in rejection slips—I doubt if I'd have had the courage to continue submitting this book. So the short stories serve another purpose: they help to toughen a writer's skin.

To get the most out of your apprenticeship, cultivate a professional attitude toward your work. One of the marks of the professional is *continual output*. You must learn to be ready to start on a new story the moment the old one is on its way to market. Once you drop it in the mail, it should cease to be your topmost concern, because you should now be involved with the new idea you're ready to work out. Such an attitude not only serves to maintain your output, but it also becomes a shield against the disappointments of rejection slips. Keep a number of stories circulating and you will become known among editors as a *producer*. And that is what editors want: people they can count on for repeat performances, not one-shot geniuses.

To avoid dry spells between stories, keep a stock of ideas on tap. Where to get them and how to keep track of them is discussed in the following chapter.

Chapter 4

Ideas and You

Workable ideas are the result of careful preparation. For a store-house of ideas, notebooks and card files are invaluable to the professional as well as the beginner. So is a sure knowledge of himself.

Getting to Know YOU

Before you can know others—real people and characters—well enough to write about them, you must know yourself, because all emotion and experience that you write about is first filtered through *you*: the kind of person you are, the personal values you hold dear. In this lies the secret of your individuality—and your writing style.

Are you an optimist or a pessimist? Does a partly filled jar of honey look half-full or half-empty to you? You'll do better at writing for young people if your outlook is bright. This does not mean that you can deal only in sweetness and light. Juvenile liter-ature—even for the youngest readers—can tackle realistic prob-lems.

It would be ridiculous to think that children are not aware of the seamy side of life and that they are not affected emotionally by this awareness—whether it comes from exposure to TV, movies, radio news, photo-journalism, or newspapers; not to mention what they hear and see when grownups forget or ignore the fact that they are nearby. Maybe in a bygone era there was such a thing as an over-protected child. I doubt that such innocence is possible today. So, if you want to write about alcoholism, divorce, integration, prejudice, drug addiction, street gangs, or girls and boys in deep trouble—you may—*if* you can handle such subjects skillfully. Your job as a writer for the young is to resolve this type of plot action in such a way that your story evolves on a hopeful note, though not necessarily in outright happiness.*

Your characters should be willing to fight for their goals without whining or pitying themselves over failures. Even in stories written "just for fun," the enduring human values should be very much in evidence.

The point is that your writing must say something to your readers. You will be saying what *you* believe. Be sure you know what that is—and that it reflects sound, healthy philosophies.

And what are those philosophies? This is where a notebook comes in. It should have several sections, so be sure to use index tabs or dividers. In order to be useful to you, all of your reference material must be easy to locate when you need it.

How do you want to head Section One? *"Me—in Depth"?* This book is just for you. No one else is supposed to see it. But you may want to leave it to posterity after you become famous! The important thing is to put in it exactly what *you* think, your real opinions, what makes your mental or physical hackles rise.

Whatever you believe, like, or dislike deep down inside yourself will come to the surface, because all writing is in a sense autobiographical. You can't help but inject your way of looking at life into your work. That is why it is so important for you to know about *you*.

Section Two: "What I Know." Anything you know can be adapted to stories for the young, so it is valuable source material. *Professions*—teaching, engineering, science. *Jobs*—secretary, machinist, sales clerk, delivery man, coal miner, lumberjack, Scout leader, oil

---

*See *Leap Before You Look,* by Mary Stolz; *The Empty Schoolhouse,* by Natalie Savage Carlson; *A Cup of Courage,* by Mina Lewiton; *Ellen and the Gang,* by Frieda Friedman; *Danger Beats the Drum,* by Arnold Madison; *A Girl Like Me,* by Jeannette Eyerly; *The Man Without a Face,* by Isabelle Holland; *The Watchers,* by Barbara Rinkoff; *Durango Street,* by Frank Bonham; *Senior Dropout,* by J. L. Summers.

driller, baby sitter, telephone operator. *Skills*—jewelry making, skiing, deep sea fishing, carpentry, mountain climbing.

A good place to prospect for ideas is in your own fields of interest. What are your hobbies? Do you collect or make things? Does art or music have a special meaning in your life? Are you an expert at anything?

What do you like to read? Romance, travel, history, biography, science, mystery? Your reading interests may indicate the type of things you can write, too.

How about *Backgrounds, Regional and Local?* Do you know Mouse Hollow, U.S.A., or East 88th St., New York? Paris, Rome, Bombay, Johannesburg? Small town, big town, urban, suburban, rural; north, south, east, west; desert, lake region; farm life, college life, or island living? Make a note of whatever is familiar to you.

Perhaps you know *Periods in History*—ancient Egypt, Greece, our own Old West, the Civil War period, or Colonial times. Of course you know life as it is lived this minute, wherever you are.

In your search for story material, do not overlook your own back yard. Don't discard the too-familiar because it does not seem exciting enough to you. To someone else it may be brand new and remarkable! And anyway, anything can be changed through the medium of a story situation. Suppose a bag of uncut diamonds or an old engagement ring were found while some youngsters were spading up your garden? Something like that happened in *Mystery of the Second Treasure*, by Eugenie C. Reid.

Suppose a letter were found with mysterious instructions; or a paper, with just the word "Help!" were blown through your living room window from the house next door? Or a skeleton were found in your attic—an incident I developed in my book, *Family at Seven Chimneys House*.

The familiar can produce a convincing background and life-like characters—and you'll be following the tried and true precept of *writing what you know*. But you'll add a special ingredient, your writer's imagination, and the familiar and unusual (the plot stuff you dream up) will fuse into a story.

Section Three: "What I'd Like to Know About." *Interesting Jobs and Professions*—Did you ever long to be an actress, an adventurer, a detective, a nurse, a doctor, a model, a dress designer, or a lawyer? Might you like to be a ballet dancer, a scuba diver, an astronaut, a submariner, a fireman, a band leader? The list of other people's businesses can be a never-ending, fascinating source of story possibilities. Add to it *Places and Backgrounds*—anywhere in the world—that you'd like to know well enough to be able to write about.

A sure way to get your material noticed is to use some unusual subject in your story, or a background that's really different, or a hero who is a real individualist. In one of my short stories, "Rajah and the Sacred Tooth," I used a Ceylon setting, with a celebration honoring Buddha's Tooth. The facts were researched, while the human situation was my own invention. This story sold at once to *Junior Scholastic*, was later reprinted in a collection of stories, and included in a school reader.

Whales are not exactly backyard beasts, and ambergris is not usually found in New Jersey, where I live. But some research equipped me to write a story called "The Affectionate Whale," which appeared in *Story Parade*, was reprinted in *My Weekly Reader*, and again in *Teen-Age Tales*, a D. C. Heath textbook. An excerpt from this story was also included in school testing material. Twelve years after it was first published, the story was reprinted again in the then new *Golden Magazine*, now called *Young World*.

One of the musts for a writer for juniors is a big bump of curiosity, because youngsters are curious about everything. Any subject that intrigues you can be a story possibility—if you're willing to do some research on it. (The how-and-where of research is detailed in Part II of this text.)

Other Sources for Ideas

Leave your desk now and then and explore the world around you. Take a trip—I don't mean a little jaunt to Spain or up the Amazon. Around the corner, downtown, or to the zoo will do. Or, you can travel armchair style, with a book or magazine; but do so with a mind open to ideas. A word, a name, a background, a picture—any and all of these can be the seeds that sprout into stories.

The idea for my *Showboat Holiday* came from an illustration in a book I was reviewing (Holling C. Holling's *Min of the Mississippi*). A wrecked paddle-wheeler was shown washed up on land, with laundry flapping from a line between the smoke stacks: someone was living aboard. I transferred my paddle-wheeler to the inland waterway of the New Jersey coast, put a modern family of kids aboard, surrounded them with plenty of obstacles, and let them solve their problems. The book was a Junior Literary Guild selection, as well as a ten-part serial in *Trailblazer*.

Names for characters are very important. A card file will make these easily available. Collect girls' names, boys' names, and possible last names. Nicknames are also useful. Collect foreign names and nicknames, properly tabbed as to nationality, so you can find them when you need them.

Don't overlook names for pets. My lists include names in English and in foreign groups. I started it after I drew a blank in naming a French poodle in one of the *Susie* series. That won't happen again!

Lists of street names, towns, and place names are also helpful.

Newspapers, magazines, books—and the telephone directory— are splendid sources for names. Or, you might buy yourself a "Name the Baby" book. I find name dictionaries immensely helpful because they give derivation and meaning of names.

Some writers keep lists of possible *titles*. These, too, can spark story ideas. Books of quotations are dependable title and theme sources. Be sure, however, to keep titles simple and indicative of what the story is about. You'll catch more readers that way.

The Idea File

Jot your ideas down on 3-by-5- or 5-by-8-inch file cards. Don't depend on remembering them; they can vanish all too easily. When you are ready to start on a new story, your idea may very well come from this file. In any event, *having* the ideas *there*, on tap, gives you a nice sense of security. You know you won't need to cast about frantically for something to write about.

The Role of Fiction

The purpose in writing fiction is to interest the reader and to make him feel something. It might be amusement, as in Eileen Rosenbaum's *Two for Trouble;* or excitement through thrilling adventure, as in Jim Kjelgaard's *Swamp Cat* or Armstrong Sperry's *Danger to Windward.* It might be a delicious tingling of the spine over a creepy mystery, like Keith Robertson's *Three Stuffed Owls,* or Phyllis Whitney's *Mystery of the Haunted Pool.*

The "feeling" might be sympathy for a character who is misunderstood, unloved, or mistreated. Or it might be inspiration and hope, making the young reader spiritually pick up his burdens and walk on with courage, because the book has given him a kinship with others who have problems which *he* has faced, such as an unhappy family life, the loss of a loved one, overwhelming shyness, or a physical disability. Books can be comforting, inspiring, informative, hilarious—and the skillful writer can run the gamut of human emotions and needs, at all levels, in his work.

But, to carry out a story idea—any story idea—the writer must create a set of characters through whom the story happens.

Chapter 5

Characters Who Make Your Story —Techniques That Tell the Tale

There is nothing more important in fiction writing than your characters. They are the center of your story. Each story stems from the main character's problem or goal and his way of solving the one or reaching the other against great odds—with suspense woven in to keep the reader reading. In capsule form, these are the elements of plot—for the short story, for the book, and for any age reader you may have in mind.

How Characters Can Help You

Everything that happens in your story springs from character action and reaction. Therefore characters *are* plot. Or, to put it another way: Plots are not possible without characters.

If your story actors become real people to *you*, with human qualities, emotions, and desires—whatever their age—they'll help you devise the plot. Their ideas, hopes, motives, and antagonisms —charged with your technical know-how—will create the situations, the problems, the complications, the climax, and the solutions you will need. Of course, when I say "real people," I mean characters to whom you have given the *illusion* of reality.

Actual children and grownups, just as they are, have no place in fiction. Their real characteristics and traits would be a hindrance rather than a help because they would not blend with the action and reaction necessary to your story plot. At some critical point your inner voice might whisper, "Aunt Helen, or Joanie, or young Mark simply wouldn't do this!" and how do you get past a block like that?

Story actors must be built to order, to fit the needs of the tale to be told. For this reason real people are good material only when they are used as composites from which the *needed* fictional characters are created.

Story characters must not be mere types or caricatures such as are sometimes found on our TV screens; silly, gum-chomping "juveniles" who seem afflicted with some kind of nerve disease and squeaky vocal chords or precocious children who talk like miniature adults. Hackneyed characterizations are found in adult actors too: "hard-boiled" reporters and slick, trench-coated detectives. Avoid stock characters in your writing. They're sure to bring rejection slips. Enrich your characterizing skill with study of the more truthful examples from fine literature and from personal observation.

How to "Collect" Characters

Carrying a small notebook with you always, in your pocket or purse, along with a reliable ballpoint pen will enable you to jot down spot observations and quick character sketches before the first sharp impressions fade away. You'll need all kinds of story actors, because even picture books can include a wide range of ages, relationships, occupations, and nationalities. Learn to observe and analyze swiftly, wherever you are.

"Characters" are all around you. You have been looking at them all your life, but it may be that until now you have not really *seen* them as story material. This is what you should look for in people—that first impression they create, then the individual features that contribute to that impression. The way they talk, gesture, walk, and even smell. All sensory details are important reflections of character. Note facial expressions under varying circumstances, tone of voice, ways people of all ages move under different conditions or disabilities.

Note differences among people in the same occupation or social groups and in family relationships. Being aware of human variety will help you to make individuals of your characters instead of stock types. Grandmothers come short, tall, thin, fat. Some are loving, some are doting, some are full of chuckles, and some are not. Store clerks are different from each other. How are they different? Janitors, too, differ from one another, as do doctors, judges, school principals, ladies next door, teachers, librarians, little boys, big and little sisters. Real people are individuals—and so must your story people be.

Your brief notations, legibly transferred into your loose leaf notebook or in a card file, under suitable headings, will then be at your fingertips whenever you need them for character composites. They serve the writer as sketchbooks serve the artist.

Characterization for Different Age Levels

Characterization in books for very young children is, of course, the very simplest. The child is named, the age is given, or more likely, indicated in pictures.

Books for the six to eight age group continue with the uncomplicated, but lively, character who does not change greatly from start to finish. He may learn to accomplish something, perhaps to overcome a fear, or he may have an adventure, but essentially he does not change.

In books for eight- to twelve-year-olds, the character is more complex, reacting strongly to his world, himself, his problems, and the people around him. He must have a number of character traits, a definite personality. Your reader should feel that if he met him on the street, he would recognize him. Many a fan letter to the author of a convincing character in this age bracket asks for an address, "so I can visit or write him/her."

In the teen-age book, whether for girls or for boys, the characters are as fully developed as in adult writing. The only difference between the adult and the quality junior book now is the kinds of problems the main characters face and the kinds of situations into which they are plunged.

Until you learn to handle all the elements of the writer's craft, avoid creating a thoroughly unlikable character—an anti-hero—in the main role, regardless of the age group for which you are writing.° The reader wants to identify himself with the hero and he isn't going to do so with a nasty person. Neither should the main character be a goody-goody; the normal boy or girl is equally unwilling to identify with *too* virtuous a character. No one is perfect, and the reader certainly knows *he* isn't, having been told so often enough by those around him.

Selecting and Individualizing Your Story People

Use only the number of characters absolutely necessary to carry out your story action, but never limit your list to *one*. It takes two to tangle—and tangles make the most interesting reading.

However few or many characters you have, be sure to vary their personalities. Joan must never be exactly like Kate, even if they are twins. Twins may be mirror-images of each other, but their inner selves must be different. Each character must be an individual, unmistakable person in his or her own right.

FLAT and ROUNDED Characters

Your *total character* is the combination of all the qualities or *traits* that distinguish him as an individual. Short story limitations allow only for the *flat* delineation of a type. The character exhibits a single trait or perhaps two, which are distinct and make him different from his story fellows. (He might be *timid*, but have a *strong sense of responsibility* that causes him to overcome his fears in the end.)

The *rounded* character is for booklengths. He should have a number of traits, and these may even be somewhat inconsistent—as in real life. He is brave—but not always. He is loyal—but perhaps a bit envious. He is honest—most of the time. He may be rather relaxed when it comes to causes that excite his young

---

°See: *The Dream Watcher*, by Barbara Wersba; and *The Bully of Barkham Street*, by Mary Stolz.

friends. Yet when goaded into action (perhaps by injustice) he leaps into the fray. If he is your hero, he can be richly endowed with character traits. But if his role is a minor one, his traits must be trimmed down to bare essentials.

Character traits make possible the variety of personalities and the contrasts that lend color and interest to a story. If one character is careful, make another careless. If one is loud, make another soft-spoken. Gay-sad; cruel-kind; thoughtful-thoughtless; ambitious-lazy; brave-timid; neat-sloppy; wildly imaginative or earthbound-practical.

A copy of *Roget's Thesaurus of Words and Phrases* is an indispensable part of your writing equipment. When you are thinking up characters in contrast to each other, a thesaurus will provide you with a quantity of descriptive words which may serve as character trait leads. And when you have selected the traits, you will also have a vocabulary with which to convey them to the reader.

For the gay character you will find at least a dozen words to convey the impression: joyous, gleeful, light-hearted, merry, carefree. If sad, you will find: sorrowful, downcast, unhappy, low-spirited, moody. Use defining words judiciously, however, to stamp him on the reader's mind, make his actions prove the point.

There is a latent danger in secondary characters. No matter how necessary he or she is to the plot, never make a minor character so interesting that he steals the show away from your main character. It can happen—and the hero ends by standing around watching the minor character perform. *It is an absolute rule that heroes must be doers, not people watchers.* Should this happen in your story, tone the offending character down at once. If this show-stealer is that interesting, make him the lead in your next story.

Although for the best character interpretation the writer should "step into a character's skin," the writer in real life seldom thinks or acts the way his character does in any given circumstance. In the course of writing, you are every character you portray, but every character is not you, as you naturally are. This is an important fact to remember. When dealing with characters and situations not your own, you must shed your personal views and take on those of the time and place in your story.

Tagging Your Characters

Tags are devices by which a character may be identified each time he appears on the scene. A tag might be a gesture, a characteristic mannerism such as tossing the head, snuffling, touching a finger to the side of the nose in thought, or flaring the nostrils in anger. A character might habitually pull down on an ear lobe, crack his knuckles, swing a key chain, or chew on a strand of hair. He might collect string, or pick threads off himself or others, or brush imaginary specks of dust from his (probably irate) friends. Smacking the lips before or after speaking might also be an annoying tag. A girl might think that to flick her tongue out is cute, unaware that she reminds others of a frog, fly-hunting. Or worse, a snake.

A character might give a little hop when he walks, indicating a physical disability. Posture can be used as a characteristic tag. When someone usually portrayed as brisk and erect is shown with slumped shoulders and dragging feet, the reader instantly knows something is wrong. The possibilities for using tags are infinite and anything that *individualizes* your story actor is to the good.

You might want to use a speech tag, such as tone of voice or manner of speaking. Or your character might use some expression repeatedly. A bubbly teen-age girl might breathlessly exclaim, "Fantabulous!" while a boy might spout cliches (which is one way to get them out of *your* system), or utter terrible puns.

A character might sing or whistle one particular song, and this habit, later on, could be used to play a significant part in the plot. Tags are not hung on the characters willy-nilly, but for story purposes. Choose them as carefully as you choose traits and names for your story people.

Naming Your Characters

Your character becomes more of a person as soon as you name him or her. For this reason, do not name characters who have only walk-on parts in the story. The receptionist, the druggist, the storekeeper may be necessary to a scene, but unless they play active roles, more particular identification is not needed.

Names help to characterize and individualize your story people. They help you and your readers to visualize your characters. And names also help to contrast characters.

If you find any difficulty in naming your story people, it is probably because they are not yet fully realized in your own mind. When you know your story actors and begin to juggle names in your mind, the right combination will click into place for you.

Characters must be christened appropriately. A girl named Minnie Mushmouth might conceivably win a beauty contest in real life, but *never* convincingly in a book, nor would a boy called Clarence make a likely football hero. Nicknames, which include personal characteristics, can save yards of description, especially for minor characters: Gloomy Gus, Turtle, Speedy, Fats, Whistler. Avoid fancy names that may detract from the effectiveness of your story. Don't be afraid of common names like Janie, Susie, Barbara, Dick, and Bill, but do not overdo simplicity and make all your characters Johns and Marys. Variety adds interest to everything.

Do not have two or more names beginning with the same letter, as John, Jean, Jill, Jodie, or the reader will soon be very mixed up. Vary the number of syllables in the names as well as the beginning letters, especially for your leading actors.

Even the sound of names must be considered, because readers "hear" as well as see them. The difference in the sound helps characters to stand out and not meld into an undistinguishable mass. Harsh consonants in a name, for example, give the impression of ruggedness.

Incidentally, did you know that in the original version of *Gone with the Wind*, the heroine was called *Pansy* instead of *Scarlett* O'Hara? What a difference the name makes in our mental picture of the heroine! A rose may smell as sweet by any other name— but what euphonious appeal would *Romeo and Teresa* have? All the romantic bell-tones would be reduced to a dull thunk. The names of story characters are indeed important.

Chapter 6

The Hero . . . the Villain
. . . and the Vital Viewpoint

Generally your hero or heroine should be a fairly familiar type, with motives, desires, and traits common to most young people. At the same time, there should be a streak of the unusual in his or her makeup—the potential for whatever hero-action that will be called for later. He must be defined clearly, as an interesting individual to whom things happen—and who *makes* things happen.

To create a main character, who promises the reader never a dull moment, *you* must have a clear mental image of him. Get inside his mind so that you know what he thinks, how he feels, and what he hopes to achieve in *this* story. Choose one major and two or three minor characterizing traits for him very carefully because it is these traits that will determine the course of your story.

If your heroine is to win a singing contest in the end, some-where among her attributes must be a good voice, or a voice capable of being trained. The other attributes you give her should make her way to success possible—the drive of ambition, the initiative to take a job to pay for expensive lessons. At the same time, these very qualities can make her path more difficult—ambition might make her trample over other people (until she learns better); she might work to the point of exhaustion, endan-gering her voice. Such complications, the opposition a plot re-quires, might make for a really gripping story.

If a boy hero must, in a tight spot, be able to throw an object and hit the mark, somewhere along the line you'd better give him some athletic skill—and let the reader *see* him demonstrate it—so he can then convincingly accomplish the necessary feat.

Your main characters, those who *make* things happen, must have a function and an ability to perform it. Determine what it is they must do, then endow them with the necessary skill. And don't overlook a logical supply of the weapon or tool with which they must perform this action—as in the story of the boy who always overloaded himself on hikes. When he insisted on taking along a coil of rope, his friend said it was a dumb thing to do because they didn't need it. But they did, for the friend fell over a cliff and had to be rescued—and there was the rope, logically provided at the start of the story.

Now then, *who is your main character? How old is he?* Age is an important means of characterization. Be sure to edge it toward the top of the specific bracket for which you're writing, in order to insure maximum reader-interest. Establish the age of your character as soon as possible in the beginning. People at different age levels react differently to given situations and emotional impacts, so determining age at the start will aid you in your plotting.

What does your hero or heroine look like? What sort of person is he or she? What kind of hero or heroine do you *need* to solve the problems or reach the goal through individual effort in this story? The hero or heroine must win out in the end—but only through his or her own actions.

The truly appealing character is not wholly good or wholly bad, but possesses a balance of positive (good) and negative (bad) qualities. In the hero, the good outweighs the bad—but the negative traits, just as the positive ones, must be chosen with care since they, too, should affect the course of the story. Because of these negative traits the character acts or reacts in a certain significant way and thus affects the plot. So the "faults" selected by the author are chosen for this purpose. Faults might be impulsiveness, exaggeration, procrastination—weaknesses which will also make the leading character appear human and likable, because the reader can identify with this sort of "imperfect" person and sympathize with his predicaments.

Especially appealing to young people are lively heroes and heroines who leap before they look, who speak before they think.

Overhelpfulness is a major trait of Mary Malone's ubiquitous hero of *Here's Howie*. A character's over-active imagination can be fun for the reader, too, as in Beverly Cleary's *Emily's Runaway Imagination*. See also *Ellen Grae*, by Vera and Bill Cleaver.

To SHOW or TELL

The worst possible way of characterizing any story actor, major or minor, is to *tell* the reader that he is this or that kind of person; that he is high-spirited, inventive, or scatterbrained, kind, or unkind. This sort of *telling* will have the reader yawning and reaching for the TV switch. To hold his attention and keep him reading, you must continually *show* him in word pictures.

Don't, for example, say anything as vague and colorless as this: "Tommy came into the house and put his books on the hall table," if the kind of boy Tommy really is in your story would be more likely to provide action like this:

> The door opened with a whoosh and Tommy skidded on the hall rug as he flung his books on the table. *Arithmetic for the Fifth Year* thudded on the floor. Tommy leaped over it and rushed through the house toward the back porch . . .

Tommy is characterized at once as a lively, none-too-careful youngster. His age is suggested rather than stated. Readers will assume that he's ten or eleven, because of the fifth grade book he dropped. They will also wonder why he is in such a hurry. What's on the porch?

Unless a description of a character comes alive with detail, it is likely to bog down a story: "Amy Kendall was ten years old. She had brown eyes and brown hair which she wore in pigtails . . . " Amy might as well be made of wood.

This is how Amy really appears in *The Family at Seven Chimneys House*:

> . . . the outside door burst open and ten-year-old Amy staggered in.
>
> Her brown eyes were sparkling, her flyaway brown hair stuck out in saucy pigtails. Under one arm, pressed close to her side, she had two books. Under the other was a bunched-

up flower-printed cloth, like a slipcover. Awkwardly she held the handle of a large cage, inside which a big, cross-looking parrot rocked and glared.

You don't need an avalanche of details to build a picture of a character. Avoid cataloguing your character's features, as if you were taking an inventory. Use a few details to create that first impression. Give a glimpse of each character who enters upon the scene. As the story develops, you gradually build out the characters, too.

Your story should have movement, and every detail you present should keep it flowing in a steady stream. Your character descriptions should be a part of that stream.

The Villain

Even as you think over the word, your eyes narrow and you tense a bit. For "villain" is a base and wicked person, a scoundrel. He's the one who makes life difficult for your hero. But what would a story be without difficulties? Without opposition to the hero's straight flight toward his goal? I can tell you: it would be dull reading.

Without a powerful villain you will not have a dramatic, suspenseful plot action. If your villain is a paper tiger there can be no question of your hero's easy success—and easy winnings are no fun to read about. The villain must be strong and cunning— he must on several occasions outwit or even clobber the brave, struggling hero. In fact, the hero should have some healthy qualms about going on with his quest, in the face of this opposition. But, after licking his wounds, and thinking things over, he *does* because a hero *must*.

How to characterize your villain? Consider his function. *What does he want?* What must he *do* to maintain his villain status? How must he be able to compete with your hero's strength, skill, or cleverness?

When you know this, endow the villain with the necessary character traits so that the conflict between your "good" hero and your "bad" villain will be interesting to watch. The two must appear to be almost equally matched—but the faults and flaws in the character of the villain, and the high purpose, courage, and perseverance on the hero's part are what bring defeat to the one and victory to the other.

Modern villains are not wholly evil, although their negative qualities do outweigh the positive ones. I manage to gray my villains up a bit by allowing them to be kind to animals—or very small children—or old people. But not too often! They must not be allowed to run around doing a whole string of good deeds, or they lose their credibility as the bad eggs of the script.

At the same time, in your efforts to prove that your hero has some well-rounded human flaws, do not allow him to buzz around flaunting them because he, too, will lose his standing and support from the reader. One or two unworthy thoughts or deeds should fill the quota.

Incidentally, usually it's best to avoid casting Mother or Dad in a really mean role. However, aunts, uncles, cousins, and even grandparents can serve in "meanie" roles. Mother and Dad may not "understand" the young hero or heroine—they may be absolutely *staid* and frustrating—but somewhere at the end, generation gap notwithstanding, it should be admitted by their youthful progeny that they're not so impossible after all.

Stepmothers have suffered much defamation since the earliest days of Cinderella, so a wicked one today might be considered a stock character. In modern fiction it is often the well-meaning stepmother who needs the love and understanding of her antagonistic new family.

Naming the Villains

In naming my villains I exercise a personal idiosyncrasy: I try to avoid giving my "bad people" common names, so that no Bill or Jim or Dick or Janie will pick up one of my books or stories and find himself cast in the role of a major villain.

Choose the names of your "meanies" with care, being sure they suit the character. *Astrea* fits the ruthless girl in my book, *Dance to My Measure*. For her a cozy, friendly name like *Babs* or *Susie* would never do. In christening your characters, consider the effect of name association.

The WHY of Villains

Villains are villains because of their poor characters—not because of the way they look, or the job or profession they may have, or because of their race or religion. They are *individuals* and their villainy never casts aspersions on the group from which they spring. If an artist does something dishonorable, it is not because artists are like that, but because *this* artist has the flaw of envy, avarice, pride, or whatever makes him act ignobly.

A well-drawn villain adds much to the excitement of your story. He must be interesting, but not so fascinating that the reader starts cheering for him instead of for the hero! If you make it clear *why* he or she is the nasty person he is, you and the reader may even sympathize with him. But don't overdo it. It's very well to understand villains and their villainy, but they still have to be foiled and the hero must win.

Since villains are part of plot and conflict, they will be further discussed in later chapters.

Viewpoint

Some writers have difficulty understanding what is meant by *viewpoint* in a story. This term does not mean *which person* (author, hero, onlooker) tells the story, but *through whose eyes and heart the story is told.* Once you understand this important distinction, selecting and maintaining the proper viewpoint should not be difficult.

A story for young people should be told from the viewpoint of the main character—your hero or heroine—the person with the problem to solve or the goal to reach, and therefore, the most involved emotionally. Everything that happens in the story should be presented through his/her eyes, senses, feelings, and thoughts. This is called the *single viewpoint,* and most successful writers use it.

> Bonnie Parker was out of breath by the time she reached
> the third-floor landing. One more flight to go with this heavy
> bag of groceries. . . . She leaned against the cool wall of the
> hallway for a rest. This was so different from their house in

Long Valley. But then, here in Grove City, everything was different from the country home they had left a week ago. And that included the Junior High four blocks away, which would open next Tuesday.

It was so huge—and she wouldn't know a soul there. Her brother didn't count, of course. Jimmie was only twelve and in seventh grade. Besides, Jimmie had the knack for making instant friends—and she certainly did not. Bonnie sighed. She would have to face a mob of strangers all by herself . . .

Be sure that you are telling the story of one person, one central character—who may be surrounded by a number of other people, but it is in this important one that the reader takes the greatest interest. It is with him or her that the reader identifies himself, and it is for him or her that he sheds tears or shouts cheers right through to the final outcome of the plot. Begin the story with him and end it with him.

There are several possible viewpoints, which you will learn to handle as you become more proficient in your craft—and some you should never attempt.

To be avoided is the *omniscient*, the all-knowing multiple viewpoint, which is a god-like revelation of the thoughts and feelings of any and all characters, at will. Some writers of adult fiction do use this device, but it tends to make spectators instead of participants of the readers, unless the writer is especially skilled or is dealing with an especially fascinating subject. Many old classics are written in this way, with the addition of editorial (author's) opinions and comments addressed directly to the "Dear Reader." This was popular in Dickens' time; it is no longer. The best modern story tellers, like Daphne DuMaurier and Mary Stewart, always write in the single viewpoint—and so do the best writers in the junior field—and it is difficult to put their books down, once begun.

The straight *objective viewpoint* is another one to do without in fiction, because this is the reporter's approach to his kind of writing. Properly he tells only what he sees or hears, without bias, without expressing any opinions or delving into anybody's emotions. The reader simply gets the facts. But the reader of fiction wants more than that. He wants to know how facts affect the feelings of the story people, especially those of the main character. A story without *feelings*—emotion—is no story at all.

A *skipping viewpoint* can be purely awful—jerking the reader this way and that. I've had stories submitted where everybody's viewpoint was given—even the dog's! Never jump from one character's viewpoint to another, nor from one problem to another, as in the following horrible example:

> Betty sprawled in the living room chair and stared out of the window. Rain—in buckets. Yesterday it would have been all right because she and Dot had gone to the movies. But today Sally was supposed to come and play tennis. What a mess the weather could be . . .

> Her brother, Chuck, went whistling through the hall and then raced up the stairs, two at a time. A rainy weekend was fine with him, he thought. You couldn't cut lawn in the rain. Instead he would go to his room and start on that new rocket model. Maybe if he could finish it by Monday he could show it to Mr. Foster, the science teacher. Mr. Foster said . . .

> Mrs. Howard stood in the foyer looking from Betty to Chuck. She sighed. Teen-agers were such a problem. Betty was sitting there all arms and legs, mooning over something. She hoped it wasn't over that new boy in the neighborhood. And Chuck—what a mess his model kits made in his room. Chuck's father always said . . .

The reader has no idea whose story this is—or what the problem is. He cannot get emotionally involved or *care* about any one particular character, identify himself with him or her. This is the main reason for avoiding the use of "everybody's" viewpoint: it's the perfect way to make your story nobody's.

In juvenile fiction it is permissible to break viewpoint once in a while, but the technical reason for it must be very, very good. Sometimes the viewpoint is given to another character in a chapter all his own for purposes of story clarification. But no matter how skillfully this is done, all the rapport, the emotional tone previously built up for the main character, is lost as the interest shifts to the mind and heart of another person.

One more viewpoint to avoid is that of "they." This is usually exposed to the reader in characters' thoughts.

"It's a surprise," *they* thought, when Father entered with
the large package.

But, one of "them" might have thought: "What a big box!" or
"Where did that come from?" or "What is that?"

The only time a writer can legitimately use the "they" viewpoint, is when two (or more) minds have a single thought under
the stress or impact of some tragic, comic, or moving event which
brings on a joint or mass reaction. For example, each time the
astronauts return from the moon, millions of people heave a
collective sigh of relief as *they* think, "Thank God those fellows
have come back safely." However, in usual circumstances, each
of us thinks as an individual. If your characters entertain
the same thoughts *all* the time, there's something wrong with
them, or you're writing mind-manipulating science or occult
fiction. In real life no one can really know what another person
thinks or feels—and no group of people can convincingly think
the same thoughts, like some sort of silent Greek chorus. In beginner's stories, twins, brothers, and sisters often are allowed to
think as "they." Nobody really thinks that way, not even Siamese
twins.

The *first person viewpoint* with "I" as the story teller may be
used, but it not only has limitations, it also establishes prejudices
in that all-important person, the reader, and this is especially
true of the younger child. First of all, technically, nothing but
that which the "I" sees and feels can be told. In order to tell his
story, "I" has to be the lead character, and *everything* has to
happen to him. If he is the hero and tells about his heroism *sub-
jectively,* in the light of his own feelings and self-concern, the
reader may take offense at his lack of modesty.

To avoid this problem, "I" is sometimes relegated to the role
of observing someone else's story which he then tells. This puts
a further strain on the viewpoint. In order to see it all happen
so "I" can tell about it, the first person narrator really has to
get around; in such cases, the author may find himself in a
corner. So, be wary of the "I" viewpoint—the perpendicular pronoun. But also keep in mind that teens and 'tweens, who are apt
to be more interested in subjective thoughts, do respond favor-
ably to first person tales in short stories and books such as this:

Are you there God? It's me, Margaret. We're moving today. I'm so scared God. I've never lived anywhere but here. Suppose I hate my new school? Suppose everybody there hates me? Please help me God. Don't let New Jersey be too horrible. Thank you.*

Humorous situations often "work" better in first person, as with a bumbling character who sets out to help someone else, or to extricate himself from a dilemma.† The rule to follow, as with all rules in writing: choose the best way to tell *this* particular story.

The most popular and serviceable viewpoint is that of the third person, subjective. (See example used with single viewpoint discussion.) Here, although the main character's name is used, and the pronoun *he* or *she,* the single viewpoint makes everything seem to happen to the reader. The perfect climate for that ideal reader-identification, this method of narration allows him not only to *look* on the scene, but also to get into the mind and body of the main character and *live* the adventure with him.

To effect this perfect union through the single viewpoint, the author must not ever leave the mind of the main character to tell what some other character is thinking or feeling.

The *third person objective viewpoint* is used for all other story people. They are seen and thought about through the eyes and mind of the viewpoint character (as Bonnie's brother, Jimmie, is). Only through action and dialogue can they reveal their feelings.

First Aid for an Ailing Viewpoint

If you find it difficult to maintain a single viewpoint, try writing your story in first person, and then rewrite it properly in third. One or two such practice experiments should teach you the mental trick involved.

---

*From the book, *Are You There God? It's Me, Margaret,* by Judy Blume.

†Read: *Me, Cassie,* by Anita Feagles; *The Great Brain,* by John D. Fitzgerald; and the *Rupert Piper* stories by Ehthelyn Parkinson, for rollicking humor; and *Edgar Allan,* by John Neufeld, for a heart-wrenching contemporary theme.

Describing the Viewpoint Character

Your viewpoint character is the hardest of all to describe—without resorting to plate glass windows and mirrors. I'm sure you've read many a story where the character—female usually—looks at herself in some shiny surface and thinks about what she sees. Editors have "looked" at this sort of description thousands of times, and they're heartily sick of it. Do yourself a literary favor and stay away from mirrors. And where does that leave you? In a perfectly fine spot—with a "camera" and what is called "the camera view."

At the very beginning of your story you can stand off and describe the scene or situation, then zoom in on a close-up of the main character entering upon it. But, once your character thinks or speaks or feels, you immediately get into his viewpoint and stay there. The following example is from Phyllis Whitney's book, *Mystery of the Black Diamonds*:

> There was a sign at the foot of the canyon and Angie Wetheral stopped to read it. The morning sun of Colorado was already hot upon her bare head. It touched the shiny red of short curls and brightened a sprinkling of freckles across her nose.

The author goes on to describe brother Mark, younger but taller than Angie and dark, like their father (which takes care of him, too). Angie speaks and from then on *she* carries the viewpoint ball.

In your own writing, remember that you cannot characterize (describe) your story actors once and for all the duration of the book or story, expecting the reader to remember what you said. He won't—and neither will he go back through the pages to find out just who Betty is and what she looks like. You have to re-portray and re-identify your actors as the story progresses, not repeating what you said the first time, but making some reference to an oustanding characteristic. The major traits of your main character must be stressed again and again—his bravery or loyalty or cleverness—so that when the trait is needed to accomplish his purpose or goal, the reader will have been prepared for it. The character will not seem to "come brave all over" all at once, or become suddenly talented in some field.

Character Growth

In a short story or a picture book the characters do not have to show growth development; there simply isn't word-room for it. They attain their goals and that is that. But in a book, the main character should change in the course of the story. In young people's fiction, characters must grow, develop, mature, become better adjusted to life, circumstances, to growing up, or to whatever their problem happens to be.

Life is never static. Its impacts change people—at all social and age levels. All experiences, new friendships, successes, or losses should have an effect on the story characters involved, too. The changes should not be sudden. The reader should see them happening gradually in the course of the story. Gradual character development contributes to the reality of your story illusion.

Part of the fun of writing is creating characters. In creating story people *you* can be anybody or anything, of any age, time, social condition, or vocation, sampling any life you choose. And when you're plotting a story (while you're working on characters, you *are* plotting), and the characters suddenly spring into life and become "real," you may be sure you'll have no difficulty in getting them down on paper. You'll just have to write faster!

Chapter 7

Dialogue

Have you ever watched a youngster pick a book from the library shelves? One of the first things he looks for is quotation marks, the signs of dialogue. The little symbols mean people, at least two of them, talking about something—maybe planning an adventure or unraveling a mystery. Having discovered the "conversation," the prospective book borrower will read over a few passages. If the conversation is lively, "like real kids talking," and filled with promise of exciting things to come, he'll take the book out.

Dialogue is a means of catching your reader—but to be effective it must sound natural. To sound natural, it must bear out whatever traits you have given your story actors. It is one of the most useful mediums for characterization. Yet in many beginners' stories all the characters sound exactly alike. This weakness can only stem from poor acquaintance with one's story people, along with insufficient skill in effective writing technique.

Listen!

As you study people—grownups and children—listen to them speak. Cultivate an ear for dialogue from your reading and from the live models around you.

What your story people say can be every bit as interesting as what they do. *What* they say and *how* they say it not only reveals the kind of people they are, but speech presented convincingly also lends reality to your tale. So, listen, read, study, and learn to adapt spoken words to your own fictional needs.

You've heard people talking all your life, but have you ever paused to analyze their speech? Have you considered the *tone of voice* used, the *choice of words,* or the *tempo* at which they were spoken? All these affect the characterization of your story people.

Before long your observations will make clear to you that everyone speaks somewhat differently. What is said and how it is said is affected by the speaker's age, his emotional state at that moment, his family and cultural background, his job, profession or occupation—and by whether the speaker is male or female. Even tiny boys have a definitely masculine way of expressing themselves, just as little girls express themselves in a clearly feminine manner.

When you first meet a stranger, you quickly observe his physical appearance, and you immediately draw certain conclusions about his personality. The moment this person *speaks,* you begin to find out how right or wrong you were. The first thing that jars or charms you is the tone of voice. Is it pleasant, well modulated? Or is it nasal, twangy, similar in sound to a foghorn? In my book *Bonnie,* the "opposition," Toni Reo, speaks in a purr—and I use this as a double-edged description, for Toni soon proves that she has "claws," too.

The voice quality you choose for a character must be in keeping with the kind of person that character is. A sweet, motherly woman would not be given a stentorian bellow. Your boy lead would not wheeze and whine; your heroine would not screech every time she opens her mouth.

As for the story actor's vocabulary—my Tommy-in-a-hurry, introduced some pages back—probably would not use impeccable English. A tough character would not speak as a sensitive, carefully reared lad. The boy interested only in sports would lace his speech with terms related to his activities. The budding scientist might also be interested in sports, but not to the degree of the athlete—and his talk should show it. A Puerto Rican girl, new to the United States, would not talk like an American Professor's daughter. To write about her, you'd have to *know* how Puerto Ricans talk.

A Touch of Flavor—Foreign and Domestic

If you think you'd like to use foreign-born persons in your stories, you might prepare yourself ahead of time by collecting foreign words and phrases which can be immediately understood or explained. I like to use Italian, French, Spanish, German, and Russian characters, with a sprinkling of Orientals, usually as secondary or minor actors. For this reason I have "Talk Cards" in my file with typical sample words and phrases. Even something so small as a "*Si*," a "*Da*," a "*Non, non!*" or an "*Ach!*" can lend flavor to a scene. Foreign dictionaries and phrase books, plus an attentive eye and ear tell me all I need to know for my story people.

One way of characterizing a foreigner who has learned English is to have him express himself in stilted phrases, without contractions, idioms, or slang: "Excuse please that I am taking the liberty to write you. I am a Nigerian boy seeking a pen pal friend in the United States . . . My hobbies are foot-balling and swimming . . ."

Don't attempt to reproduce foreign dialogue or regional dialect exactly—it will make awkward reading—and never attempt it at all, unless you are truly familiar with it. It is not necessary to drop "g's" or pepper your story with hard-to-read contractions. Instead, depend on the idioms and speech patterns typical of certain regions, races, or countries. This will mean research and study, but it will be well worth it, for the added flavor to your narrative will contribute to its "realness" and authenticity.

Beware of slang, especially in short stories. Magazine editors frown upon it, though in book form a small amount is allowed. The real danger of using slang is that it changes quickly; even while it is current the same expressions do not always mean the same thing in all parts of the country. But most important, your stories are sure to outlive the slang—which will then either "date" your work, destroying its sense of here-and-now immediacy, or make it incomprehensible to the new crop of readers. So confine yourself to such expressions as have become a part of our language, or coin some phrases tailored to your particular character —and use in moderation. Your story actors can speak *in character*, even without the tinsel riches of a slang wardrobe.

When Your Characters Speak

Good dialogue, when it captures the reader's attention, becomes so real that the author seems to vanish and the characters to move under their own power. The reader feels he *hears* them and believes in their reality. Dialogue is the breath of life for your story people.

It is good practice to read your dialogue aloud when your scene or story is complete. This is the acid test: *Do the words sound natural on the tongue?* If slow or stilted, the fault will then show up. If you are too close to your creation, perhaps you can ask someone else to read the material to you. It may be easier for you then to be more critical. Often, when I read manuscripts in class, a student's ungrateful brain child seems to develop a serpent's tooth. I see the author writhe—and draw a step closer to a professional attitude toward his work. When you can recognize the flaws, you can learn to correct them.

Real Talk and Dialogue

Written dialogue only simulates the talk of actual people. Real talk can be vague, or terse. It can wander in and out among clauses, drop into "well's," or grunt and grind along on "er's." It can also last for hours.

Written dialogue not only must be meaningful to the story, but it must be telescoped—condensed—to keep the reader's interest at high pitch. Neither in life nor in a book does anyone (and the young reader especially) want to be talked numb. While story conversations must serve a definite purpose, they do not need to be completed to the last good-bye, as they are in life. You can stop them at any point and finish whatever needs to be finished by some writer's device at your command—perhaps in the main character's thought, or by a bit of physical action, or narration, or a few words of transition that lead the reader smoothly into the next scene.

No character should be allowed to talk too long without a break. Thick paragraphs of monologue are just as unattractive to the reader as blocks of description. If a character must tell about something at length, be sure to have someone break in from time to time with a question, a comment, an exclamation. Or fit in some sort of action—at least a pause, in which the speaker looks around his audience, sighs, draws a deep breath, groans, laughs, or does whatever is appropriate. Anything that will alleviate the solid, dull look of the page is to the good—provided it fits smoothly into the story flow.

A word of caution about the use of dialogue: No matter how charming and witty the conversations you've devised may be, unless dialogue advances the plot it has no place in the story.

How Dialogue Can Move Your Story Forward

Fictional dialogue can serve many purposes and your skillful use of it reflects your ability as a writer. Besides *characterizing the speakers,* it can *inform* the reader of facts that the speakers already know and that the author wishes revealed to the reader. Dialogue can also *further the action of the plot* by having some change like a decision or a quarrel take place during the conversation. In addition, it can *reveal the emotional state* of the speakers or point up conflict and thus build *suspense* as to what will happen next. Dialogue can also *characterize other people* in the story more convincingly than can expository statements.

Note how all the above items—and more—are illustrated at the beginning of Chapter One of *Chip Nelson and the Contrary Indians.*°

> "Gee whiz, Mom, does Chip *have* to come here and live with us?" George Nelson asked for the eleventh time during breakfast on Saturday morning. "And for a whole year! *Whee-ee* . . ." He sighed like a bicycle pump leaking air, and stirred his dry cereal into a mush.
>
> Across the table, his sister Sally, who was almost nine, watched him with disapproval. " 'Course he does, doesn't he, Mommy?" she asked, her honey-colored pony tail bobbing.

———————

°Because this story will be used to illustrate other points of technique, it is quoted at some length here.

"Yes," Mrs. Nelson said wearily. "We have been all through that this past week."

"And the subject is closed as of right now!" Mr. Nelson set down his spoon and dabbed at his lips with a napkin. "I want to hear no more complaints from you, young man. Your Uncle Jim has an important engineering job to do in the jungles of Brazil. Although Aunt Nell is going with him, it is no place for an eight-year-old boy like Chip. It's nice that your cousin can come here to Riverledge and stay with us."

"Huh! Nice for whom?" George grumbled.

"Geo-rge!" his father said warningly.

George ducked his head. The top of it was like a thick, stubby, black brush. "Well, if Chip wasn't such a coward—" he began.

"I'm ashamed of you, George!" his mother said. "Now finish your cereal, march right upstairs, and start cleaning up your room!" . . .

. . . "I don't want that crybaby in *my* room!" George howled. "He's afraid of thunder and lightning worse than Sally. Mom, you can't *do* this to me!"

"George Meredith Nelson," Father began in that special slow way. "Not another word. Do you hear?" He pushed back his chair and glared at his son.

George gulped down his cereal and milk, excused himself, and scooted out of the room. But all the way up the stairs he grunted and groaned and thumped his feet as if he were carrying an elephant on his back . . .

His parents now discuss the situation a bit more, and sister Sally asks a few pertinent questions and comments further on their coming guest:

"I wish Chip were a girl," Sally said. "It would be like having a sister. I'd like sharing my room with a sister. Boys aren't much fun. Except Chip isn't too bad. At least he isn't when he comes to visit us. He always plays with me. But I guess that's because George won't play with him much . . ."

. . . After the dishes were put away, Sally ran upstairs to investigate the thumps and bumps in her brother's room . . .

George is still very cross and uncooperative. Mother comes up and reinforces previous orders and suggests that he store his overflowing belongings in the attic space over the family garage. Sally says:

"I'll help you carry this stuff over . . ."

"Aw—all right. But be careful. I suppose Chip will tag along everywhere I go. I suppose he'll want to join my Indian Club and everything."

"Will you let him?" Sally asked.

George stared at her as if she'd lost her mind. "I should say not! We'd as soon have a *girl* in the club as that scaredy-cat cousin of mine."

Sally's face turned bright pink. George let her go into the small attic space over the garage sometimes, because Mother made him. But he never allowed her to come anywhere near his precious Indian tepee set up among the apple trees in the back field where the Indian Club met. And now he wasn't going to let Chip in, either.

"Phooey to Chip Nelson," George said, clattering down the stairs with four airplanes and a feathered Indian head-dress trailing over his arm. "I'm going to take all my Indian stuff out, too, so your friend, Chip, won't get any ideas right off. Anyhow, he's only eight years old and in the third grade!" George said it as if that were a crime, just because he was a big, husky ten-year-old in the fifth grade. "And don't you go telling him about our Indian Club, either," he hollered back to Sally over his shoulder.

And so, almost entirely through conversation, the stage is set for poor Chip's arrival as an unwelcome guest, at least as far as his cousin is concerned. (The whole chapter is a kind of "camera view" of the scene and situation before Chip comes on and takes over as the viewpoint character.)

We know the boy is timid—he's afraid of thunder and lightning, and George has called him a sissy. We suspect that this will cause all sorts of problems and conflicts, not the least of which will be the efforts and frustrations to gain membership in the Indian Club, since it has been frequently mentioned. And, though very little physical description has been used, each of the characters has begun to emerge as a certain kind of individual—through dialogue.

Some Don'ts and Do's

Don't have conversations taking place in empty space. Weave in background details of where the action (dialogue is a form of "action") is taking place. Don't have invisible people talking, either. Let the reader *see* them as they speak—their facial expressions and gestures. And by all means, "cue" the speeches to the speakers.

Tag Lines to Conversations

Never have a page of dialogue—even between only two characters—where the person speaking is not identified from time to time. The reader never wants to grope back and start all over again to find out whether it was Andy or Jack who spoke in the sixth paragraph.

To preface or conclude every speech with the word "said" is dull, but vary with care. An over-zealous beginner with a thesaurus syndrome might achieve a hair-raising effect like this: asked, inquired, rejoined, asserted, retorted, remarked, insinuated, mumbled, muttered, grumbled, bawled, shrieked, whispered, thundered, cried, howled, yelled, hissed—and maybe ululated, for good measure. While this assortment in a single tale might have a horrid fascination for the reader, it will never get by a sober editor.

Notice how in the preceding excerpt the dialogue was tagged with "said" and a few synonyms, and how sometimes it was leavened by a bit of action or emotion, placed before a speech instead of after it, to change the pattern on the page and to relieve the reader's eye and mental ear.

Here are some tags to avoid because they create an incongruous effect which may distract the reader from the flow of your story. Time and again I've stopped in reading student manuscripts in which a character performs like this: " 'I don't know,' he *shrugged*"—or, " 'Never!' she *seethed*"—or " 'Don't do it,' she *hissed*." You can't possibly *hiss* that last word with sibilants—"s" sounds. And, if you wish to have a smile or a shrug accompany a line of dialogue, put a decent little period at the end of the speech, and then say: "He smiled." Or—without the period—"he said, smiling."

Beware of characters who are so happy or so good-natured that they "beam" their remarks. Quite an impossible feat, you know. Instead of writing, " 'Oh, thank you,' Sally beamed," say " 'Oh, thank you.' (Period) Sally beamed."

If your character "laughs" a remark, first be sure it is something to laugh about. Quite often, in beginners' stories, it is not. And even if it is, take care to use the word smoothly. " 'How funny,' Joan said, and laughed" reads better than "laughed Joan." Pay attention to small details, and the results will be better writing and less risk of jolting the reader out of the illusion of your story—possibly for keeps.

To involve readers in their story, some writers prefer to set the stage, bring on the story actors, give them something to do to catch the reader's attention, *and then have their people speak.* However, a catchy opening can be created with dialogue too, if the very first speech indicates that there is an interesting problem or situation confronting the characters. In a short story a dialogue opening can save a lot of words and plunge the reader right into the heart of the matter.

First Aid for Ailing Dialogue

If you experience difficulty in writing dialogue, read some plays and try your hand at writing one. The dramatist is entirely dependent on the spoken word to carry the action along and reveal the ramifications of the plot. Such a procedure might free your own gift for creating dialogue. Since you are concerned with writing for young people, read plays written especially for them.

However you do it, master dialogue you must, for dialogue is one of the most useful techniques of fiction because it can perform so many story-telling tasks. Study, read, observe. Work on your characters until they come alive—then let *them* do the talking!

Chapter 8

The Story Problem . . .
Motivation . . . and Significance

If a character has no problem to solve, there is no point in writing about him. It is the urgent problem confronting your main character and how he goes about solving it—against stalwart opposition, of course—that gives him appeal and involves the reader in your tale.

What does your main character want? *What vitally important thing must he have that he cannot easily get?* This you must decide early in your story planning, because his *want* or *need* will not only indicate the kind of main character he will be, but also what other people will do to support or oppose him.

In writing for juniors, the conflict must interest the children of the age for which you are writing. The teen-age girl will be much more interested in problems involving the social success of the storybook heroine, in her romances or career ambitions, than she will be in getting the heroine's maiden aunt married. The ten-year-old will be more intrigued by a book dealing with a "Horse for Keeps," than in getting great-uncle Henry a fancy chess set. The easy-to-read-age lad will be more interested in a story of how the neighborhood's kids got themselves a clubhouse than in how somebody's big sister got herself a prom date with the football captain. Tailor your problems to your potential audience; make them the kind that children of that age can conceivably solve.

Three Types of Problems You Might Use

1. *Purpose Problem.* The character has a goal. He knows what he wants. It might be a career, a place on the team, the lead in a play, or a chance to take ballet lessons. It might be a dog or a horse, perhaps a bicycle or a car (for a specific worthy purpose). Whatever it is, it must be something he'll be willing to fight for with tremendous drive and force.

2. *Situation Problem.* The main character wants to change an existing situation, or a situation brought about at the beginning of the story. He does so with a great deal of discouraging struggle and effort.

The situation might be caused by moving into a new neighborhood, going away to school, losing one's parents, having a parent remarry, or suffering a serious accident, which destroys the young person's original goal in life (as in my book, *Ballet Teacher*).

3. *Decision Problems.* Here the main character must decide which way to go, right or left, up or down. Often a moral decision is involved in this kind of conflict—personal integrity, or the effect such a decision will have on others. It should be similar to a tug-of-war, and for greatest reader interest and suspense, the pulls should be equal, so that the final decision will be very hard to make—and is made, in the end, only because of the strengths with which you have endowed your hero.

Beware of letting your characters have cheap or trivial goals. The boy who merely wants to humiliate someone is not worthy of being a hero. The new girl who longs to be liked by her classmates can be made a sympathetic heroine—and all the more if she is awkward in her attempts; but the vain girl who sets out to steal boy friends from other girls is cheap and petty and does not deserve to be made the heroine of a story. (But she might make good opposition and the reader can dislike her heartily.)

Why must the main character get whatever it is he's after? What would happen if he failed? The consequences of failure should be serious, as the reader (and the character) should be well aware. Thus the problem should be a vital one to your hero or heroine. (*Vital* comes from the Latin word *vitalis,* meaning "life." Therefore the problem in your story should be—relatively —one of "life and death" importance.) Upon its solution should depend the main character's happiness; and you should involve your reader so thoroughly that he will cheer for, fear for, and support the hero to the last period in your manuscript.

Motivation—The WHY Behind the WHAT

If a boy wants a dog because everybody else on the block has one, or if a girl wants a fancy poodle only because she thinks they're "cute," the action of the story will be weakly motivated. The reader will not care if these characters get what they want, and certainly it will make no real difference in the lives of either one.

On the other hand, if a boy wants a dog because he is a lonely orphan being reared as a "duty" by a cold, strict aunt or uncle, his motivation becomes more meaningful. The dog would fill the boy's need for a playmate and friend. The motives for this boy's efforts would be strong, and the reader would be entirely in sympathy with him.

One of the basic truths of which the experienced writer and editor are aware is that *strong motives make for strong, convincing stories and weak motives make for weak and unconvincing tales.* Your main character's problem, want, or need must not only be something worth fighting for, but it must also be the sort of thing *this* particular character might *logically* need and want and fight for. The conviction that lies behind the logic is backed up by *motivation—the reason that prompts your character to take action to get what he wants.*

Motives are urges, conscious or subconscious, that lie behind everything we do. These urges stem from our personalities which, psychologically speaking, are the sum of all our physical, mental, emotional, and social characteristics. Some of these urges are instinctive, some emotional—and some are fostered by cold logic and design. All of them can furnish motives for the problems and upheavals created in fictional lives.

Three Powerful Urges—for All Ages

The life urge, the drive for self-preservation or survival, heads the list. The struggle to maintain life might be a problem, and certainly a powerful motivation, in a hair-raising adventure tale or a mystery.

Love in all its forms, among children as well as adults is strong motivation for many actions. This *includes* loyalty as well as pity. Youthful romance can present many problems and poignant heartaches—and puppy love can be a painful experience.

The power urge can be used both positively and negatively in stories. Your hero might long for a certain high office because of a genuine desire to serve. The antagonist or villain fights for the same office, but his motive is a desire to dominate, to use the office to further his own selfish ends.

There are many other urgent motivating factors, but these are enough to give you an idea of how they can be used. In the course of the story, the writer must let the reader know the motives or forces driving his characters. Then the reader will be able to recognize the *significance* of the various actions in the working out of the story problem.

To understand what makes certain people want certain things, you need to know something about human psychology—but not so much that you wind up writing psychological treatises and fictional case histories instead of stories.

Your own life experience and common sense can be a reliable guide for your writing, but it is also reassuring to have the backing of experts for your own beliefs and conclusions. To that end, you might read *Psychology Made Simple,* by Abraham P. Sperling, Ph.D., for a broad view of the subject. Several chapters deal with childhood and adolescence, and many others are of considerable value to the writer.

Youth, the Years from Ten to Sixteen, by Dr. Gesell and his associates, is a goldmine for the juvenile writer. Don't attempt to wade through the entire tome. Select the age bracket in which you are working and read about it. It's all in layman's language. Dr. Gesell covers the first five years of life and the years from five to ten in a similar manner.

Between Parent and Child, Between Parent and Teen-Ager,

Between Teacher and Child, by Dr. Haim G. Ginott, psychologist, is a guidance trio filled with warmth and wisdom and love of people—especially children. These books will give you a better understanding of today's young people—and the grownups around them. They can also provide you with a practically endless fund of characters, characteristics, themes, problems, incidents, and motivations that can lead straight to successful story plots. Dr. Ginott delivers his wisdom simply, practically, with a leavening of humor. If you learn nothing more from him than that "Mistakes are for correcting"—by everybody, young and old—you will have learned a spirit-freeing, uncrippling truth you can expound again and again in storyform. These books are available in Avon paperbacks. Don't walk, *run* for your copies.

Be alert, always, to new books and articles by children's specialists, and to radio and TV discussions. Browse through the child guidance shelves of your community library and your local bookstore. And remember, no matter what you know, you can demonstrate it to your readers only by means of a story. So, become aware, but not bogged down with knowledge.

Significance—Having Something to Say

In order to have something to say, it is no more necessary to have travelled the whole world—physically—or to have undergone unusual experiences and the gamut of emotions—personally—than it is necessary to commit murder in order to write a murder mystery. You need only to live in a world of people, with all your senses tuned, and to observe everyone and everything about you with sensitivity and compassion.

In my *Reader's Digest Encyclopedic Dictionary,* the word *compassion* is defined as "pity for the suffering or distress of another, with the desire to help or spare." The cool and detached attitude is not for the writer—and woe to you if it creeps into your writing. Instead of significance, your writing will then reflect indifference, even callousness, which will chill your reader.

Having "something to say" does not mean you must have some earth-shaking revelation. It means, simply, that you have a very strong interest in your subject and are sufficiently informed about it—and skilled in your craft—to write about it meaningfully for the reader.

Theme and Variations

Story significance, besides reflecting basic human needs, also involves a lesson in living, in human attitudes; it might point up a "moral"—the kind found in Aesop, and in books or proverbs or epigrams—*but never stated in words.* Your theme must come through the action and reaction of your story characters.

These themes—proverbs, maxims, epigrams, wise-saws—are a crystallization of wide-spread human experience. That is precisely what makes them interesting and understandable to the reader. The common experience they summarize makes it possible for him to identify with the story characters. So, here is another addition to that helpful file of yours, a section labeled "Themes." From now on, distill the stories you read to their basic theme and jot this down. When you're casting about for story material, one of these may prove a springboard to a sparkling, fresh idea.

In one of my short stories with a Korean background, *"Donkey Cough"* (the Korean term for whooping cough), I used the theme that *Understanding and helpfulness overcome suspicion and distrust and lead to friendship.* If you break down this thought, you'll see that it contains the capsule synopsis of a story. *Understanding and helpfulness* suggests the characters; *suspicion and distrust* suggests the problem; *overcome,* the conflict and the outcome; and *lead to friendship,* the resolution and happy ending.

Although I wrote of an American missionary family and an influential Korean family, and practical medicine as opposed to superstition to illustrate my theme, that same theme can be used again and again with variations. All that is necessary is a change of location, people, and the specific problem. The end result would be the same, and yet it would be an entirely different story.

This is where the value of a theme you can state to yourself lies: when you break it down so that it suggests characters, problems, action, and a solution, all you need to do is create the characters to carry it out, or *prove* the statement. To be useful to you in this way, the basic theme should be stated in such a way that it suggests action-conflict. *Honesty is the best policy* may be true, but it does not suggest a definite course of story action. Stated as *Honesty can triumph over dishonesty*, you immediately have an honest and a dishonest character to work with. *Triumph* suggests conflict as well as the outcome for the honest character.

Actually it might be said that all stories have a theme, an underlying idea. As Arthur Sullivant Hoffman puts it:

> . . . there can be no course of action that does not illustrate life-truths, however commonplace they may be . . . Even the most elementary plot illustrates such general truths as 'Faint heart ne'er won fair lady' or the coveted job or the buried treasure . . .

And, he points out, such themes come so naturally that neither the author nor the reader gives conscious thought to them.

You don't need to strain for a meaningful theme before you write your story; if you have strong ethical convictions, they will come through in your writing. If you believe that a small boy should not be tormented by a bully, you will create a story in which the little fellow will somehow get the best of the big meany. (Theme: Through wit and courage, the small and weak *can* overcome the big and bad.) David and Goliath, along with any number of old fairy tales, illustrates this popular theme. Basic story themes are not original—only the variations on the theme are.

Theme is your melody, the motive, the dominant *idea* you develop through your story. This is what the story is *about*. At the same time, in the larger, universal sense, theme is the nugget of human wisdom illuminated by your story. It can be expressed through a familiar proverb or paraphrased to mean the same thing—if you are required to define it. This is what is meant when you are asked to *tell what your story is about in a single sentence*. Editors are always on the alert for stories which deftly handle meaningful universal themes because these are the plus features which make stories worthwhile. Sound themes make for profitable, long-lasting books and stories which live on in anthologies and school reading texts.

A writer must believe in what his story is about. If he doesn't, his writing will be thin, not convincing, as rejection slips will be quick to confirm. Significant factors cannot be tacked on to make a story "worthwhile."

Even the youngest children are concerned with story themes of universal significance. In her book, *Writing for Young Children*, Claudia Lewis says:

> Children . . . begin almost as soon as they are born to touch the problems, the concerns, the themes, that become the mainstreams of our lives . . .
>
> Stories that present, either realistically or symbolically, the problems and emotional situations faced by real children in and out of their families, at different stages of their growth; stories of warmth; of . . . courage . . . that lead even the small and weak, or the old and worn-out, to successful achievement; stories of the overcoming of fear and danger; stories that bring new perspectives and discoveries flashing onto the page, with surprise or suspense, or adventurous turns and twists; stories made for laughter and peopled with ourselves, as we are, and as we would like to be—these are essentially what all children are looking for . . .

The Basic Needs

Children's fundamental needs are no different from yours and mine—or from the concerns of the teen-age boy or girl.

1. *The Need to Love and Be Loved.* Everyone, in all times and places, has the need to be loved and to love in return. No one ever outgrows the need for love. Children deprived of love do not develop into well-balanced human beings. Whether this basic emotional need is fulfilled or not affects our relationships and attitudes toward others. Stories of deep and moving significance can be woven around this subject.

2. *The Need to Belong.* First to be accepted by one's family, then by one's peers, is often desperately desired by children of all ages. In some cases there is only wistful, inarticulate longing—as in Eleanor Estes' *The Hundred Dresses.* Or sheer determination,

as shown by Nan Gilbert's trio of high school sufferers in *The Unchosen*, girls bound together by their "outness" and vying for a place in the exclusive, happy "in" world. Trying to fulfill this need can lead youngsters to all sorts of extremes in conduct such as "showing off," becoming a toady, or joining a street gang. Becoming a "rebel," a hippie, or whatever happens to be the *in* thing to be when you're *out* and deeply hurt and resentful, is another compensation taken by frustrated young people. However, positive acts as well as negative ones can result from rejection.

3. *The Need to Achieve.* To *do* or *be* something, which not only gives one a feeling of personal satisfaction and worth, but also elicits respect from others, is a built-in hunger in many people. Sometimes rejection by one's peers becomes ambition's spur and the victim strives to excel in some field in order to prove himself before others. Achievement is a useful theme for stories, and my books, *Bonnie,* and *Beth Hilton, Model,* are built around it.

Overcoming physical handicaps can also provide important fiction themes, especially if the character has to learn to live with them, and not feel sorry for himself. It is also important for the whole in body not to show pity for the handicapped. One of the best treatments of this subject to come across my review desk is Phyllis Whitney's *Secret of the Emerald Star*. Every child who reads this book will ever after regard blind people with new understanding and respect.

4. *The Need for Security—Material, Emotional, Spiritual.* To be secure means to be free from anxieties and fears—a utopian dream on a par with the lip-happy formula for contentment: to have a million dollars. No one is completely free of anxieties or fears. *How* these are faced, or not faced, provides innumerable story themes for the writer.

Youngsters can be caught in the middle of adult strivings for *material* wealth—or even bare existence—and suffer from the attendant anxiety and fear, resentment, envy, and frustration. The youthful character can be badly warped by such tensions, or tempered and strengthened by adversity—depending on the influences he comes under.

Children can thrive under the most adverse physical and social conditions if the home atmosphere is happy—and the writer can demonstrate this truth, as Sydney Taylor did in her prize-winner, *All of a Kind Family,* a book about immigrants with very little money, five little girls, a full quota of vicissitudes, yet a rich and satisfying life in New York's lower east side.

And, since today's stories for children do not shrink away from realism, the opposite picture can be drawn of the result of a lack of family unity.

Emotional security involves and depends on all the other needs.

Spiritual security. A sense of values and moral purpose often comes from religious faith, but in fiction, moral and spiritual considerations are best illustrated within the framework of family life and through character action and reaction. Such stories can serve as guideposts for courses of action contemplated or taken by young readers.

5. *The Need to Know* has filled our bookshelves with tomes on every conceivable subject. Even quiz books, those fascinating grab bags of interesting facts, fall into this important category. Small children show their curiosity when they lie on their stomachs and inspect blades of grass and study insect life most adults walk over unheeding. People from time immemorial have sought to know the *how* and *why* of things. This need is responsible for inventions and discoveries and flights into space—*and it is your reason for reading this book!*

If you use any of the fundamental needs of all people everywhere, no matter what their age or station in life, you have a powerful magnet for holding the reader's interest, because the basic needs you dramatize are his needs also. But have a care. As Emerson put it, "The universal does not attract us until housed in an individual." Ralph Bunche distilled the thought further, by saying, "If you want to put an idea across, wrap it up in a man."

Significance and emotion are tied together so closely that one springs from the other. If you want the reader to have a strong emotional reaction to your story, you must have something to say. But evoking emotion also depends upon the quality of your writing. The techniques you can use to obtain that emotional response I shall take up in the next chapter.

Chapter 9

Making the Reader Feel
Emotion . . . Mood . . . Atmosphere

To be moved—to "get a feeling" or an *emotional experience*—is the reader's chief goal in reading fiction; though he may not realize it, *you* must! Any book or story which leaves the reader unmoved is not likely to be a success.

It is the magic of fiction that allows the young reader to "escape" from his ordinary day-to-day doings and to live more fully in a heightened, high-lighted version of life, with adventure possible at every turn of the page. The reader's emotional involvement in a story effects this escape because to feel it is to experience. Your job is to *make him feel*, but not in a free-fall tumble into any emotion. He must feel *what* you want him to feel, *where* you want him to feel it, and *when*. His emotions must be under your control, and that control is exercised by the choice of words you use. This choice, in turn, is governed by what you know about human emotion, and what you know of your craft.

The books recommended in the previous chapter will be helpful in the study of emotions, too. But as a writer you are not concerned with the clinical aspects of emotion. You do not analyze it for the reader, you dramatize it. What you need is a practical understanding of children and grownups, an awareness of how they are apt to feel and appear under the stress of varying circumstances. For this understanding you have the best possible source of observation: *yourself.*

The Basic Emotions

In the course of your life you have felt many emotions, major and minor, and observed them in others. No one is a stranger to love, anger, fear, hope, despair, grief, joy. These are fundamental and universal. And so are the minor ones, which include jealousy, envy, loneliness, self-pity, vanity, ambition, greed, humility, stubbornness, courage, timidity, boredom, amusement, pride, suspicion, shame, guilt, gratitude. In some degree everyone, even the small child, has experienced these.

Remember the classics mentioned earlier? What makes these books live on and on? It is their appeal to human emotions, their genuine portrayal of people and their feelings. In every era people differ greatly in their thoughts and particular wants—the things they believe indispensable to their happiness, the gods they worship, and the customs they follow. But *basic emotions are universal, and physical sensations are common to every man, regardless of his age or the time in which he lives.* You can always count on reaching your reader through the primary emotions.

Yet it isn't all that simple. You know what these emotions are. But to *know* is not enough for the writer. *You must be able to express the emotion in words,* for it is only through words that you can transmit the feeling to your reader. And these must not be glib cliches ("She was bursting with happiness," "The air was charged with anger"), but carefully chosen words which make the emotion poignant, understandable, "see-able" and "feel-able" to your young audience.

To have an element of reality, your story people must also feel, as well as think and act, and they must react to the emotions of those around them.

William MacKeller's book, *Wee Joseph*, deals with a familiar topic—a boy and his dog. But there is vigor and a Highland freshness in the treatment, a delicate sensitivity and a complete absence of sentimentality. It's a book well worth studying.

Young Davie Cambell is about to acquire a dog—of sorts—for a sixpence, and he is overjoyed:

> . . . A slow pounding came from under his blue wool
> jersey where his heart was . . . He put out his hands. The

farmer placed the little dog between the cupped fingers. For a long moment Davie just stood, too filled with emotion to speak. Gently he eased his forefinger down the little dog's back . . .

But when he brings the puppy home, his father is anything but pleased; to him the dog is worthless. A less skilled writer might have said, "His father was furiously angry." But this is how Mr. MacKeller puts it:

> The silence was thick in the kitchen. It seemed to drip from the very beams in the ceiling. Then it was torn asunder by the sound of his father's voice . . . The voice was a terrible loudness in Davie's ears. It was hard to think. There was a queer spinning and tumbling in his mind, and it was impossible to sort the words out. The words that needed to be spoken if Joseph were to stay . . .

Wee Joseph is intended for the child aged eight to twelve, but a reader of any age can appreciate this crackling, crushing anger and Davie's desperate confusion and fright.

Emotions—from Experience

Emotion never stops touching our lives. It springs from many causes, and we are affected by it every waking moment. Train yourself to observe the signs of emotion in people of all ages, small children at play or in fights or frights or temper tantrums; expressions you catch on the faces of friends, neighbors, strangers in a crowd. How do they *look?* What exactly do they *do? say?* What is the look of anger, tenderness, compassion, tension?

How did *you* feel when you were waiting for someone very dear to you and the hours dragged by and the person did not come? Or the telephone did not ring? Did you make up waiting games to occupy your mind, or did you pace about, wringing your hands?

Analyzing your own past experiences—when you're sufficiently distant from the happening to see it outside yourself as well as from the inside—will help you understand how other people might feel under similar circumstances, and help you tell the reader, so he too will understand. Everything is grist for that writing mill of ours—the remembrance of the report card we hated to show Dad, the loss of a pet, that very first invitation to a dance, even a car smashup you might have been in. I adapted my vivid recollection of an auto accident for *Ballet Teacher,* and readers have told me how *real* it seemed. It was!

In your reading of published material, note how the authors create their effects, how they catch at your feelings and involve you to the point where you're living the story right along with the main character—*empathizing* with him.

Sympathy and Empathy

The sympathetic rapport between the writer and his character should be so great that to all intents and purposes *he* becomes that character. He can then think, feel, see, smell, touch, *and react* to everything that affects that character as if it were all happening to himself. This kind of entering into another's being is called *empathy*: feeling *as* the subject, or character. *Sympathy*, however, is a different degree of emotional response. If you sympathize with someone, you feel *for* that person, but the twinges are not nearly so strong.

Facts and Feelings

If the story has a vital problem, the emotion will grow out of the dramatic situation—out of your story people—and how they feel about what is happening. A story is composed of *facts*—the happenings—and *feelings*—the emotional effect these happenings have on the story actors involved.

This is where the author takes control of the reader through technique—the know-how of his craft.

As you list the characters in planning your story, write down opposite the name of each character the specific emotion you want the reader to feel toward him. This will help you be consistent in your characterization, too.

How the story people feel toward each other depends on the

course of the plot. Feelings can create all sorts of clashes which result in story drama: younger sister Chris may have love and admiration for her older sister, Helen; but secretly shy, introverted Helen is jealous of the younger girl who makes friends easily wherever she goes.* The dominant traits with which you endow your story actors affect not only the action, but also the emotional tone of the story. And you must devise incidents and situations that will allow these character traits, and their corresponding emotions, full scope for expression.

You cannot merely name an emotion and have the reader see and feel it. The reader must be *shown* the emotion in action and reaction before he can "experience" it himself through his reading. He will see it if you give him John's outward signs of anger to look at, and he will *feel with* the character as you tell how John feels inside and what he does as a result:

> John stared up into Butch Jones' sneering face and his stomach tightened. His legs began to shake. His hands curled into fists, the nails biting into the flesh. The blood began to pound in his head and his chest felt so tight, he could scarcely breathe. He saw the towering big bully through a kind of red haze. And then, without thinking of the consequences he lunged at Butch, both arms flailing . . .

That's *anger.* You know it and the reader knows it. And even with this economy of words you know that John is small because Butch "towers" over him, and yet anger—which ignores logic—makes the smaller boy "lunge" at the "big bully."

Whenever I read this passage in class someone always asks, "What happened? Did John get the best of the bully?"

I don't know. This is not from a story. It's just a made-up passage to illustrate a point. But the question proves that it has enough *feeling* in it to generate interest.

Learn to know the visible and audible signs of different emotions, the physical way in which they are expressed, and use these correctly. If you were to say: "Susie jumped up and down *hopelessly*" your reader would recognize it at once as nonsense. People jump for joy, in impatience. But without hope, the whole body droops and there's no impulse to jump.

---

*See *Five in a Tent,* by Victoria Furman.

"Her eyes *flashed* indifference . . ." is from a student manuscript. But *flash* indicates a lively emotion—anger, suspicion, interest perhaps, rather than "indifference," which has a lackluster quality.

In an angry quarrel you do not say, "Kindly close that wideopen orifice from which all that nasty language is coming." You say instead, "SHUT UP!" Could anything be clearer? The choice of words is governed by emotion also. If you know and *feel* the emotion yourself while you are writing, the chances are you'll use the right words.

To demonstrate emotion in your story characters you can use dialogue; thoughts—of the viewpoint character, of course; and descriptive action. You can heighten the whole effect through the *mood* you create.

Your Story's Mood and Atmosphere

Some pages back I said that your story's theme might be called its "melody." Following this analogy, we might then call your story's *mood* its "key"—high, low; major, minor. The mood or "key" sets your story's tone. Is it gay, comic, fantastic, sharp with strife, or somber with painful social problems? A story should have an over-all mood: romantic, mysterious, serious, adventurous, humorous—and although the action and emotion in different scenes may vary greatly, the story as a whole must never lose its pervading dominant air. Whatever setting, description, dialogue, or characterization is used, it should be unified with the mood you want to create and with the emotion you want to rouse in your reader.

In life chance and coincidence are often present; all sorts of things happen without logic. But a story is an *illusion* of real life, and therefore it must be a unified, artistic presentation, with nothing left to the vagaries of chance, not even the weather. *All story effects must be pre-planned for that over-all effect you want.* Knowing how to plan and what to plan and why makes all the difference between a professional and an amateur literary performance.

Chapter 10

Sensory Details
and What They Do to Feelings

All that we know about our world, whatever our age, has been learned through our five senses: sight, hearing, touch, taste, smell—and the "sixth sense"—our reaction to what the other five have told us. Wherever we go, we take our senses—and the reactions which affect our feelings—with us.

How often have you said, "I can't help how I feel, can I?" We are all apt to see things through the filter of our emotional state at a given moment, and this personal mood can color our attitude toward everything around us. *Moods can—and should—color your characters' thinking and responses, too.*

Children react strongly to the color, size, shape, sound, smell, and *feel* of things. And, as Ursula Nordstrom of Harper and Row says, "We must remember that children are *new,* and the whole world is new to them." Therefore writers must learn to see the world with young eyes and through the filter of young moods, in order to present youthful adventures through the viewpoint of young story people.

A flash of light—sudden darkness; heat—cold; something rough to the touch—something soft or smooth; sweet—sour—bitter; pleasing scents—disagreeable odors; a loud noise—a tinkle of melody. What are these sensory impressions *like*—to young people?

Too often beginning writers assume that they *know,* until the moment of truth when they must put their "knowledge" down in words. Then they suddenly find their minds cluttered with stereotypes and blocked to original thought. To exercise your word-picture-making imagination, gather sensory impressions and practice writing them down in colorful, fresh phrases and figures of speech. File them for easy reference, and they'll be there, ready for tailoring to a particular story and its characters. Use words which will create images in the minds of readers for whom your writing is intended. Flat, colorless statements won't do it. To a grownup, his leg may be asleep, but to a child "it feels like gingerale, all tingley."* Compare the following passages for sensory detail and appeal:

> The day became cloudy. The waves began to roll on the beach. Later it grew foggy. And then the awful noise came . . .

The sensory details are nil, and the only sentence that carries a smidgen of interest is the last one. Note the effect when the reader does have something to go on:

> The day which had been so bright and sunny abruptly clouded over. The cove became gray, with whitecaps rushing in and breaking on the beach . . . As the wind freshened, the waves slapped against the stern of the *Showboat*, frothing upward as if they wanted to come aboard. Then the wind died and fog rolled in. It was as if great rolls of gray cotton were being fanned shoreward by some unseen giant . . .
>
> When it grew dark the fog became oppressive, wet and mushy like damp cotton. The Taylors could hear distant bellows of foghorns on passing ships outside the cove. They sounded like monsters with belly-aches, Ginny said . . . Then, all at once, a dreadful noise burst through the fog, quite near the *Showboat*. It was a shrieking, wailing, quite the loudest sound they had ever heard . . . †

When You CAN Do Something About the Weather

Everybody talks about the weather—but a writer can *do* something about it. He can make his own. Story weather can play an important role by helping to set an emotional mood or even pro-

---

*See the sections on figures of speech in Chapter 18.
†From *Showboat Holiday*.

viding a climax for your tale. Notice how often mystery and suspense stories utilize the terrors of nature, uncontrollable by man,
with all the stops out and all the sound effects turned up full blast.

When you use weather in a story, your imagination will come
to your aid *if* you give it experience to feed upon. An English
proverb states: "Seeing is believing, but feeling is the naked
truth." To get at that "naked truth," *you* must look, listen, touch,
sniff, taste, then strip the sensory perception down to the "naked
truth," and tell your reader about it in such precise and colorful
terms that he will experience the same feeling also.

Study the elements. Rain, snow, wind, fog—all these oblig-
ingly repeat themselves. Next time it storms, get yourself a writing sample. See how a storm blows up, how it breaks, how it
blows away. What is it like seen from outdoors? From shelter
inside the house? How might a child, a teen-age boy, an old
woman feel about a blizzard or a hurricane? How do you react
to being caught in the rain? Though I'm not suggesting you go
out and catch pneumonia, if you should, pay attention! Remember what it was *like*—reconstruct it as soon as you can after you're
on the mend—and jot it down, just in case one of your characters
ever has to have it in the course of your story plot.

An ice storm that left us without electric power for eight days
has served me a number of times in stories—as a thing of beauty
in *Buttons and Beaux*, and as a dreadful ordeal in *Beth Hilton,
Model*:

> . . . The rain had changed to sleet and . . . it grew colder
> . . . with an increasing roar of wind . . . Evergreens were
> tossing their ice-coated branches and bending over like giants
> in agony. As Beth watched, [from a window] a huge ball of
> earth came up . . . a tree fell with a thunderous crash . . . and
> then another and another . . .

Later, when the group of storm-marooned models need ice for
the non-functioning refrigerator and for drinking water, Beth
ventures outside:

> She had taken a piece of wood from the fireplace and now
> gave a thick icicle a whack. It cracked off and tumbled down
> —only she wasn't fast enough to duck and it caught her on the
> head. A black curtain seemed to drop before her eyes, and
> then a shower of stars sprayed over it . . .

I can vouch for every star! Personal experience is of great value, but as a writer you don't need to go to the lengths that I did. You can invent and expand and imagine a great deal.

A Calendar of Weather and Other Useful Facts

Much of the material mentioned in this chapter came from a loose-leaf notebook bristling with index tabs that I've kept over the years as a catch-all for random observations. Once, riding through a hilly countryside, I saw the contour-plowed fields as "rivers of chocolate," to the delight of a small, sweet-toothed companion. Another time, looking out the windows of my mother's apartment in New York, on a foggy afternoon in March, I had "a strange feeling of being suspended in fog over the city—and the top of the Empire State Building floating toward me out of the haze . . . "

Helen R. Sattley must have seen something like this and had a similar reaction, because she captured it in a picture story, *The Day the Empire State Building Went Visiting*. So you see how useful such impressions can be.

Summer . . . Fall . . . Winter . . . Spring . . . What are they *like?* The whole round of the seasons—at home, abroad, in the country, city, at the seashore or the mountains, or the desert, has over the years found its way into my notebook. The words help me recapture the feelings I need—the searing heat of sun on bare skin—on a freezing mid-winter day—or the dry crunching squeak of snow under boots—in June!

The mere act of setting down impressions fixes them more firmly in the mind. It is the sort of knowledge that helps to put sureness and speed into a writer's fingers as they fly over the typewriter keys, building a bridge of words to the reader's mind and heart.

Background—a Sense of Place

To have reality for the reader, your story must happen some-where on the globe—in a certain country, in a particular city, village, farm, or wilderness. This is your *place*. The more you can narrow the place down to a particular spot, the better, because always it is the particular, not the general, that transmits a sense of here and now reality to your reader.

This particular place, then, must have a definite *background setting*, against which the action will be visualized. And it must be complete with all the things of life likely to surround your characters: a house, or castle, or hovel, or tent; appropriate scenery, flora and fauna; particular views from different windows; furniture and bric-a-brac; pots and pans and strings and things—the objects which tie the story people to life as it is lived in their time, place, and social atmosphere.

Social environment means a manner of life as well as the background setting in your story. In writing for young people, you will usually have some sort of family life. Is the family rich, poor, middle class? Are they city people, small-town folk, farm dwellers, seafarers, mountain people, ranchers, migrant workers?

The WHERE of It

Wherever and however you choose to locate your story, make the setting vivid. But avoid piling on too many details. The modern reader is not pleased by lengthy passages of "scenery" which slow down the story. His reaction in such instances is to skip—and if he skips too much, he may skip right out of your story and turn on the TV. Hold him by building descriptive detail into the action of your story people.

If the location you've selected is an actual place, read up on it (see the chapters on research in Part II). This information will be a plus feature. Many a book has been firmly entrenched on important buying lists because of such extra background research.

No one can doubt the authority of a descriptive setting like this or miss the atmosphere it exudes or wonder about the *where* of it:

> The city that rose beyond them shimmered, almost drained of color, in the glare of Egyptian noon. Doorways were blue-black in white buildings, alleys were plunged in shadow; the gay colors of the sails and hulls that crowded the harbor seemed faded and

indistinct, and even the green of the Nile was overlaid by a blinding surface glitter. Only the sky was vivid, curving in a high blue arch over ancient Menfe . . .*

Time—the WHEN of It

Unless the reader is told almost at once *when* the story is taking place, he will assume that it is the present. So if on page eleven he suddenly discovers that the year is 1820 he'll become understandably confused. The mental images he's made will disintegrate, and with them, quite possibly, all interest in the story.

Properly handled, your story's *time* helps to establish the atmosphere. It can affect the story's mood and its emotional tone; certainly the kind of characters you use and how you characterize them (as present day or period people or historical characters); and the background against which the action takes place and all the "things of life" with which you fill it.

Authors, realizing the importance of establishing the time especially when it is not the present, occasionally state it in their very first sentence: "It was May, 1918, that a new friend and companion came into my life . . ." Sterling North begins in *Rascal.*

When Too Much Is Too Bad

Sensory, emotion-producing material must be kept under control. No matter how moving the scene you're writing, you must develop the ability to be both *inside,* in a state of complete empathy, and at the same time *outside,* looking on and describing. If your tendency is to overwrite, to spill over with emotion and cry right into your typewriter, be prepared to cut copiously when you revise.

The most important emotion the writer must aim for in his story as a whole is the reader's complete satisfaction with the way it all turned out. Sometimes this response is a wistful sigh because the story did end, and the reader has had to say good-

*From *Mara, Daughter of the Nile,* by Eloise Jarvis McGraw.

bye to all those delightful story people. Then you're likely to get letters asking you to continue Bonnie's or Chip's adventures.

But beware of stirring feelings too deeply. The reader's purpose in reading is to "escape" his everyday world, to live more excitingly—but not to wallow in grief, or experience too much unhappiness or pain. Be sparing in your details of accidents, bereavements, operations, and amputations.

Some tenderhearted children will not read animal stories, "because something terrible always happens to them"; and even though reading experience has shown that usually "everything turns out all right in the end," for some, this assurance is not reason enough for the agony in between. Even I, a veteran book reviewer, sometimes find I have to "escape" from an animal tale because it's just too, too much.

"Escape" for the reader is a revolving door. He is perfectly willing to go book-adventuring, because he knows that he can always "save" himself if things get too rough. By the simple expedient of closing the book he can escape right back into his safe everyday world. Consider this fact also in your writing.

Chapter 11

Conflict, Opposition, Suspense
—How to Keep the Reader Reading

The writer of fiction might well follow the example of Shakespeare's redoubtable witches in *Macbeth* when cooking up conflicts and calamities for his story characters. "Double, double toil and trouble," is a reliable recipe for holding the reader's interest.

Life without adversities may be pleasant to contemplate, but it makes dull reading. It's not the kind of "living" a reader looks for in a story. *The course of fictional life must never run smoothly.* This advice has come to us from the oldest story tellers. "There is nothing better fitted to delight the reader than changes of circumstances and varieties of fortune," said the Roman philosopher, Cicero, sometime between 106 and 43 B.C.—and the rule was ancient then.

No trouble—no story. Without problems, conflicts, opposition, there is no suspense; and without suspense a reader won't keep reading. It is this important element that you must build into a story once you have created a leading character so interesting and appealing that the reader *cares* what happens to him.

Conflict is the struggle of your leading character against opposition. The outcome of this struggle should never seem to be a "sure thing." Despite the reader's assurance from his previous experiences that the hero usually wins in the end, he must lack absolute certainty to keep him turning the pages.

How to Build Suspense

You must rouse the reader's *curiosity*. He must wonder: What is going to happen next? You must also rouse his anxiety. He must *worry* about your main character: How in the world will he get out of *this* predicament?

To reduce this phase of writing technique to a formula: *Character plus anxiety equals suspense.* Your reader should bristle with anxious questions about the welfare of your main character—with whom he now identifies himself—but he should not be able to guess the outcome.

If you feel that the outcome of your story may perhaps be obvious, rework it. You may have given away too much information or been too generous with clues foreshadowing the conclusion. You may have made the opposition too weak, the path to attainment all too easy for your hero. Develop a receptive ear to the voice of your own built-in critic. All too often it gives sound advice which the writer refuses to hear—because it means more work! But professional writing success requires hard work, a fact you might as well face. There is no future for the lazy.

Realize also that the brilliant, easy ideas for conflict and complications that first flash into your mind are apt to glitter with fool's gold. Screen those "instant inspirations" carefully. With additional thought you may come up with something more effective for harassment of your story people. Always reverse the Golden Rule when it comes to making trouble for them; you do *not* do unto them as you would be done to!

Your success as a writer depends on your ability to think up problems, harrowing complications, and satisfying solutions for your story actors.

Obstacles and Oppositions

The obstacles and oppositions which cause your main character's struggle must not be teacup tempests or flimsy misunderstandings which a few words of explanation at any point could clear up. His struggle must not be simply delayed action for a measured number of scenes ("He doesn't succeed, he doesn't succeed, he's beginning to succeed, he succeds"). That's too obvious and dull a pattern even for the youngest child. Today's young people are knowledgeable readers with no scarcity of books from which to choose. They will read your story only if you offer them something fresh, entertaining, and exciting.

Your story problem must be a real one and important for the hero to solve. His goal must be worthwhile and troublesome to reach. His struggles and conflicts must appear to be difficult ones, not mere postponements to the final triumph.

Money-raising stories are likely to fall into the postponement-of-success category. The idea has been used just too often to be convincing or suspenseful. The reader *knows* the necessary amount will be raised in the end—unless *you* can think up some fresh twist to the whole situation.

Conflict

Opposition means conflict. Your main character can be in conflict with his environment, with others, or with himself. Having given your hero some desire or dissatisfaction with things as they are, you can heighten suspense by making it necessary for him to accomplish his purpose within a certain length of time.

Although trouble is of utmost importance, remember that in a child's story you can't pour it on as in a soap opera; and it can't be the kind of trouble a child or young adult is unable to face or surmount realistically. So temper the afflictions of your characters, but also avoid stories awash in sweetness and light.

Three Types of Conflict

Generally speaking, there are three types of conflict that can be used singly or in combination.

1. *Man against nature.* This kind of conflict involves any natural phenomenon as the "enemy" or opposition: a blizzard, a hurricane, a fire, a flood, a wild beast. A story character might be trapped on a mountain, lost in the woods, or adrift and helpless

on the ocean. He might be caught at the bottom of the sea with fouled diving gear, or he might be whirling in space, out of control.

Any of these situations can be very exciting but also difficult to write about, especially at length. A short story might be built around a youngster left in charge of the family farm, for example, with an unexpected blizzard or flood cutting him off completely from help. How he copes with the situation is the story. But it is not easy to keep a reader interested in the doings of a single character, even in a short tale. If your story involves a conflict with nature, plan to use at least two, and preferably more characters for contrast of personalities, reactions, and additional conflict and suspense.

2. *Man against himself.* This type of conflict is bound to have psychological overtones, the struggle arising from the strengths and weaknesses and the war between good and evil within the character himself. Such a story will inevitably include a great deal of "think stuff" which is slow-paced and generally uninteresting to the young reader. He prefers *action* and lots of it!

3. *Man against man.* This is usually the most absorbing form of conflict because the greatest interest of most readers is what happens to other people—especially if they can identify with them—regardless of the time or place of the story.

Vary the Obstacle Course

Be sure that the obstacles or difficulties which prevent your hero from getting what he wants are not all of one type. To maintain the highest peak of interest, your hero must not always nearly drown in the same ocean, or flounder through one desert after another, or be clobbered continually by the same opponent. That would be about as gripping as having one flat tire after another.

Conflict and adversity test the mettle of your story people and show them for what they really are. How they meet disaster, grapple with it, deal with an opponent, and overcome the obstacles in their way *must* be part of your story planning. Things must never "just happen" to your main character—or to anyone else in your tale.

The Right Proportion

Conflict, opposition, suspense must be used in the right proportion; too much of any of these, like too much seasoning in a stew, spoil the effect. Any prolonged periods of action or tension should be broken with rest periods for your reader, so that he can take up the story action again with renewed zest and interest. "Think stuff" slows the pace—so here is the place to use it. Let your character mull over his situation—which will, in effect, recap for the reader what has been gained or lost, reminding him of what the story is all about. A brief, quiet scene is all you need.

So far I have dealt with the ingredients that go into a story and with some of the mechanics of the writing craft. Now let's see how these can be put together most effectively.

Chapter 12

Plot and Plotting

A well-constructed story is never written "off the top of the head" with a happy-go-lucky trust that "everything will come out right," that it will jell and sell; 99 times out of 100 it won't. Anybody can have an idea, but an idea that has not been executed with professional competence might as well have never been born. That is why *plot* and *plotting* are so important.

What IS Plot?

Often the word strikes terror in a writer's heart and numbs his mind. Don't let *plot* discumbobulate you! Everything that you have been reading in this book has been preparing you to plot. What you read now will tell you how to go about it an an organized manner. Commit the following definition to memory and never allow yourself to forget it: *Plot is a plan of action devised to achieve a definite and much desired end—through cause and effect.*

In a plotted story, *cause* sets your main character off to take certain action to solve his problem, get out of a situation, or reach a certain goal. The *effect* is what happens to him *as a result* of the action he takes. He must struggle to get what he wants—and he must be opposed vigorously, either by someone who wants the same thing, or by circumstances that stand in the way of his goal.

The odds must grow against your hero so that his goal appears more and more unattainable, no matter how he struggles toward it, until he reaches a black moment where all seems lost. But the hero makes one more super-human effort, and emerges victorious.

You have seen this plot demonstrated again and again on your TV screen. Every Western, every spy drama, every adventure yarn uses this tried-and-true method for achieving drama, for holding the viewer's interest through the final scene—and every suspenseful, interest-gripping book and story uses it, though you may not recognize it so readily in print.

Plotting means planning. All planning, regardless of what it is for—a route for a six-week motor journey or a picnic supper in your back yard—has to begin with a solid period of thinking. Just so, in plotting a story you need thinking time to *devise* a course of events that lead to a resounding climax. Events which happen *because* of something that occurred before. In other words, yours must be a *cause and effect* sort of thinking.

"This happens and this happens and this happens" is not a plot. It is a string of unconnected incidents, even if they do happen to the same person. But when you have *this happen* because *that happened,* you have plot. Cause and effect is in operation.

The Inseparables—Plot and Character

There is no single component of a story that is more important than another component, unless it is *character.* But even even character, given nothing to do, might as well be a heap of sand. So another important part is *action.* But action which is not devised to further the plot to a planned conclusion might as equally well be a heap of sand—with the wind blowing it in all directions.

Character plus meaningful, directed action toward a previously planned desired end—that is the meaning and purpose of plot.

The desired end is what the character wants.

Writers go about plotting in different ways. How I start depends on the kind of story I'm planning to write. For a career romance I begin with the occupational background, which then produces the kind of heroine that career calls for. The heroine of *Lady Architect* had a logical mind and lots of courage to stand up against competition in a field where women are in the minority. *Beth Hilton, Model* had a potential of beauty which was realized in the course of the story.

Bonnie began with a situation: the heroine's family moved from a country town to a city. Shelley Andrews, in *Dance to My Measure*, had to adjust her personal life and dance study plans from a smooth arrangement in Philadelphia to a very doubtful one in New York. The young hero of *Chip Nelson and the Contrary Indians* was also transplanted from one place to another, and all kinds of fireworks were the result because he was not welcome.

If you take a character from one area or situation where he is content and place him in another area or situation where he is not, problems are bound to generate. Immediately there is a state of unrest, conflict, all kinds of story stuff—especially if your character decides to do something to improve his lot, gain his ends, or assert himself in some way.

The "What If . . . ?" Formula

Before you can begin to plot you must have an idea that sets your creative wheels in motion. Your idea file, suggested earlier, may provide one, or you may prefer to cast about for ideas. In the latter case you can bait your hook with the "What If . . . ?" formula. It spurs creative thinking through many writing problems.

What if a girl wanted to become an architect? What if a promising ballerina were suddenly crippled and could never dance again? What if a boy and his grandmother suddenly inherited a trained ostrich? What if a modern family lived in a castle—in New Jersey—and the children found an ancient, left-over dragon in one of the towers . . . a girl dragon . . . named Amelia? What if two children received a baby chick and a baby duck for Easter—and unlike the usual fate of such pets—they survived . . . in a city apartment . . . and grew . . . and grew . . . and then the kids added other pets . . a talking parrot from a white elephant sale . . . a baby pig, won at a country fair . . .

At various times, every one of these *what ifs* has started a successful short story or a book for me.

The thing to do is narrow down your thinking to the one idea that intrigues you most. *Never undertake to write about something which interests you only mildly*—especially if you are contemplating a book. The subject will certainly not interest the reader if you, yourself, are not excited about it.

Twelve Point Recipe for Plotting

Having settled on the idea, consider the "what if . . . ?" possibilities that apply directly to it—and soon your story will begin to emerge. Characters, situations, backgrounds, conflicts will spring into your mind. These are the *makings* of a plot, and when you organize the action into its most effective order, you will have a story. But first you must ask yourself some pertinent questions—*and answer them on paper.* These will form your *Twelve Point Recipe for Plotting*:

1. Who is the main character?

2. Who (or what) is the antagonist?

3. Who are the other people in the story?

4. What does the main character want? Why? What is his problem, goal, situation, greatest need? (This *need* or *want* will govern the kind of person he must be in your story. It must be suitable to his age and attainable—but only through considerable effort on his part.)

5. How important is it for him to get what he wants? (It should be vital. A great deal should be at stake, with serious consequences if he fails.)

6. How does the antagonist prevent the main character from getting what he wants? (This is the conflict, the opposition—the character himself, another person, a situation.)

7. What does the main character *do* about this obstacle? (Our heroes, big and little, male and female, must be *doers*, not people-watchers. They must win through their own power, not through luck or coincidence. *It is their doing something about the situation* that starts the story action.)

8. What are the results of his initial action? (Here complications should set in—new difficulties that make the main character's situation worse than before, intensifying his struggles.)

9. What do these struggles lead to? (This is the crisis, the crucial point for the main character. Things just can't get any worse; here consider his possible Black Moment.)

10. What is the climax? (This is the moment of decision, the point of no return, where intensity and interest in the story have reached their highest pitch. The main character must decide which way he will go *because of the kind of person you have made him.* His action now governs the answer to the next question.)

11. Does the main character accomplish his purpose or does he abandon it in favor of something else? (This is the story outcome, the resolution or *denouement.*)

12. What is the theme? What basic truth have you illustrated through your characters' action and reaction?

All the foregoing chapters will help you answer these important questions, and the ones that follow will show you how to carry the story through to the end.

Before You Write, Outline!—and Why

The answers to the preceding twelve points in plotting will provide you with a basic outline for your story. Beginning writers often rebel at the thought of outlining, for it seems such drudgery. But what they really mind is the discipline. The purpose of an outline is to clarify your thinking, to guide you through an orderly sequence of events and keep you from wandering off at tangents the moment something new streaks into your mind.

A complete outline gives you something else: your story's ending. In the various courses I have given, I've had many students tell me that they have dozens of unfinished manuscripts stashed away in their desks or attics, unfinished because they did not know how to end them! They wasted time and effort because they embarked on the heady crest of a new-born idea without thinking it through in orderly outline form. *Never begin writing a story before you know how it will end.* And never fail to outline your story, however sketchily, before you begin to write it!

The Short Story Synopsis

With the twelve point outline before you, your characters, situations, and ending clear in mind, write out a *brief*, note-style synopsis of your story. Put down a general account of *what happens* from the opening scene through to the end, making the main problem clear as early as possible in the ideas you will develop into opening paragraphs. *Write in the present tense* so that this preliminary sketch of your story will feel distinctly different from your actual writing. The synopsis might go something like this:

> Shelley Andrews arranges to pay for ballet lessons by working in Mlle. Renee's dance studio in Phila. But father announces move to NYC. Shel. in despair—never arrange anything like that in strange town. Father does not approve of dance as profession. Won't pay for lessons.
>
> Talks over sit. with Mlle. R—learns of Theater Arts H. S. in NYC—public school—limited enrollment by audition—must live in NYC. Exam stiff . . .
>
> . . . Arrives at school and runs smack into Astrea de Rioso also competing for admission. A. very sure of self . . . ruthless . . . shakes Shelley's confidence . . . Five girls audition—only one will be taken . . .

Study your story in this kind of written synopsis. Are you satisfied with it? The opening situation, the course of action, the complications, the climax, the solution? Give yourself plenty of time to consider it from all angles.

The synopsis is not graven in marble. Change it if you get better ideas for the story line. Once you are completely satisfied, go ahead and write. With your story so thoroughly planned, you should be able to get it down fast.

Nine and Sixty Ways

Writing is an intensely personal form of communication. That is what gives it variety, freshness, interest, and surprise. No single method can be proclaimed *the* one to use. No writer should be forced to use another's method, no matter how successful that method is for that writer. Even the way a story is initially considered varies from writer to writer.

Do you like to talk your stories over beforehand? Do they seem to jell better if you discuss them first? If so, talk away. But many writers cannot discuss their stories and then write them. Other people's criticism smothers the project or exhausts the need for communication with the reader—and that's the end of that tale. Analyze yourself on this score, and if you must be a clam, *be* a clam. It may also be that you have an extraordinarily logical mind and retentive memory. You may be able to think every detail through entirely in your head. Well and good. The proof of the pudding is your success in selling stories. If the percentage is impressive, then don't change your method. But if your stories fail to sell, do try the plot plan I suggest.

Chapter 13

How to Organize a Book

No matter how brilliant your mental faculties, you cannot carry in your mind the multitude of details that go into the writing of a full-length book.

You have a larger cast of characters whose main problem is more complex. There are secondary themes involving additional people who are involved with the main problem. And there are more scenes—and more word space for you to move around in, which is part of the fun of writing a book. You don't feel cramped by the number of words in which to tell your tale.

At the same time, the sheer quantity of the words you are allowed can prove awesome to someone who has written only short stories. I grew up to full-length books by writing three, four, and five-part serials. Learning how to think these through, outline and synopsize them helped me to develop an organized book plan.

Is Your Idea Book-Worthy?

Before embarking on a book project, test your idea for its worth. *Is it big enough for a book?*

It would be difficult to stretch a girl's concern with "a date for the junior prom" into a full-length book, but with a fresh twist the idea might make a fine short story. On the other hand, the story of a girl who comes to New York to make a career in fashion could scarcely be covered in 3,000 words. It *requires* book-length treatment.

How to Think BOOK

Full-length junior books usually run from 20,000 to 60,000 words, depending on the age level you're aiming for. But don't let the number of words terrify you. Don't even think of the number of pages you must produce if such thoughts bother you. Instead, consider the ten to twelve pages you have been accustomed to write for a short story. That's about the length of a chapter: 2,500 to 3,000 words. *Think of your book a chapter at a time.* Even if you plan twenty chapters, by writing one chapter a week you will have a book in twenty weeks. Viewed in this way the whole prospect becomes less frightening.

Your Current Project

Once you have chosen your book project, label a file folder with the working title of your project. Into this folder put all the odds and ends pertaining to it—newspaper clippings, articles, pictures, brochures, and notes that you don't know what to do with—yet. Collect any books, magazines or other reference material that you'll need close to your working area. A small bookcase on wheels or a serving table with two or three tiers is handy for this purpose.

Your Work Book

Select a loose-leaf notebook of a convenient size, with large rings so that you can put lots of paper into it. My favorite takes 6 by 9½ inch fillers. Use linen tabs that you can cut yourself, or notebook dividers that come in different colors to index the various departments. —

Below is a description of how I divide my work book, but you may decide to label and organize the sections differently. Every professional writer eventually develops his own system for ordering his work.

Tab 1. Title—I use a page to list titles as they come to mind, even when I begin with one; along the way something better may present itself.

Then I use a page for a variety of pertinent data:

a. *Deadline*: the date when I hope to have the manuscript completed. (Since I usually work under contract now, my target date is a positive one; however, under any circumstances, it is psychologically advisable to establish a deadline for yourself. Like a professional, you work toward a definite goal.

b. *Length*: Skipping a couple of lines, I set down the number of words this book should have: 30, 40, 50, 60,000. This is to plant the figure in my subconscious, but not to brood upon. Some of my editors like short books, others long ones. The average is about 200 pages and about 50,000 words.

c. *Theme*: Again skipping a few lines, I leave a space to write in theme—when it is clear to me. (See Chapter 8 for guidance on this point.)

d. *Chapters*: The number of chapters I expect to have—usually I aim for twenty, but the result may be as few as eighteen or as many as twenty-two.

e. *Date when actual writing is begun*:

f. *Date when first draft is finished*: (As a matter of statistics, it is interesting to have a record of how long it has taken you to write your various books. Besides, after you are published, people will ask you.)

If you are very methodical, you may want a separate page for a work log, a record of your day-by-day output. This may be simply a date and the number of words written on that day, with a total for the week.

What should be your quota? That depends on you—your creativity, your experience—not to mention your typing skill. Usually I can do better than 2,000 words a day, and once I wrote a 40,000-word book in ten days, but that was a kind of miracle! (In nonfiction I work much more slowly. And Elizabeth George Speare, two-time winner of the Newbery award, told me that she considers herself lucky if she gets 500 words done in a day. Each of us must work at his own pace.)

How many hours should you spend writing? That again depends on your personal makeup and circumstances. Many literary successes in the juvenile and adult fields actually write only three hours a day. But as Somerset Maugham once commented:

> . . . the author does not only write when he is at his desk; he writes all day long, when he is thinking, when he is reading, when he is experiencing; everything he sees and feels is significant to his purpose and, consciously or unconsciously, he is forever storing his impressions.

Tab 2. Plot—the story plan. When this is clear to me, I type it in here in synopsis form. To me, the synopsis is what the preliminary sketch is to an artist. I set down only the essential features of my story in a brief, general account. But long before I write even a trial synopsis, I start working in the other sections of my work book.

Tab 3. Situation—The several pages included in this section usually get written first, for here I put down the things that happen before my story actually takes off. These are the circumstances that *cause* my main character to take action: the difficulties that set up a pattern of discontent, the desire or challenge to accomplish some aim. These are the bits and pieces from which my beginning will spring.

And here lies a *difference between the short story and the book*: In the short story the problem is stated at once and the main character goes to work on it immediately. But in the full-length book the reasons which lead up to the problem are usually built up first; then the problem is stated, and the main character proceeds to solve it.

Tab 4. Problem(s)—Here I detail the main problem of my main character—the thing the story is about—the thing he or she must solve through personal effort and against almost overwhelming odds. Please notice the *almost*. No matter how serious the problem, or how close to life-or-death the struggle, the problem should be one the main character *can* do something about. In stories for young people, our characters are not usually allowed to beat their heads against the granite walls of impossible odds. There should be a chink in the wall of opposition which the main character can find and widen for the triumphant leap to victory.*

Into this section I also put all sorts of incidents and other problems and complications and developments that might be used in the course of the story. Not chronologically, but just as they occur to me. Some of these will be used, some discarded, but all are useful in getting me wound up in my story. These are the items I refer to constantly as I begin to develop my story. I take the pages out of the loose-leaf binder, shuffle them about, and whenever I use an item, I cross it out, thus reducing the bulk of notes.

Tab 5. Chapters—In this section I write down the numerals from one through twenty (or whatever number of chapters I think I'll have), with a few lines between on the page and a *wide*, two-inch margin at the left. (The margin is for a specific purpose, so keep it in mind.) Next to the numerals I shall eventually put either a chapter heading or a working title to serve as a clue to what the chapter is about, should I need to look up some point in the manuscript.

Then I allow a page for each individual chapter, where I can put down what might happen. But until my plot is set these ideas are very tentative, subject to change or discard. Once the plot is set, I become more positive about the chapter happenings—but not inflexible! Characters have a way of taking over the story, once you breathe life into them. They can work out their own destinies, a phenomenon of which the author should take advantage.

I do not include any dialogue unless it is something especially witty that I don't want to forget.

While setting down chapter incidents, I try to think in terms of drama, scene interest, setting, action, emotion. I write in detail

---

*Since all rules seem to have exceptions, I must add that some current "realistic" books and stories do not observe the rule for happy endings, or even the one for ending on a note of hope. Unhappy endings are acceptable, if the emotional impact is sufficient to warrant them. And sometimes, when the subject matter and writing are exceptional, a story ends without a rounded-out plot, usually because it has none, but is rather a spinning out of an episode—long or short—in the life of a character. It's like a slice of life—a wedge cut out from a whole, not a story which moves full circle from a problem or goal to a satisfying solution.

about a third or even half of the chapters before beginning to write the story. The last half can be outlined later, based on how the book evolves. But of course, before I ever get to this writing stage, I must know the ending and the probable climax scene. Otherwise there cannot be a complete plot outline to work from.

Although chapter titles are almost always used in books for young children, they are not necessary for teenagers. Whenever you do use them, don't give away the story through chapter headings which are too revealing, such as "Kip Finds the Treasure," or "Judy Wins the Prize." Even the youngest child is annoyed when suspense is ruined in this way.

Time—In your planning, decide on the length of time your story will cover. *Make this as short as possible, because a short period (or a time limit to accomplish what must be done) intensifies interest and drama.* It also automatically affects the pace in which you write. A brisk pace conveys the sense of immediacy, of urgency, and is always preferable to the slow, leisurely one.

Books for young people should not have long time lapses covering years in the main character's life. A month, a year, one summer, even a period of a few days is far more likely to hold the reader's interest. The exception applies to career books, where the main character's success must be kept within the realm of plausibility. Too rapid a success for your hero will make your story unbelievable. (See Chapter 16 for a discussion of how to handle time transitions in novels that cover several years in time.)

Be sure to establish the historical period in which your story takes place—past, present, or future (as in a fantasy); and the chronological time that will be involved, as "from May to December." Jot down the time covered in every chapter; the season, the month, the day of the week, even the hour(s), if pertinent. *Making the reader aware of the passage of time adds to the reality of your story.*

For a quick check of the time involved at any point, note it in the *wide* margin to the left of your numerical chapter listing, or use an extra work book page to list the time sequences as your story develops. In that case make an extra tab and put this just before the chapter tab so you can find it easily. The important thing is not to slip into Friday if your action is taking place on Tuesday, or into May if your action is still taking place in April.

Historicals—If yours is a story about a period in history, you must be especially careful of the chronology. (See the chapters on research in Part II.) In this case, put in a tab labeled *Historical Chronology* and consult it frequently during the planning and writing.

Tab 6. Characters—As my characters evolve, I make a list of them in order of their importance, choosing their names with the greatest of care and juggling these until I feel they are exactly right for the people in *this* story. (See the section on names in Chapter 5.)

Then I assemble them into family groups on another page, for easy reference.

Next I allow a page or more for each important character's delineation. Half a page may do for minor story actors. At the top of each character's page, I tabulate pertinent data such as age, coloring, eyes, hair, build, physical characteristics—so that I can find them quickly if I should forget what someone on page seventy-five looks like when I want to insert a bit of description to refresh the reader's memory.

Then I jot down chronology of birth, and anything important that might have happened to the story actors to color their personalities, create their social attitudes, establish their goals, and in short, make them what they are at the opening of the story. (Refer to Chapters 5, 6, 7.)

Finally I write the individual character sketches which I hope will change my "types" into flesh-and-blood people, with problems, goals, emotions, and reatcions to all the other characters around them. It is important to know exactly what each character thinks and feels about every other character in the story. In each character sketch I immerse myself in that particular person and view the rest of his world through his eyes.

Working with the characters in this way can be most fruitful plot-wise. Each one can make a spontaneous contribution—and with the *Problem(s)* and *Situations* sections in the work book, none of these ideas will be lost.

Tab 7. Background—Here I note down everything that I'll need for the setting of my story in general, and for the individual chapters and scenes. This may include layout sketches of grounds, streets, towns, topography of the land, house-plans—the arrangement and furnishings of rooms—the things of life. (See Chapter 10 for details on this topic.)

Tab 8. Research—The importance of this section cannot be overemphasized. It is what makes your story "authentic," whether the setting is in the immediate present or the very distant past. Usually, I prefer to use a separate notebook (as suggested in the chapters on research in Part II). However, if comparatively few notes are required for a project, the research can go directly into the work book, along with a page for bibliography and one for authorities, listing all the books and people I may have consulted while preparing to write.

Tab 9. Check—Even the most careful research can leave a trail of question marks in the actual writing. Rather than stop the creative flow to look anything up or re-check a fact that I've put down somewhere, I make a note in this section and find the answer at a more convenient time. Once I write the question down, it no longer nags and I can go on with the work I should be doing.

Tab 10. Inserts—This is for additional useful information that I think of after I have started the actual writing. Background details, some bit of character business, anything at all that I may want to put already written into the story is safe here until I'm ready to use it.

Tab 11. Words and Phrases—This, too, is a "safe deposit" section—for anything that might add sparkle to my writing: figures of speech, which do not always occur to the writer at the moment he needs them; bits of dialogue that can make the characters sound more witty; quotations; etc.

. . . *And One to Grow On!*

There is one more section—at the *back* of my work book. It is a duplicate set of the front tabs, for the capture of any ideas I may get for my *next* project while working on *this* one. As a professional writer, I always have plans for at least one book beyond the one in work. Whenever I finish the current project, I simply move the back section into the front, and make ready another set of tabs for the project to follow!

The work book is not only a more efficient project organizer, but it is also an idea generator. By providing yourself with definite sections to work in, you always have a place to put down whatever comes into your mind. As you write in the different sections you can *see* and *feel* your story grow and develop and quicken with life. The characters clamor to be released to their adventuring, and at last *you* are ready and eager to let them— and *write!*

Chapter 14

The Actual Writing—
the Good Days and the Bad

With the organization work finished, you can recapture your original excitement as you merge yourself with your characters and their lives. Now is the time to stop thinking of the "rules" and allow your imagination to take wing. If you have grounded yourself thoroughly in the writing of short stories, you have absorbed the necessary pointers on technique—and you have your book plan to guide you.

Allow no doubts of your ability to enter your mind at this stage. Creative people thrive on a positive attitude. If any signs point to a flagging self-confidence, here is a quote from that many-sided genius, Goethe, to elevate your spirits and (I hope) galvanize you into action:

> Are you in earnest?
> Seize this very minute!
> What you can do, or dream you can, begin it!
> Boldness has genius, power and magic in it.
> *Only engage, and then the mind grows heated.*
> BEGIN, and then the work will be completed.

Consider the wisdom of these lines. They state a psychological principle: *Interest follows action.* You begin to work—*to write*—to engage the gears of your mind. Interest awakens, your imagination is freed, ideas begin to flow. This does not happen the other way around. If you sit and stew and wait for "inspiration" it may never come! Such pressure is more likely to block off creative thought.

Some Don'ts and Do's

Do not attempt to analyze or perfect your words while you are getting them down in the first draft. Write as fast as you are able, letting spontaneity take over. The time to criticize and take apart comes later—when the work is inescapably on paper.

No matter how engrossed you are in your project, do not work at it every day until you're limp. More is involved in this kind of creation than the physical act of pounding the typewriter. "Living" through every scene you write can be exhausting, and so, too, is the intense concentration you give your work. You can drive yourself just so far, and if you overdo repeatedly, your subconscious will build up such a resistance that you won't want to go back to your desk.

Be sensible about your work. Along with a set time for writing, decide on the number of pages you should do each day and *do* them, but don't push too much beyond that limit. In fact, it is often best to stop in the middle of some interesting scene. Jot down the next action in a note to yourself and stop writing. (Some writers stop in the middle of a paragraph or sentence.) Leave your desk and do something else. When your next writing session rolls around, it will be easy to recapture the mood and plunge into the story with freshness and vigor.

There is sound psychology behind this advice. Finished business can be forgotten, but something left undone will linger in your mind—and your subconscious will helpfully churn away at it. Yet there's no need for *you* to be restless, because the act of writing a note on what's to happen next frees your conscious mind of the problem until you're ready to return to it.

Catching the emotional mood of your story is hardest during the first half hour or so of your writing session. I frequently begin my new day's work with a "wastebasket exercise"—retyping the last page or two written the day before. In this way I wind myself into the mood of the story quickly and am ready to go on with the new action and developments.

You can also catch the mood by reading over what you have written. However, do not read any more than the previous day's output, and only enough of that to enable you to go on from where you left off.

With my book plan completed, I usually embark on the writing of four to six chapters, and this brings the whole thing to life; the book takes a definite shape and direction. When these chapters are done, I go back, reread and revise them until I am satisfied with this beginning. Sometimes this "trial flight" suggests significant changes in character and plot, as it shows me the book in a different light. In that case *I make the changes, both in the synopsis and the outline, to avoid possible confusion later.* However, such changes should be made only after serious consideration.

Chapter lengths are not arbitrary, either. When a chapter runs too long you can divide it into two chapters. Sometimes you may find that chapter events can be condensed for a better effect and story pace; two chapters may need to become one. This letting out or tucking in is to be done later, however—in revision—when the technical tests should be applied to what you have written.

Don't let worry over sentence length, construction or vocabulary hamper the writing of your first draft. Just write naturally. Incidentally, use smooth, 16-pound paper for typing your first draft. You'll be able to work on it with pen or pencil during revision, scratching out or erasing without having the paper disintegrate under pressure. Double space, and allow wide margins for corrections and interpolations.

With one chapter finished, read over the outline of the next and think about it with quiet confidence. Read over the character sketches, the background notes, the various situations as you've jotted them down. Don't forget these aids in the organized sections of your work book.

Do not attempt to polish your writing while you're creating the story. This is wasteful, and every interruption will make it harder to plunge ahead with your original zeal. Enthusiasm must last a long time for a book! And yet you can't expect it to remain at the same high pitch all through the writing.

Action scenes are less apt to give you trouble. Often they seem to write themselves out of your own absorption and excitement in what is happening. But "think stuff," descriptions, and transition scenes frequently must be labored over and hauled and tugged out on paper.

Overcoming Writer's Blocks

You must be prepared to work on the bad days, when nothing seems to come right, as well as the good, productive ones. At such times, your professional attitude must see you through—with some help from your work book.

If you hit a block, it often means that you have not given enough thought to that particular part of the story. Don't fret and stew—unproductively. Instead, consult your work book and *think constructively*, confident that the solution will come to you. Check over the outline, the characters and their problems, the opposition, the complications. Use the "What if . . . ?" method until the right answer comes to you—and then the words will flow again.

Chapter 15

The Beginning—Getting Your Story Off to a Running Start

How you begin depends on the kind of story you want to tell.

If it is to be an *action tale*—an adventure—think up an arresting incident with which to start it off. If you are going to rely heavily on the *mood*, then play up the interesting or exotic setting. Should yours be a *character* story, present the main character in a fresh, exciting way. Make him sound like someone around whom things happen.

The beginning is your chance to catch the interest of the reader, at a moment when he is most curious about what you have to offer. At the same time, he is not yet involved with your story people, or what happens to them. Before the reader's attention strays to something else, you must seize and hold it.

No matter what exciting things *you* know are going to happen on page five or ten or fifty, your reader (and your first reader is that important someone in the editor's office) will not stay with you that long unless you snag him on page one and lure him into reading on.

What You Must Accomplish in Your Story Opening

1. *Catch the Interest of Your Reader.* The most important consideration in working out your opening is the audience for whom your story is intended. With this in mind, present characters in whom your particular reader is likely to be interested, doing

something which is likely to interest him. If your opening action concerns characters much older or much younger than he is, he'll reach for another book on the shelf.

2. *Introduce the Characters.* Since the young reader tends to identify himself with the first character he meets in a story, the first one introduced should usually be the hero—the viewpoint character—unless there is an excellent reason for not doing so, as in *Chip Nelson and the Contrary Indians.* (See this story's beginning in Chapter 7.) Here I had to set the stage and provide the motivation for the conflict and opposition before I could bring on my hero.

It is seldom possible or necessary to introduce or even to mention all the characters in the beginning, but the existence of each one should be indicated in some way as soon as practical. This rule applies more to the short story than to a book, where even important characters may not appear until the middle or the end of the book. In my *Slipper Under Glass,* a motivating character did not appear until the last quarter of the book; and in *Dance to My Measure,* the romantic lead did not step on the stage until the last half.

So get the main character in. Introduce him by name—*all of it*. Indicate his personality or background quality. The first glimpse of your hero should put the reader in sympathy with him. Show him as a likeable person, with some human weaknesses and troubles, but willing to fight his own battles.

If you must open your story with just one character on the scene, be sure to show him *doing* something interesting before you allow him to think about anything. You can simplify the job of characterizing him by having an animal with him, a creature he can talk to or pet. (See Chapters 5, 6 and 7, dealing with the creation of characters. Take special note of the "camera view" for describing your viewpoint character, in Chapter 6.)

3. *Set the Stage.* The reader must know what the setting is: the time, place, and social atmosphere. You must let him know at once if you are dealing with the present or if this is a period piece, a space opera, or some other kind of fantasy. (See Chapter 10.)

4. *Introduce the Problem* or the situation that will bring on the

problem—the sooner the better in a book; right away in a short story:

> Merlin Jones was the saddest magician in the world. He had lost his magic.*

5. *Set the Mood.* Letting the reader know what kind of emotional tone will dominate your story is one of the best means to catch his interest. (See Chapter 9.) Indicate quickly whether he may expect to laugh or cry, feel romantic, brave with adventure, or all shivery over a mystery. You can do this with some typical dialogue, a characterization, or your description of the setting. Here is a good example, with the "mood" words in italics:

> The night was clear and *crisp*, with only the *ghost* of a breeze to stir the dust in the road and rustle the *dead leaves* along the hedgerows. A brilliant moon cast *weird, wavery shadows in the fence corners*. As the group of boys walked along the country road, *they stayed close together, and they looked behind them more than once.*
>
> "Billy," asked Jim Allen in a *low voice, "did you bring the spade?"*†

6. *Suggest the Complications.* Begin to reveal the story gradually by hinting at the various things to come—not necessarily the main problem, for it may take time to develop and reveal it (in a book), but indicate some difficulties that beset your hero or heroine.

7. *Hint at the Solution.* Even in the beginning, the final solution of your hero's dilemma must be prepared for, so that when it comes, it will be convincing.

One way to make fiction believable is to *show* the reader how things happen and *prepare him* for things that *might* happen. Such preparation beforehand consists of two literary devices called *plants* and *pointers*.

When an author *plants* something, he lets the reader know that certain conditions exist. He might *plant* the knowledge of certain skills his character has, or equip him with special characteristics—courage, stubborn perseverance, or a lively curiosity—

---

*From *The Magic of Merlin Jones,* by Barbara Hutchenrider.
†From *Halloween Is for Adventure,* by Marcia Morgan.

which will then lead him into or out of certain situations. (See Chapter 6.)

Your beginning should be full of *plants* which unobtrusively inform the reader and make everything that happens in your story later sound plausible to him.

To *point* or *foreshadow* is to indicate that a certain thing might, could, or will happen later on in the story. This device differs from the *plant* in that it suggests an *event* that will follow.

In my book, *On Your Toes, Susie!* the studio cat is chased up a tall tree by a pet monkey. Terrified, the cat will not come down and the fire department is called. The cat is rescued, but the firemen say they will not come again because a new rule has been made on animal rescues. Later in the story, when the monkey's leash is caught high up in the tree branches and he is in danger of being strangled, Susie knows it will be useless to call the fire department, so she climbs up herself. The result brings on the climax of the story, which, although it is surprising, is believable because of the *pointers*—the foreshadowing—used before.

The seven points of the opening, as I have outlined them for you, must be covered quickly and effectively, in an interesting manner. They need not be used in the order in which I have given them, but until they are covered, your beginning is not complete.

How to Write Your Opening

There are various ways to write your story beginning. Narrative exposition is the poorest, because it just tells and explains, without *showing* the characters in action or allowing them to say a word. A much sounder way to begin a story is to show your main character in an interesting setting, doing something of interest to the reader, and talking with at least one other story actor. Be sure to mix thought, action, and dialogue—and never use any of these unless they move the story forward.

Incidentally, when you begin with action, don't throw a terrific slam-bang scene at the reader before he knows who is fighting whom for what and with which! The reader should never stand on the sidelines and wonder which side to cheer. He should always cheer for the hero—so let him know as quickly as possible who the hero is and what worthy cause he is fighting for.

The best place to begin your story is where the flow of events leads directly into the action your main character must take in order to get what he wants. Whatever the story, the beginning should have lots of dramatic potentials, and then a turning point for contrast—anticipation of one thing and getting something else, for example.

A sense of change is highly desirable. Journey beginnings are often used because they get the story moving. Going from one place to another brings on new faces, new things to see, new experiences. Here's an example from my *Silver Yankee*:

> . . . The excitement with which Perk Hilton had boarded the southbound train from New York was still with her as the cars raced through the flatlands of New Jersey and into Pennsylvania. She had been staring out the window for an hour, but instead of seeing the June countryside, her mind kept making pictures of a South Carolina river plantation as she imagined it. Gracious lawns sloping down to the water, a great white house with wide porches and tall columns, moss-hung trees . . .

Compare that beginning to this:

> Perk Hilton was excited because she was going to South Carolina to a river plantation.

Even this holds some interest, because it suggests, however flatly, an unusual background, a change; but it scarcely grips the reader and he can easily escape.

As for the quick reversal to heighten interest through contrast: Perk's plantation turns out to be a dilapidated old mansion with unkempt grounds—and instead of gracious hospitality she finds hostility and downright dislike in the girl who meets her on the rickety veranda. Conflict and opposition are off to a running start!

But this is still only the introduction to the real story, a *who, what, when, where* orientation for the reader (with the *why* and *how* to come, and the *therefore* to state the resolution and tie things up at the end. Even while the author concentrates on the story parts, he must be conscious of the story as a whole).

The beginning extends to the point where the problem confronting your main character is clear to the reader.

Now the main character should decide to *do* something about his problem or goal, or he should be precipitated into doing something about it by some outside influence or force.

This is the real take-off point for your story: *the day that is different,* the day your hero is no longer content to put up with the situation. And this brings *you* into the problem of your story's middle.

Chapter 16

And Then . . . ?
Problems of Your Story's Middle

Now you must begin to fulfill the interesting promises of your story opening as you clarify the *why* (motivation) of your main character and reveal *how* he copes with his situations.

The moment he leaves his safety island of "things as they are" he must be confronted by a barrier of opposition. Each obstacle, whatever its form, presents a problem to be solved, a disaster to be averted, or an opponent to be overcome. But such is the nature of successful story-telling that the solving of one problem must immediately bring on more difficulties. The hero must leap from the frying pan into the fire.

In your story middle you must have a course of ups and downs—of "furtherances" toward the hero's ultimate goal, and of "hindrances" which thwart and frustrate his attempts to succeed in his purpose. These must occur at irregular intervals, so that the reader will not be able to anticipate success or failure on your hero's part and lose the excitement of suspense and curiosity as to how it will all come out. He will never stop reading as long as there is an incompleted situation before him.

One simple device which will keep him reading from chapter to chapter is never to end a chapter on a completed incident. Break it off at a crucial, suspenseful moment, and pick it up again in the next chapter. Like this:

> Whoever—whatever was moaning and sighing was in her room. She could hear it *breathing.*
>
> With a loud yell Amy sprang out of bed and ran in the

direction where she thought her door was. The yell changed
into a piercing shriek when the Thing grabbed her and
knocked her down.

The reader (of *Family at Seven Chimneys House*) has to turn
the page to see what happens next.

A review of Chapter 11 will help you chart the middle of your
story. And, as an exercise to accompany the study of this text,
make marginal notes and underscore passages in a book of your
own that illustrates the different points of technique discussed
here. Such an exercise will also help to develop your own critical
faculties.

Your Story—Scene by Scene

Scenes expand your story synopsis or outline into dramatized
units of action. A story should be divided into different scenes to
give the reader action as well as a change of setting.

In a short story you must be wary of skipping around and
thereby creating a jerky effect. But in a book you have far greater
freedom. A chapter might require three, four, or more scenes to
complete its purpose. But in either story form, once your main
character has set about solving his problem, *every subsequent
scene should reveal some sort of struggle or conflict, or the solving of a problem, with a carry-over of interest which makes one
scene flow into another with unbroken continuity.*

Make a practice of thinking your story through in scenes—
like segments of your main character's life, each against its own
definite background.

Each scene must move your story forward. Its action must be
an outgrowth of what went before, and in itself, support and
cause or *affect* the action that will follow. The story line must
move in a direct course, and there must not be any side trips
to admire the view or chase the butterflies of unrelated thought.
This is the test of a scene's importance to the story: *If it is really
vital to the plot, it cannot be cut out without damaging the story.*
The removal of a *necessary* scene would leave a gaping hole in
your story tapestry, as jarring to the eye as the leaving out of a
bar of music from a familiar melody would be to the ear.

Transitions

Characters and readers must often be moved from place to place, from one time to another, and from one emotion to another mood. The device for such changes is called the *transition*. It may consist of only a few words, but sometimes a paragraph or a longer passage may be involved when several of these objectives must be accomplished, or when some thinking needs to be done by a character after a period of particularly lively action. The reader cannot sustain the same high pitch of interest indefinitely. Like your main actor, *he* needs a rest scene now and then. This is where the transition can take the form of a "think-over," a recapitulation of events that went before, and perhaps a reaffirmation of the goal ahead.

Lazy or inexperienced writers sometimes avoid the transition and plunge the reader from one event or time to another by the easy device of leaving three or four lines of blank space between paragraphs. *Don't!* The abrupt change of thought or scene is bound to jolt the reader out of your story's life. As he "comes to" and notices the white space and maybe looks at the clock, he may also say, "Here's a good place to put the book (or story) down." For keeps! And no author wants to put such a notion into his reader's head. On the contrary, what you want him to feel, is that he can't possibly put your story down—not until he has finished it and knows how it all came out. "When I would sit down to read only a few pages of *Candy Stripers,* I would end up reading fifty," a young Chicago girl wrote me. "I would have read more, but my mother came and hollered at me to go out."

White space between paragraphs may be left to make the page more attractive, but the reader should be "floated" over on transition.

Smooth, easy transitions make scenes dovetail and continuity remain unbroken, even though one sentence can move the story forward a day, an hour, or a year. For clarity, it is best to put transition words first; use very little detail; summarize quickly and get on with the story:

> *On Saturday,* the four Kendalls and Grandpa boarded a
> big blue bus in the terminal and rumbled out of New York

City. They whisked through a long white tunnel under the Hudson River, whizzed over wide concrete highways, past some cities and then some towns. Finally they rolled to the edge of Spring Valley, which was all fields and farmhouses and trees—and a huge fairground (their objective), with a fence behind which stood dozens and dozens of tents.

This excerpt from *The Family at Seven Chimneys House* takes place almost a week after the scene before it, and moves the characters from one place to another briskly enough for a book. But if this were a short story, I probably would have used fewer than half the words for the transition:

On Saturday, the four Kendalls and Grandpa boarded a bus and rumbled out of New York City. An hour later they rolled into the Spring Valley fair grounds . . .

Then I would have begun the scene at the fair by having one of the children say something about the tents or the ferris wheel. Transitions can do away with gobs of in-between details. They can bring people on—and take them away:

The sound of crunching gravel on the drive sent Gini to the window. "Mother's home!" she announced, and rushed out of Beth's room and downstairs.

A transition can help set the scene for a change of mood:

In the midst of these happy preparations (the Kendalls were sure they would win the Unusual Pet Prize) their house agent, Mr. Wallace, arrived . . . Mrs. Kendall invited him to eat with them and Amy hurried to put another place setting on the table.

Mr. Wallace refused firmly. "I'm sorry," he said, "But I'm afraid I have bad news for you. I didn't mean to catch you at supper—but since I'm here, I might as well tell it."

When he told his news, nobody had any appetite to eat.

[The "news" is in the next chapter, next scene.]

In time transitions it is permissible to use the simplest phrases: "that night"; "the next day"; "two weeks later." But do avoid tired cliches and florid phrases: "time passed"; "winter came at last"; "the day dawned bright and clear."

There are many ways to word a transition. Add the search for samples to your study of published material. And remember, *the object of the transition is the same as that of a shortcut: to get from here to there—fast.*

Flashbacks

When it is necessary to retell some background event or experience which *now* motivates the hero's actions or clarifies his present attitude toward something, the device used is called a *flashback.* It must be used skillfully, or it will bring the present action of the story to a grinding halt. The young reader is far more interested in what is happening *now* and in what is going to happen *next* than in what occurred last summer, or last year, or ten years ago. The necessary flashback must be worked into the story line imperceptibly, so that the reader is in and out of it—and properly informed—without being aware of the literary maneuver.

Sometimes bits of what went before can be woven into the story, as in the following example:

> *Beth Hilton, Model.* It was a shock to come across the childish scrawl now, at seventeen—especially when it was so far from the truth.
>
> *Beth had been ten when she wrote that in the Five Year Diary someone had given her . . . Naturally it was because of Lisa, the Lovely Child Model . . . Beth's hazel eyes narrowed with remembering* as she sat on the floor, her long slim legs tucked under her and the straight, soft chestnut hair pushed behind her ears.
>
> *. . . Her cousin Lisa had been six when she was "discovered" in the New York subway. Someone from a model agency had spotted her . . . and that's how it began . . .*
>
> *Sometimes, posing before a mirror, Beth had pretended she was a child model, too. But all these sessions usually ended the same way—with angry tears or horrid face-making . . .*
>
> That sort of dreaming was over, of course. But the perfect model-groomed Lisa could still make Beth feel terribly awk-

ward—as if she had three legs, and arms to the floor. At this moment Lisa was also making Beth angry. Did she have to snag Pete right from under her nose?

Note how the story moves along, blending the present and the past, the *then* and the *now;* and how cousin Lisa begins to emerge as a catalyst in Beth's life.

In *Chip Nelson* a flashback is necessary to make clear *why* the boy is so terrified of thunderstorms, because this is the source of most of his present troubles and motivates not only his current actions but also everything that happens in the big, dramatic climax at the end.

> . . . But what had awakened him? . . . A brilliant zig-zaggy flash in the sky, followed by a tremendous clap of thunder gave him a sudden answer . . . Chip buried his head under his pillow and began to cry . . . *He had been terrified of thunderstorms ever since he'd seen a tree split in half by lightning.*
>
> *It had been a school picnic and lots of fun, till the storm roared in. Chip and some of the others started to run under the big, spreading oak tree. But their teacher shouted to them to come back.*
>
> *"Never stand under a tree during a thunderstorm . . ." she made them crawl under the picnic tables in the park clearing . . .*
>
> *And then the lightning hit that oak tree.* Ever since whenever there was a bad storm like this, Chip saw that oak tree being struck by lightning. Only . . . *he* was under it . . .
>
> "Oh my gosh," he heard George's disgusted voice in the bunk below. "Are you at it again? It's nothin' but an old thunderstorm. It wont hurt you!"

Here the flashback is presented as a vivid and terrifying, though not very articulate, emotional experience—the way an eight-year-old like Chip would feel it.

Sometimes the "past" can be revealed in dialogue, or in answer to a question. In the following excerpt from *The Timid Dragon,* note how the dialogue is "skimmed" for just the needed details:

> During the night, the dragon got lonely and crept into Janie's room and nuzzled her hand. She woke up and they

talked a bit, and Janie learned a great deal about dragons. She also learned that the dragon's name was Amelia, and how it happened to be hiding in her great-grandfather's castle.

"You see," the creature said, "when the Dragon Age was over, all the dragons were supposed to fly to Dragonland. We had to cross an ocean and it was so tremendous . . . I took one look at it and I was terrified. It was then that I shrank to the size of a lizard and hid in the crack of that stone in Blodget Castle."

Janie said she understood perfectly because she was even a little afraid herself sometimes. She patted the green scales comfortingly. "You don't have to worry about it any more," she said.

Something a character sees can trigger off a flashback in his mind, as the diary did for Beth. Any object can become a symbol that jogs the memory: a photograph, a doll, an old clipping, a top, jewelry, an odor, or the glimpse of some view. On occasion you may want to use a letter or a document to shed light on the past important to the story now. This is the test for the need of a flashback: *does it clarify or intensify what is happening now?* If it does not, you don't need a flashback, or even a "think-over" reminiscence. But if it does, then "flash" it in briskly. Dramatize it as much as possible, and then get back into the current flow of the story.

Chapter 17

Climax Scene and Ending

Every scene in your story should lead up to the dramatic final climax. Your main character's path should become increasingly difficult—with the main problem or goal still out of his reach—when he arrives at the point where he *must make a decision.*

Depending on what your story is about, the decision might be to fight or flee; to abandon a goal or press on. Under certain circumstances it might even involve the sacrifice of some hard-won prize, as in *Beth Hilton, Model,* where the heroine wins the coveted title of the *American Miss Abroad* only to realize she simply cannot fly off on a world tour and leave Amos Burr, the young photographer she loves. She is about to renounce her prize (while the young reader wrings her hands) when the story is happily and romantically resolved through another surprising development.

The necessity to make a fateful decision should bring on a *crisis* in the main character's affairs—"life or death" for all his desires. He is plunged into his blackest of black moments. Success or failure hangs in the balance, and only *he* can take the decisive step. *What will he do?*

Here must come the most intense struggle for the main character—and the highest point of interest in the story—the *climax.* The reader should want the hero to succeed, to make the right decision. Sometimes the reader knows what that should be. But will the hero know? The eagerness to find out should make the reader take a firmer grip on the book. A good climax will not allow him to let go and do something else. How often have you delayed some task because you just *had* to finish a story you were reading? That's the sort of climax you should try to write!

The MUSTS of a Successful Climax

Exploit every possibility for a smashing emotional outburst among your story actors. And above all, don't get lazy and skip the big explosion altogether! I have seen this done not only in student manuscripts but also in some that I have read for publishers—and rejected. Some writers bring their leading character to the brink of disaster—then blithely skip a few lines and show the main character being congratulated for solving the problem.

"Afterwards he couldn't tell exactly how it had happened, but there he was, safely at the bottom of the cliff" simply will not do. The reader always wants to know *how* it happened. Not only that, he wants to *see* it happen—and even *be there* vicariously when it does.

Play Fair with the Reader

Never cheat your reader by dabbling in plots which deliberately set out to deceive him, such as harrowing adventure tales or mysteries chopped off at the climax with the revelation that it's all been a dream. Editors do not look kindly on such shenanigans.

The same holds true for "surprise twists" too surprising to be believed and stories where the author leaves the ending up to the reader. My grudge against Frank Stockton and "The Lady, or the Tiger?" dates back to sixth grade! Even Paul Gallico's poignant "Small Miracle" leaves something to be desired—a positive and conclusive ending.

The reader should be left with a sense of completeness, a sense of rightness, instead of with restless questions in his mind. It is the author's job to finish a story, not the reader's.

The story problem that is finally solved must not be a mistake or a misunderstanding which could have been cleared up anywhere along the line by a sensible main character. Such pseudo-problems can be made to come off in short stories, but it would be difficult, if not impossible, to hold the reader's interest with much ado about nothing for the length of a book. A humorous story can revolve around a comedy of errors caused by misunderstanding, but a more serious piece can only suffer from it.

Climax and Character

Since the solving of the main problem is of greatest importance to your main character, he is the one most affected by the climax. Thus, you must never show a minor character taking the lead at this point, for that would not only diminish your hero or heroine, but it would also destroy the unity of purpose in your story by shifting the spotlight to the wrong person.

It is the concentration on *the* problem—the constant "spotting" of the main character's goal—that brings him and the other story people into focus and makes all the action meaningful. It gives your story or book a definite beginning, a middle, a climax, and an end.

The main characters must get what they deserve, and they must get it in a rousing, dramatic fashion. At this stage, that very necessary ingredient, suspense, arises from the balanced struggle between the hero and the circumstances he must overcome, whether these be physical or mental. Suspense is sustained by the reader's uncertainty as to what the hero will do in the critical climax. It is heightened by the conflict of emotions in the hero's heart and mind that keep him and the reader sticking to the problem and fighting it out together, as in *Chip Nelson and the Contrary Indians*:

All along Chip has been thwarted in his desire to join his cousin's Indian Club. He'd belonged to the YMCA Indian Guides at home, and now that he's come to stay in Riverledge while his parents are away on business, his dearest wish is to be one of the fellows who seem to have so much fun in the backyard tent. But to Cousin George, Chip is an unwelcome guest and he resents sharing his room with him. The fact that Chip is terrified by lightning and thunder gives George not only an excuse to keep Chip out of the Club but also an opportunity to tease him unmercifully.

Then on a class outing to find Indian artifacts, Mr. Maddox, the social studies teacher, teams George up with Chip and the two are assigned the trail along the river. They find a cave at the water's edge and climb down into it to explore. While they're down there, a storm which has threatened all day, breaks. (This event was foreshadowed—*pointed*—in an earlier scene, before the boys were *planted* in the danger spot. And of course Chip's fear and the cause behind it have already been made clear.) Now Chip crouches at the entrance, his hands clenched into fists, his body shaking. George grabs Chip's shirt-tail and hauls him back.

> "Aw come on inside . . . You're white as a sheet and your freckles look like they're going to jump right off you into the rain . . . I'll protect you."
> *If he laughs,* Chip thought, *I'm going to hit him, big as he is.* [Our little worm is turning!]

There is a struggle, and then a section of the cave ceiling crashes down, "leaving nothing but his cousin's head and one hand visible under a pile of earth and stone," and we're rolling up to the black moment for Chip. The boy can't dig George out, and soon he discovers that water is creeping in through the cave opening. *Chip must get help—but there's the storm outside!*

> "I'll drown!" George bellowed. "Help me, Chip! Help me!"
> "I can't, I don't know how!" Chip was crying now, tearing at the earth and stone until his fingers were raw and bleeding.
> "Get somebody!" George yelled. "Get Mr. Maddox!"
> . . . Chip shook so hard that his teeth chattered. He couldn't go out into the storm with the lightning snaking about. But . . . the water was up to his ankles already! . . .
> Maybe Mr. Maddox was in the picnic area—taking shelter under the big tables—just the way Chip and his classmates had done during that other storm. [Remember the Flashback example in Chapter 16?]
> But to go out in it now . . . Behind him, George was blubbering . . . would there be time to find Mr. Maddox and get back? There was already eight inches of water sloshing in the cave.
> Chip knelt beside his cousin. "George," he said, " . . . I

have to get help. I can't move this stone alone. I'll get Mr. Maddox."

But George had changed his mind. "Don't leave me!" he begged . . . He clutched at Chip's sleeve. [George has been such a stinker that the reader is happy to hear him whine—although of course he doesn't want him actually drowned!]

Chip unfastened his cousin's fingers and stepped out of reach. "I *have* to go, George . . . We'll get you out . . . " Chip was babbling, but he wasn't going to let himself think of what would happen if he didn't get back with help—in time. [Our hero is emerging through his own action.]

Ducking his head, he rushed out of the cave. He was soaked to the skin within seconds. Darts of lightning zipped all around him and the thunder sounded as if the whole earth was cracking. Chip's heart thudded against his ribs. He slipped and slithered and clawed his way up the streaming bank, got his bearings, and ran off through the rain.

A huge tree barred his path, the trunk black and cracked and steaming. Chip stopped, frozen . . .

Suppose the lightning hit another tree! Suppose he was right under it! He held his arms tight to his body and tried to shrink inside his own shivering self . . . but suppose George drowned because he was afraid to run and get help!

. . . He couldn't let George drown—not because of an old thunderstorm. [Decision—but not easy.] Chip tried to remember all the things he'd heard about taking care of yourself during a thunderstorm . . . Up ahead was a bunch of little trees—not the kind likely to be struck. Behind him was George, pinned into a cave. And yet Chip stood, rooted to the spot.

Maybe if he yelled, the way Indians yelled to frighten enemies and give themselves courage . . . The storm was his enemy—and he certainly needed courage. Chip opened his mouth, took a deep breath, and let out a series of Indian Guide whoops. It seemed to him, that at the sound of his loud voice, even the storm seemed to pause and listen . . . Without giving himself another moment to think about it, Chip took off and ran blindly through the rain, like a terrified deer.

His breath was coming in rasping gasps when he thought he heard . . . voices. *"Over here! Over here!"* they seemed to scream at him . . .

Chip does find Mr. Maddox and the others at the picnic area.

> It took the teacher a while to get the story, and then call-
> ing out to Stew Withers and Egg Hanley, he followed Chip to
> the river bank.
> When Chip saw how high the river had risen, his heart
> almost stopped beating.
> "Where *is* the cave?" Mr. Maddox asked, gripping Chip's
> shoulder.
> "There—no—over there. No, *here!*" Chip shouted, spotting
> the black opening. It was half under water! More than half!
> The river seemed to turn upside down before Chip's eyes
> to stand on end and engulf him in a terrible smash of water.
> Chips knees buckled . . .

But that's permissible now. He's done his part and behaved
like a hero. In the next chapter Chip is revived, George is saved
—in the nickiest nick of time—and later there is a very satisfying
scene when Chip visits George in the hospital. His cousin is
quite subdued—and properly grateful.

> "You see," George said softly, "I guess I know better than
> anybody what it meant·to you to go out in all that lightning
> and thunder."

Chip has grown as a person and outgrown a fear. He has
been praised for his action both by grownups and his peers—and
most important, by his erstwhile enemy, cousin George. And of
course he gets into the Indian Club. So the hero's purpose is
accomplished.

The Come-to-Realize Ending

But all climax situations are not like that. Often, in stories for
young people, there is a *come-to-realize climax and ending.*

This must be handled with special care. It will be weak and
unconvincing if the main character *comes-to-realize* whatever it
is he should do or avoid doing *by himself*—by thinking things
out and making a decision, for example, by reading a letter. A
climax will also be weak if someone tells the main character
that he ought to change his ways, and he does. Real people

simply don't behave that way and every young reader knows it.

The best method for resolving this kind of an ending is to have something happen to your main character to *make* him "come-to-realize." It should be some powerful personal experience that shocks him, rocks him, or even floors him. Whatever it is, it must have a terrific impact on him. A scene with these elements is bound to produce action and drama and an emotional involvement for the reader. Then you should have a quiet scene, for the change in the main character must in no way resemble instant magic. The hero should think over what has happened and realize the impact and implications, and resolve to change course or mend his ways. The reader will not leave him, because now he will have another question in his mind: *Does he mean it?*

Next comes the clincher for this kind of ending: you must devise a scene in which the hero can *prove* that he has indeed changed. This is absolutely essential. Worked out this way, the "come-to-realize" ending is effective and satisfying.

Conclusion

Stop when your story ends! Once the hero or heroine has surmounted all difficulties and solved his problems, your story is over. The original situation has changed considerably, and so has the character—and it was all brought about by the events in the story. If you handled the writing technique properly, your reader *saw* it happen; he even *lived* through it. So don't rehash everything over again in a compulsive summation. The reader is no longer in your grip, once the suspense element of "how will it all come out" is gone. Let him go with a graceful parting.

Your story really ends with the climax, you know, but because the reader doesn't want to leave the delightful people in your book, he stays around for the *resolution*, the final disentanglement and outcome of the character's affairs. So tie up the little ends, and close the story *inside* the main character, in his thoughts, which reveal his true feelings.

Never end the story with a scene between minor characters. All secondary plot threads should be tied up before the big climax. In the conclusion, be brisk, be brief, and be gone.

Chapter 18

How to Revise . . . and Polish

No story or book should ever go to a publisher hot off the type-writer. What may seem flawless to you in the heat of creation can turn out to be anything but—in the cool of reason a month or so later. Never send out anything that is not your absolute best. It may not be perfect—even the work of our most distinguished writers isn't always that—but *it must be the best of which you are capable at that moment in your writing career.*

It's not writing but *rewriting* that makes a smooth-flowing tale. And although many writers groan over revision, it is easier than creation. You have something to work *on;* you are not pulling a story out of imagination's skein. And you are not working in marble, but on paper. Words can be easily changed.

Your just-completed short story (a book is another matter) must be put away to cool in a file folder, *and you should get busy immediately on your next project.* When that is finished, proceed with the next one, and perhaps the one after that, so you have two or more stories "on ice" and something in work before you attempt to read and revise the first one. Your subconscious may continue to flash out ideas for all sorts of changes and interpolations in the completed stories. Jot these down, slip them into the proper story folders for consideration later, *and go on with whatever you're currently writing.*

This enforced cooling-off period will sharpen your critical faculties. If you read your first draft immediately on completion, you may become enchanted with the sheer beauty of your words, the splendid delineation of your characters, the remarkable ramifications of your plot, and the terrific climax, to say nothing of the Monumental Significance of the whole opus!

On the other hand, you may go to the opposite extreme and decide that the manuscript is worthless—and tear it up. Every now and then a student admits to such an act of waste and foolishness. Never, never allow yourself to destroy an irreplaceable draft in a fit of hypercritical melancholy, caused by a lack of proper perspective.

The mind works faster than the hand; that's why the brilliant passages we compose in our heads are often disappointing when we view them on paper. Something gets lost in the transcription to type—but in revision we have a second chance to recapture the magic of the original concept, and improve upon it.

With a long book, however, there's no need to wait. By the time the project is finished, you should be able to read it from the beginning with a fairly level head.

Common Faults of First Drafts

Book or short story, most first drafts are wordy and can be improved by cutting and pruning. Sentences are likely to be long and involved. These should be untangled and simplified. For very easy reading, experts recommend sentences of eight or ten words, or less. Relatively easy reading calls for sentences of no more than eleven to fourteen words. The standard length for sixth, seventh, and eighth grades is seventeen to twenty words, while anything over that falls into the "difficult" category. This does not mean that you can't have an occasional extra long sentence.

Difficult words which can be understood in the context of the sentence may be used here and there, but too many will prove stumbling blocks to the reader. Nothing should interfere with the flow of your story. Check such words and find easier substitutes for them.

The healthiest attitude you can cultivate toward your work is one which admits that nothing you've set down on paper is sacred or unchangeable. Such an attitude is one of the marked differences between the professional and the amateur. The "pro" willingly discards pages, even chapters, shifts his scenes for the best effects, and rewords "finished" writing again and again.

Skillful revision can make the difference between salable and unsalable material, so it is very much to your advantage to master every step of this process. The best preparation for revision is familiarity with effective writing technique and the components of story structure—and these have been progressively detailed in every chapter of this text.

Four-Step Plan for Revision

I revise and rewrite to some extent all through the first draft of a book. Whenever I reread the previous day's output, I inevitably find some things I want to change. With the book finished, I'm ready for the "Four-Step Plan," which can also be adapted for revising short stories:

1. A quick, silent reading, for an over-all impression—and I try to be as beady-eyed and objective as possible. Whenever I come to a passage that jars me even slightly, I make a marginal check next to it. I do not stop to analyze and correct then and there. Continuity and pace are the most important factors in this reading.

2. Next I analyze my reactions. Does the main character stand out as an interesting individual? Is it possible to identify with him? Do all the story actors who surround him appear to be real people? Is the main character's problem or goal important and worth struggling for? Is it a problem that is suitable for a young person of his age? Will it concern the young readers for whom this story is intended?

What about conflict? Is the opposition strong? Are there enough complications thwarting the main character's struggles to solve his problem or reach his goal? Or are there so many that the story sounds like soap opera? How about background details, atmosphere, a sense of movement? Will the reader feel enough suspense to keep turning the pages to the very end to see how it all comes out?

Descriptions get a thorough scrutiny. Are they interwoven with characterization, dialogue, action? Are the five senses utilized to heighten the reality of the details? Has the *effect* of the sensation on the characters been described instead of dull, declarative statements given that make the reader yawn?

If questions like these raise doubts in your mind about *your* story, jot them on a work sheet, and then track down the technique for handling them in the various chapters of this text.

3. In step three I concentrate on the structural components of my story: the beginning, middle, climax, and end. Is each part of my story (or book) handled in the most effective way possible?

Have I begun at the right point? Have I begun as close as possible to the "day that is different"? Have I covered the seven points of the story opening as outlined in Chapter 15?

When you come to this point in revising your material, make a check list based on the contents of Chapters 15, 16, and 17 and consider your story accordingly. Questions raised in your mind now may lead you farther back into the text, to the chapters on plotting, sensory details, or dialogue.

Now you should read parts of the manuscript *aloud* to yourself, with a minimum of "expression" which might deflect your attention from flaws in the writing. You can catch many problems by ear—poor, awkward phrasing, unrealistic dialogue, slow-paced action.

Do not work on more than two or three chapters a day. You must be fresh and alert to do your best. If you stay too long at revision, you'll tire. As your mind grows less clear, you'll become permissive and allow all kinds of rough spots to get by.

If your work requires a great deal of rewriting, limit yourself to no more than two hours at a stretch. At the end of a set work period, leave your desk and occupy yourself with something entirely different for half an hour or so—some physical action, a household task, perhaps a short brisk walk. You'll return refreshed, and your manuscript will benefit from it.

4. With this step we come to the final processing of the manuscript—the polishing: word-editing, the grace notes, the literary embellishments which give professional tone, sparkle, and *style* to your writing.

You and Your Style

Next to plot, *style* rates as the number two mystery word for many writers. What is it? How can you acquire it?

A writer's style is indicated by his selection and arrangement of words. It depends on his personality, his outlook on life, the quality of his imagination; environment, family and social background (past and present); education (which continues to the end of his days, through life experience if nothing else); beliefs, ethics, ambitions, and frustrations; and subject matter.

Your writing style is you, modified by the type of expression your subject calls for. If you write on a variety of subjects, or about different kinds of people in many fields and circumstances, your *style*—your choice of words and their arrangement—is bound to vary with each story.

Never strain for "style." Never imitate the writing of some author you admire. Your style will emerge when you learn your craft and write with natural ease, a ready vocabulary, and an apt turn of phrase. With each piece you write strive to be clear, unselfconscious.

The Indispensable Word Finders

Now, as you polish, is the time to use a good dictionary and your *Roget's Thesaurus,* a word finder most writers rely on. It comes in paperback, but the book gets such a workout that a hardbound edition is more practical.

The Fine-Tooth Comb

Make sure you have used the right word in the right place for maximum effect. Check the meaning of the words if you have any doubts as to their accuracy.

Do your words help to create the mood required by the different scenes in your story? Dreamy, romantic, adventurous, terrifying, elated, despairing—your words can, and must, convey what you want the reader to feel.

Clarity is achieved through the use of the familiar word in preference to the unfamiliar, as *hero,* instead of *protagonist; thin,* instead of *attenuated.* Short words are preferable to long, erudite words, which merely seem labored and affected. Always use the concrete word instead of a general term; *shotgun,* rather than *weapon,* which might be anything from a club to a stiletto.

The single word is preferable to a phrase as a rule: instead of "Jill *ran quickly* across the courtyard," say "Jill *raced . . .* " It even sounds faster!

Take out the extra words in sentences which only clutter, not clarify what you are trying to say. Delete excessive adverbs and beloved adjectives (which Clifton Fadiman calls the "banana peels" of our language). Instead of weak modifiers, use strong, colorful action verbs which will make for tighter, more vigorous writing. Analyze the action you want and then find the verb to convey the proper image to the reader's mind. If you mean that "Tony *limped* into the room," don't say, "Tony walked in slowly."

Beware of flat-wheeled, non-descriptive verbs such as *came, ran, walked.* There are dozens of substitutes for this imageless collection; all you need to know is the exact *action* of your character. What did he do? Stride, strut, trudge, clump, thump, stagger, drag, fumble, stalk, hurtle, fly, thunder, float, dance, mince, dart, creep, sweep, hobble, whirl? There are many more, and certainly the right one for your need.

As Mark Twain put it: *The difference between the right word and the almost right word is the difference between lightning and the lightning bug.*

Words which evoke no images in the mind of the reader are useless to the writer. Words which bring up the wrong images can destroy the story. Your story is an illusion—an imagined experience for the reader. Never jolt him out of the illusion by the use of the wrong word or phrase. If you find the illusion broken at any point get rid of that sentence, that word, that phrase.

Some Do's and Don'ts for the Invisible Storyteller

At all times remain the invisible storyteller, for therein lies your most powerful magic. Never break into the story flow with:

"Now what do you suppose happened next?" Bringing the reader out of the story like that isn't fair. *Whom* is he to answer? *You* are not supposed to be there while your reader is reading!

Do not inject your opinions. If you feel strongly about something, wrap your ideas around the characters and let them voice the opinions and show them in action—but only if both the ideas and the action *belong* in the story.

Avoid redundancy—the use of needless words to express an idea, as "a blonde girl with light yellow hair." Snow is usually white, so there's no more need to say "white snow" than there is to say "green grass." If trees or mountains seem to reach the sky, the reader will assume they're tall. A four-foot man *is* short and a six-footer tall, so if you give the footage of either one, there is no need to say "short" or "tall" as well.

Watch out for silly actions that stop the reader cold. I once edited a manuscript in which a character "put on her glasses in order to hear better"—only this was long before they built hearing aids into the ear pieces. Here are some other gems that were caught in revision—and some, alas, that got by and were published:

> Betty took her head out of the locker and grinned.

> . . . Almost as a reward for being amiable, Sue Tyler announced a much pleasanter job a few days later. A bride *shot* in front of a little uptown church . . . [It was nothing fatal. The shooting was with a camera!]

> And he had a big sister who wore lipstick, a big bouncey dog, and a big piano . . . [My goodness. How big was she?]

The published classic of them all is probably this one:

> Lincoln crossed his right leg over his left knee, *and planted both feet solidly on the ground.* [Quite a feat!]

Eyes are sometimes required to perform strange feats also:

> The nurse looked at him with *calm, horror-stricken eyes* . . . [And as if that weren't bad enough] she fell into position at the side of the bed.

> The girl ran down to the water's edge *and cast her eyes* out to sea . . . [A favorite example in the classroom, but here

is one just as interesting:]

> Wendy watched them, fascinated, *her eyes jumping back and forth* with the conversation, like a tennis ball in a match.

I reviewed a British book in which "Jill had to *screw up her eyes* to read . . . " but then, eyes often are subjected to painful maneuvers. They pop, fall, rivet, swivel, drop, follow, cling—all seemingly independent of the character they belong to. Watch those eyes! Let them gaze occasionally, as well as look. And don't overwork them with stares.

Word Weeding

Among the words you'll want to weed out are the following; too many of them will mark you as an amateur:

very	tiny	little
then (and then)	suddenly	oh (or, OH!)
so	but	and
look	looked	just

There may be others on your personal string, like *well, clearly,* or *problem.* Be wary of any favorites you're apt to overwork.

Cut hesitant, noncommittal wording: "she *probably* knew," "he *seemed* to think," "he *obviously* felt." As the author you know if he did or didn't. Make such statements definite.

In the "what else" category are sentences like these:

> Mike *nodded his head.* [What else could he possibly nod but his head!]

> He was ready to carry Klara down the ladder *in his arms.* [Well, he might have carried her over his shoulder—but certainly not with his feet.]

> Mrs. McBee put on her old straw hat *on her head.* [Where else?]

Catch also the overloaded, earthbound phrases which sound very much like, "About to commence to start to begin," and streamline them.

The Grace Notes

Figures of speech are the grace notes in your writing. Your ability to compose word images is a measure of your skill. Figures of speech sharpen the picture, spotlight a character or a scene so that it becomes more vivid and real. They make the reader *feel* much more intensely, heightening his emotional reaction to your story. They serve another purpose by eliminating the dozens of less colorful words it takes to get the same idea across.

Using figurative language involves the ability to see similarities between one thing and another. A thin, tall boy; an excitable girl; a tiny, nervous woman; a big, roaring bully of a man—*what does each resemble?* Sometimes comparisons flash into your mind by happy accident, but as a rule such image-making is a cultivated skill. Whenever figures of speech come to you, jot them down on file cards or in your notebook, then pull them out as you need them to strengthen passages you are polishing. Never stop the flow of creative thought to search for apt figurative language.

You have already been introduced to this process in Chapter 10, dealing with sensory details. The important thing is not to succumb to cliches, those deft phrases which have become trite through overuse.

For examples in tune with today's world, read fiction in the popular magazines. In the juvenile field, the books and short stories of James L. Summers are filled with the effervescent, colorful language of the teen world he knows so well. Poetry is full of imagery which can sensitize your mind. Browse through a good anthology now and then and see what it can do to enrich the color of your phrasing.

As an aid to developing this power-plus in your imagination, here is a brief listing of the most used figures of picturesque speech:

A *simile* is a comparison of one thing with another, linked by the words "like" or "as."

> Mr. Ormsby was as pale as a mushroom.

> The crowd closed around her like a wall.

The *metaphor* omits "like" and "as," and states boldly that one thing *is* another, which literally, it is not. This, of course, puts the matter in stronger terms and the effect is more dramatic. The metaphor may be used to characterize major and minor characters by emphasizing some personal trait:

> Oliver was a sheep. (Lacking in leadership qualities)

> A brown, shaggy bear of a man . . . (Suggests ruggedness)

Metaphor by itself, or combined with a simile, makes for effective descriptions:

> The revolving doors made Babs think of huge spools winding long strings of people in and out of the store.

> Here and there an outmoded mansion reached skyward with wooden turrets, like weary arms; hipped by porticoes, flounced in weathered carpenter's lace, the shabby finery of another day . . .

Enthusiasm for figurative language sometimes produces a Frankenstein, the *mixed* metaphor. Two or more figures are incongruously combined, resulting in a confusing or even ludicrous image. Here is a classic example:

> Let's get our ship on its feet, men. Let us put our shoulders to the wheel and iron out all the bottlenecks.

Personification gives human characteristics to inanimate objects and things in nature. The device can be used to lend color and excitement to a narrative; to set a mood; to heighten suspense or a sense of danger:

> The cloud-hung mountain glowered at the two girls laboring up its steep side. With the next crash of thunder it sent a threatening rockslide of disapproval across their path, as if warning them to come no closer to the secret buried near its jagged peak.

In an entirely different mood:

> Snuggled inside the friendly arms of the wing chair, Ellin listened as the warm summer rain whispered and chuckled in the eaves.

Whatever figure of speech is used, it must fit the mood, period, setting, and characters of your story. The comparisons must be within the range of experience of the age for which you are writing. A sea-coast story should not have figures of speech that compare anything there to life on a desert, a dairy farm, or a lumber camp. Somebody's Aunt Hetty might scream like a gull—at the seashore—and gabble like a turkey on an inland farm.

Anachronisms must be avoided in figures of speech. A 17th century sound should not be compared to the whine of a 20th century jet; the swish of nylon does not belong in a Victorian England setting.

Any number of effective word pictures can be worked out with the basic group of grace note patterns given here. A dictionary of literary terms or a book on rhetoric will detail others for you, but remember: A story top-heavy with "images" is as badly crafted as one full of cliches. Moreover, you are primarily a story-teller, not a phrase-monger. This should be a comfort to those of you who simply do not see things figuratively—or at least, not without a great deal of labored thought. The grace notes, while desirable, are not indispensable, and their absence is less likely to be noticed unfavorably than an extravagant bedecking of your prose.

The more you learn about the craft of writing, the more critical you will become of your own output. However, like all good craftsmen, you must realize that there is a point beyond which tinkering will do more harm than good. By all means revise, and by all means polish, but within reason. When you've done your best, *stop.*

Your next step is to retype your manuscript for professional submission.

Chapter 19

How to Prepare Your Manuscript
for Submission

A professional-looking manuscript suggests professional competence in the writer; make the most of this psychological advantage!

Your manuscript must be typed. Either pica or the smaller
elite type may be used, but be consistent throughout. Otherwise
it will be difficult to estimate the length of your work. Do not
use fancy type that writes everything in italics, or Old English,
or capital letters. Make sure that your machine is in good working order and that the keys are clean. Use a good *black* ribbon.

Use a good grade of white bond paper with some rag content,
for it will stand up better than the sulphite papers, on which
erasures can make holes as well as ugly blurs. My own preference
is an 8½-by-11-inch, 16-pound bond for original copies. (20-pound
costs more to buy and mail, and anything lighter will wear-and-
tear too easily.)

Although erasable papers have some advantages, I've given
in to plaintive cries from my editors and no longer use them. Penciled editorial corrections smudge, and whole lines that should
stand are too easily erased.

For carbon copies I like the inexpensive, 16-pound, smooth-
finished bond (no rag content) because it is durable, takes a clear
imprint, and does not smudge as readily as the soft finishes. In
making multiple copies I use colored sheets to make collating
simpler (yellow, green, pink). The pink copy I usually keep for
my own files.

Standard weight carbon, suitable for making as many as five copies at a time, is satisfactory. Thinner carbon curls annoyingly.

Always make at least one carbon copy of any work submitted for publication, preferably two or even three. One copy *must* go into your file; the others (especially in the case of a book) may be required for the artist, for book club consideration, or for submission for foreign rights.

Pen Names

If you decide to use a *nom de plume,* select it with care; once you have started to build a new name for yourself, you won't want to change your mind and begin all over again.

You may choose to adopt a pen name for various reasons. You might have a name that is difficult to pronounce and therefore remember; you may simply want a more euphonious name than the one you have. It may be that you want to conceal your sex: you're a woman who can write whiz-bang adventure fiction for boys, or a man who writes stories for girls. Editors have no objection to pen names, provided the writer does not hop from one to another (your "name" is important to your publisher too).

Don't hope for anonymity with a pen name, for today it is impossible. First of all, your real name and social security number must be reported to your publisher for tax purposes. Secondly, some librarians will move heaven and earth to discover your real name if they suspect you of using a pseudonym. And once they *know,* they shelve *all* your books under your real name instead of the pseudonym you have worked so hard to establish!

The legal aspects of adopting a pen name can be easily arranged. See an official at your bank to make a proper record of your professional name. Clear proof that you are *you* under two names should eliminate any problem in opening an account (or changing one) in your new name or in paying taxes on savings bank interest. A checking account in your pen name only, however, may cause trouble later for your heirs. Thus, as an extra precaution, let your lawyer know your pen name and have it duly recorded in your will.

Notify the Post Office. There you don't have to explain anything to have mail duly delivered to your new name at the same address. Before long the mailman will come to realize that you're a writer! And he'll sigh when he brings in those fat envelopes with rejected manuscripts and grin broadly when the thin (check) envelopes arrive.

The Format

A book manuscript should have a title or cover page. Short material does not require this, but it's a good idea to have it anyway because it helps to keep the script looking fresh through several submissions.

Do not decorate the cover page in any way even if you are an accomplished artist. The only things that belong on this page are your name and address in the upper left hand corner (an inch or so from the top); the approximate number of words in your manuscript on a line at the right; and halfway down the page, centered neatly, the title of your story. Two or three lines below this, center the word "by," and two or three lines below that, type your name—or pseudonym—*exactly as you want it to appear in print.* (If a pseudonym is used in your by-line, type it in parentheses under your legal name in the heading of this page so your editor won't think your real name is the name of your agent.)

If your manuscript is book length, there will usually be a table of contents and sometimes a preface of some introductory material. This is known as "front matter" and should be typed on separate sheets and numbered in the upper right hand corner in small Roman numerals. A dedication (also typed on a separate page) may be included or supplied after the book is accepted.

Your first page of text should also have your name and address (single spaced) on the left, about one-half inch from the top of the page. (This repetition is a must in case the title page should somehow be lost.) Type in the approximate number of words at top right, as shown in the sample format opposite.

Under this some people indicate the "rights" they are offering

Your Legal Name
(Pen Name)
Street Address
City, State, Zip Code   About _____ words

                        CENTER YOUR TITLE IN CAPS
                                    by
                               Your Name

     Begin your story three or four spaces below your name. Indent

paragraphs three to five spaces. Always double space your copy, and

type only on one side of the paper. Double space between paragraphs.

     Letters, telegrams, etc. used within the text should also be

double spaced and be given an extra identation.

     For pica type, margins should be 1-¼" at the top and left and

about one inch on the right and bottom. For elite type, use 1-½" on

all four sides.

     Beginning with page two, type your last name or a key word from

First Page of Text

the title in the upper left-hand corner <u>in</u> <u>small</u> <u>letters</u> and number
the pages consecutively in the upper right-hand corner.

Each chapter should begin on a new page. <u>Number</u> <u>these</u> <u>pages</u>
<u>consecutively</u>, <u>never</u> <u>as</u> <u>separate</u> <u>units</u>. Do not write "More" or any
other directions at the bottom of the page.

At the end of your story you may go down five spaces, center the
page, and tap the underlining bar a few times. But do not write "The
End," "Finis," etc. You may type your name and address at bottom left
on the last page.

Twenty-six lines per page is a good compromise between over-
crowding and too much white space. With the margins suggested, each
line (in pica type) will have about 10 words. Twenty-six lines per
page will <u>average</u> about 250 words. This makes it simple to estimate
the number of words in your manuscript. The estimate is always
approximate: to the nearest 25 or 50 words in a short story and to
the nearest 100 in a book. <u>Never</u> count every word.

Some typewriters (foreign makes especially) can adjust to a one-
and-a-half line space, which can make for a considerable line and word
count difference. Be sure to check your machine on this.

Remember that even the appearance of your typed page must come
under your scrutiny. Be sure paragraphs are of different lengths so
that the page does not have a dull, "measured off with a ruler"
appearance. Also, do not have a line of "He's" or "She's" or "Susie's"
beginning each paragraph all down the page. It can happen and it
looks terrible.

Second Page of Text

for sale. On a book manuscript, *don't*. These rights should be negotiated after the book is accepted and the editor invites you to talk over your contract. (See the chapter on markets and marketing.)

On a short story, leave out such beginner's trademarks as "For Sale," or "Usual Rights—Usual Rates." The editor knows the script is for sale, and rates are set by company policy.

The stipulation of "First Serial Rights Only" (which means the right to publish first, and once only in that particular magazine for the fee paid you), is acceptable to some magazines but not to others, whose policy is to buy all rights. In that case the editor may prefer to return the story to you unread rather than argue with you. In any event, such notices on the manuscript afford scant legal protection. *The rights specified on the check or voucher in payment for your work, which you are required to sign, constitute the legal agreement between you and the publishing company.* Rights need not be a matter of great concern, however. I have found that most magazines in the juvenile field are generous in returning unused rights after first publication, and as a rule, book rights to the story are automatically retained by you. (More detail on this subject in the next two chapters.)

Your title should be dropped about one-third of the way down the page.

It is wise, by the way, to make two or three extra copies of the first page of your manuscript, and two or three of the last page. If the story is not immediately accepted, wear and tear on these pages is inevitable even with a cover sheet, and a travel-worn appearance might prejudice an editor. After a number of submissions you can insert fresh copies, with type color to match the rest of the manuscript, and no one but you will be the wiser.

Consistency is important, so it is always wise to have your own "style sheet" handy. Some names can be spelled in several ways. On the style sheet mark down the variation you have used to avoid having *Edith, Edyth,* and *Edythe,* or *Terri, Terry,* and *Terrie* all in one story. Words like *blonde* and *blond* may be a problem. Hyphenation is optional in some cases, as in *teen-age* and *teenage.* Consistency will endear you both to your editor and her copy-editor.

Punctuation and Grammar

In dialogue *a new paragraph is required with each change of speaker.* Any gesture, action, or thought of the speaker belongs in the same paragraph as his speech:

> Migsy thought hard. "I simply can't do it," she said at last. She pulled back her hair with both hands and suddenly started to run.

Words spoken in dialogue must be enclosed in double quotation marks. Anything quoted within a speech is then enclosed in single quotes:

> "Did you hear what she said? 'I won't go and you can't make me!' Did you hear that?" Miss Price quivered with indignation.

Too many commas in a sentence suggest that it might be better to break it up and reword it. An exclamatory sentence should reveal itself to the reader through your choice of words. Resist the urge to use the exclamation mark for emphasis too often.

If you want a word, a sentence, or dialogue to have special emphasis, underline it. This means that you want it set up in italics. *Like this.* Foreign words and phrases are usually italicized. In fiction be sparing of both—the foreign words and the italics.

The possessive form of pronouns often nettles even experienced writers. *Hers, its, theirs, yours,* and *oneself* take no apostrophe before the "s." But for emphasis, it is permissible to write *one's self.*

Do not pepper your manuscript with dots (ellipses). Properly used in a story, three . . . indicate the trailing off of a speech (closed with quotation marks) or an incompleted thought or statement. If used in the body of a narrative, the dots indicate a scene shifting or a time jump. When a sentence is completed, the period is followed by three dots:

> He crawled to the edge of the cliff, utterly spent. . . .
> When he opened his eyes again, the sun was directly overhead.

The *hyphen* is used to join words, like *ten-year-olds,* or to divide a word which comes at the end of a typed line and must be carried over to the next line. Such words should be divided according to their syllables. If you're uncertain of this division, consult your dictionary.

The *dash* is used to indicate a break in thought at the end of a line or an insertion of another thought within the body of a sentence:

> Now that we're all here—except for Roger—let's get down
> to business.

In typewritten material a dash may be indicated with one stroke of the hyphen key, but then there must be one space before and after it. However, if you strike the hyphen key twice to indicate a dash in your work, no space is necessary. Whichever way you do it, be consistent throughout. A note on your personal style sheet will insure this. Be sparing in your use of dashes.

If you need more help with grammar and punctuation, consult a dictionary of English usage, or such books as *The Art of Readable Writing,* by Rudolf Flesch or *The Elements of Style,* by Strunk and White.

Proofreading the Manuscript

Your finished typescript must be proofread carefully. A blotter slid under the lines will slow down your pace and help you to spot errors more readily. Do not proofread for more than an hour at a time without a short "eye-break," or you'll begin to miss transposed letters and words inadvertently left out.

Corrections may be made in pencil, ink, or type. If a word, line, or lines should be omitted, simply draw a line through this material. A page with more than three conspicuous corrections must be retyped.

All corrections must be made on carbon copies also. The professional writer knows how important carbon copies are. Besides protecting him from a total loss of a manuscript (which does happen, though rarely) sometimes a page vanishes from material being readied for the printer. With a carbon on file, a new page can be produced easily and quickly.

How to Send Your Manuscript

Do not bind a manuscript in any way, or staple the pages; as they are turned for reading, creases inevitably will be made at the staple points. *Never* pin the pages together. Think of that rich editorial blood spilling over them and marking them forever, not to mention the editorial ire aroused by such an injury. Confine your page fastening of short works to the safe and efficient paper clip.

A manuscript of no more than four or five pages may be folded in thirds, like a business letter, and sent in a large business-size envelope (with another stamped, self-addressed envelope folded inside it for return of the material should it not be accepted).

Manuscripts of twelve to fifteen pages may be sent folded in half, in a 7-by-10-inch manilla envelope with a 6½-by-9½-inch return envelope fitted inside.

Manuscripts of more than fifteen pages must be sent flat. You may put them in a plain protective folder which has been trimmed to slip easily into a 9-by-12-inch envelope. Do not fasten the pages in any way. Send the manuscript in a 10-by-13-inch envelope, using the 9-by-12 for return. Cardboard, cut to fit the smaller envelope, will prevent mishandling in transit much more effectively than stamping "Do not bend" on the mailing piece.

Never use decorated folders for your manuscripts, either the short stories or book lengths. The effect will not be pleasing, and will scream "raw beginner" to everyone in the publishing office.

A book manuscript travels best in a box—the kind your rag bond typing paper comes in, or one bought from a writers' supplies house. Make sure that the kind you choose is easy for an editor to open and close—some of the more elaborate boxes feature interlocking tabs and slots that make removing the manuscript a five-to-ten-minute operation! Check ads on this type of service in the writers' magazines. For a sturdy outside wrap for the box, use a cut-open brown paper grocery bag, secured with package sealing tape.

Do not turn any pages upside down to determine whether your manuscript is read. This, a favorite trick among beginners, raises editorial hackles. *All* manuscripts are read because the business of editors is to find publishable stories. However, it is no more necessary for the editor to read an entire story to know that it isn't for that house, than it is to eat a whole pot of stew to discover it has too little meat.

Copyright for unpublished manuscripts cannot be secured. Since material can be copyrighted only on publication, typing "Copyrighted" on your submission is a foolish bluff that does you no credit.

Do not worry about piracy. Unpublished material is quite safe with any reputable house. (New authors sometimes go to extraordinary lengths to prevent "piracy." One editor told me of a woman who submitted only every other page of her story to make sure *her* brain child would not be stolen!) Actually you have an automatic, common-law copyright protection on your manuscript. You can validate your claim through the carbon copy of your work in your files, along with some dated material like notes, letters, or a submission record.

Letters to the Editor

Editors who spend many hours *reading* prefer not to read anything they don't have to—like superfluous letters from authors. Don't write to explain the story. Your manuscript must speak for itself. The editor also knows you've sent it because you hope to sell it, so don't include a letter stating something as obvious as that.

A letter is useful only if you have something pertinent to say about the story or yourself. If, for example, you're an expert in the field with which your story is concerned, say so. If some unusual fact is used in the plot, "document" it for authenticity. Many juvenile books are used in the classroom, so the editor must be sure that your statements are true, should a teacher or fact-happy youngster challenge them. In non-fiction and historical writing, documentation is very important, and all the references you have used should be listed at the front or back of your manuscript.

This list may be mentioned in a letter to the editor.

By all means write a letter if a well-known author or critic has suggested that you send your story to a particular editor—but make this "introduction" a simple statement. Don't say the person is wild about your tale and thinks it exactly right for that particular publisher. Editors prefer to make up their own minds —and being human, they just might resent being pressured.

If your occupation has a bearing on your material, *do* mention it—briefly. Since you are writing for young people, the fact that you are (or have been) a teacher or librarian would be of interest to the editor. Should you be in any writing field, as with an advertising agency, mention it to suggest that you'd be willing to revise without tantrums, having been already conditioned by your job.

If you have sold or published anything anywhere, even if only a filler, mention that in your letter, listing the magazines, newspapers, or book publishers. But if you have no sales to your credit, don't worry about it. Editors are eager to discover talented newcomers.

Your own printed business stationery for correspondence with editors is a good investment to help promote your "solid citizen" image. Keep it simple—your name, address, and telephone number (including the area code) are all that is needed on your letterhead. Phrases like "Author," "Free-lance Writer and Photographer," or "Specialist in Children's Literature" will mark you as an amateur.

For Your Peace of Mind

When you send the manuscript, include a stamped, self-addressed postal card, with the title of your story and the name of the publisher typed on the message side. Whoever handles the arriving manuscripts in the publisher's office will then fill in the blank spaces and drop the card into the outgoing mail, and you'll know that your material has arrived safely. (Some publishers do send company cards or letters acknowledging arrival of material, but some do not. This simple expedient will insure your knowing in either case.)

```
                                            PLACE
                                            STAMP
                                            HERE




              YOUR NAME

              Street Address

              City, State, Zip Code
```

```
TITLE OF YOUR STORY_____

Date sent_____

To:  NAME OF PUBLISHER

Received by_____

Date_____
```

Postcard Acknowledging Receipt of Manuscript

Your first submission to a magazine or book publishing house should be addressed to the editor by name. If your story is returned with a signed note of any kind by some other person in the editorial department, then address your next submission there to the person who wrote you. Most editorial departments keep an eye on promising people, and the individual who wrote you will be your "contact editor" at that office.

The Waiting Game

Magazines, on the average, take from three weeks to two months to report on a story. Book publishers take three months or more—much more, sometimes. No matter how impatient you are to *know,* do not inquire about your manuscript until two months have passed. Then expedite matters with a tracer letter to the editor. Be polite and brief:

> Dear Mr./Miss/Mrs./Ms. (Name of Editor):
>
> Would you please let me know the status of my story, (fill in title), submitted to you on (fill in date)?
>
> I am enclosing a stamped, self-addressed postal card for your convenience.
>
> > Sincerely,
> > (Sign your name)
> > Type your name

Leave the message side blank for the editor to fill in.

There is absolutely no reason not to trust the Postal Service to deliver your precious manuscript, especially if you back your faith with a carbon copy of your work safely filed at home. Postal rates and regulations change from time to time; at present the least expensive way to send a book manuscript is by "Special Fourth Class Rate." Mark the package: "Special Fourth Class Rate: Manuscript." If any message is enclosed, write: "First Class Letter Enclosed" on the package, and next to this paste the current first class stamp.

"Special Handling," for a modest additional fee, guarantees the equivalent of First Class treatment for your package. For another small fee you can *insure* the contents, something you cannot do with regular First Class mailings. Normally the insurance value should not exceed replacement (cost of retyping) of the manuscript.

Instructions for the return of the book manuscript, as well as the return postage (we do have to think negatively now and then), may be enclosed in a letter pasted on the outer wrapping of your package. Take along a small roll of Scotch tape when you go to the post office and tape the letter down right there.

With First Class, you may use Certified Mail for proof-of-delivery. There is a fee for this, plus First Class postage, plus an additional fee for a return receipt signed by the person who received the manuscript. Get details on this from your post office.

Do not deliver your manuscript in person. No editor is going to drop whatever she is doing to chat with you, or read your story while you wait. You'll only have to leave your package at the reception desk anyway. It's pointless to make a special trip to the publishing office unless you have other business in that area. Even so, it's a bit chilling to see the receptionist accept your package as if there were nothing special about it. Save yourself the ordeal and *send* your masterpiece.

But *where?*

The next chapter will give you practical guidance on markets and marketing.

Chapter 20

Markets and Marketing . . .
the Business Side of Writing

Every writer must continually study and update the market possibilities for his material. Editors and editorial needs change; new magazines and book publishers appear; some merge with other houses or suspend publication. The only way to keep up with such day-to-day trade news is to read the magazines published for writers. The two I would not be without are *Writer's Digest* and *The Writer*.

In *Writer's Digest* I always turn first to Hayes Jacobs' lively, informative and practical "New York Market Letter." Then I go through the magazine from cover to cover, culling every item that might be helpful for me or to my students or clients. These items I do not store in my head but jot down in the appropriate places in *Writer's Market*, or in the *Literary Market Place* (*LMP*), or in the Market Tips section of my own card file, which I'll tell you about presently. Market analysis must be made a routine part of the business side of your writing.

Writer's Market, a bound, thick book published by Writer's Digest, lists over 4,000 markets for free-lance writers, divided into categories, with each entry helpfully annotated. The book is revised annually and is always packed with timely tips and other helpful advice for the freelancer.

Literary Market Place, published by R. R. Bowker for publishers, editors, and the "book trade" (book store operators, salesmen, etc.), lists U.S. and Canadian publishers, their chief officers, and what kinds of books each publishes. Also an annual,

LMP. carries lists of agents; book clubs; and magazines, news-papers, and other outlets for book publicity as well.

If you are a short-story writer, you must study the magazines to which you wish to submit material. (See Chapter 2 for a general survey of this field.)

As you investigate the possibilities, *evolve your own market list—one that fits your particular kind of material.* Use a 3-by-5 card file to record pertinent data: name of publication, its ad-dress, name of the juvenile editor, preferred story subjects, word length, rate of pay. Note the ones that allow simultaneous sub-missions (submitting the same story at one time to several low-paying, denominational markets which do not have overlapping circulations). In each case, when making a simultaneous sub-mission, the writer must so inform the editor. Note also the publications which will not consider simultaneous submissions, magazines which pay good rates and expect the exclusive use of material.

There are some magazines which will buy "second rights" to stories. They reprint published material, on which the writer has sold "first rights"—rights for a one-time appearance in a publica-tion. Make a note of these markets also.

Analyze the types of stories used in the sample issues you col-lect. One of the chief editorial complaints is that authors do not bother to study specific markets but send stories out haphazardly. Here is what Adelaide Field, a former editor of *Child Life,* had to say on this subject:

> " . . . millions of dollars of postage and countless man hours are wasted annually, sending the right horse to the wrong stable. The author, who will spend weeks writing a story, will not spend a few days studying markets. Yet every magazine strives to create a hallmark, a quality peculiarly its own . . . A little study would keep the breezy story away from the moralizing magazine, the four-installment serial away from the publication that limits itself to two-chapters! And that is why editors endorse market-magazines so heartily, not only for the impetus they provide to their readers, and for their specific up-to-date information on current requirements, but also because this information, well applied, will lighten the editor's load . . . "

The Junior Book Field

Here too you must know what is being published. Waste no time in becoming a regular, card-carrying visitor of the children's and young adult rooms of your public library. You should also read the junior book reviews in the major newspapers published in your area. Some of these run special sections of reviews and articles in the spring, and also in the fall—to commemorate Children's Book Week. These sections you should keep for reference.

The Horn Book Magazine is a standard reference for librarians, teachers, and parents—and it should be yours.

There is also the *School Library Journal.* Ask your librarian about it. She may also have the *Bulletin of the Center for Children's Books,* published by the University of Chicago Graduate Library School. In these the reviewers are librarians who evaluate books from their professional point of view. Since librarians buy about 80% of our output, their views are of tremendous value to the writer who must live by his words.

You should also write for publishers' catalogs and study them. You'll discover that some houses publish nothing for younger readers, but feature only teen-age books. Others lean heavily toward factual material. But there's nothing static about your markets and you must be alert to all changes: they can spell *sales!*

Basing your choice on what you have learned, and revising it as new information filters down to you, make your own selected book market list on 3-by-5 cards, with all the details you can gather on each publisher. Arrange alphabetically and keep this sheaf of cards separate from the ones you made for magazine publishers.

The Itinerary

With your manuscript (book or short story) ready for mailing, decide on an appropriate itinerary for it. *List at least five places where you'd like to send it—now, before the manuscript leaves your hands.* This itinerary will serve a double purpose: first as a traveling guide for your brain child; second, as a morale booster if the manuscript comes back. You won't feel that the rejection spells the end of the road for it, because you'll have another publishing house already picked out—where it might fare better.

Matching your itinerary to editorial tastes is important. In a featured article, a New York agent once told *Writer's Digest* readers what subjects certain editors especially liked, what types of stories especially appealed to them. This is the kind of information you must constantly glean for yourself from the market news, wherever you come upon it, so that you can market your own material intelligently.

I recall the story of a professional client who was referred to me after having suffered considerable discouragement over her book for younger readers. She accepted my stern and lengthy criticism eagerly and creatively (she did not slavishly follow every suggestion; what I said stimulated her own creative thinking and gave freshness, zing—and the right direction—to her tale). After I saw the revised book, I suggested a handpicked editor to her. The book was accepted enthusiastically in two weeks' time, even though the market was generally thought "very difficult," "slow," "poor," and "dismal" at the time. As long as any publishing is being done, a good story will find a home. But it must be good, it must be written with professional skill, because at all times—good and bad—the competition is fierce.

Reserve a file folder for each story and book in which to keep all kinds of records and letters pertaining to that particular manuscript. The short story carbon should be kept in this folder. Since the full-length book carbon is not likely to fit into a folder, stack it safely away in a box. Keep the records and correspondence folders for your books in your file cabinet.

On the next page you will find a copy of the folder notes I made for one of my early short stories. Folders for books are made out in the same way.

This kind of record keeps me from unintentionally sending a story twice to the same editor. In the case of "Binkie," the *Story Parade* editor had said, "try us later"—which happily I did.

Notice that the story did not languish in my files between submissions. And note another important point: *I had a carbon of it in my file.* Stories seldom get lost, but mishaps do occur. Having a carbon is like taking out insurance on your story's continued life.

Sample Folder Notes

BINKIE AND THE OSTRICH

Age 8-12   2,900 words

Itinerary	Date Sent	Date Ret.	Letter or Form	Postage
1. *Story Parade*	12-2-48	12-30-48	Nice letter: *"Not buying now."*	First Class Mail 15¢ to send 12¢ return
2. *Jack & Jill*	12-30-48	1-12-49	Form	
3. *Children's Activities*	1-12-49	2-3-49	Form	
4. *JR.* (Chicago)	2-5-49	. . . MS lost!	(Thank goodness, I had carbon in this folder.)	
5. Retyped and resubmitted to *Story Parade*	5-28-49	SOLD! . . .	$50.00	
6. *Instructor*				

Published in *Story Parade*, Feb. '51 (Cut to 2,400 words)
Reprinted, *My Weekly Reader* 8-5-55 (an adaptation) $20.00
Reprinted in Betts Basic Reader,
  The ABC Adventures Here and There, (adaptation)
  Retitled: "Grandma's Ostrich" (lead story) $35.00
Reprinted, *My Weekly Reader*—Summer '61 (adaptation) $20.00
Reprinted, *My Weekly Reader*—Summer '65 (adaptation) $20.00
Reprinted, *Golden Magazine*, Mar. '67 $20.00

Did you see the notation for postage on the extreme right of my folder record? This must be calculated exactly according to the current rates; your material should never arrive with any postage due!

Trips to the post office need not be made for small, uninsured items. Get yourself a postal scale, a First Class rubber stamp, and a batch of postage stamps—and save that traveling and waiting time. *Time is your capital.* Don't waste it.

Once a story is published, I file away a complete issue of the magazine. But I also keep tearsheets from another issue in my itinerary folder, making for a complete and permanent history.

Note that your magazine stories may have a future value— considerably over and above the initial fee paid you—as picture books or reprints in anthologies. *Notify your publisher of any changes in your address,* identifying yourself by story and date of publication, if you are not a regular contributor. This will prevent frantic—and sometimes futile—hunts for you in years to come, because the Postal Service keeps track of your reported moves for only a limited time.

Don'ts and Do's on Submissions

To query or not? In fiction it is usually best to submit your completed project, especially if you're a newcomer to the trade. An editor can't possibly judge your writing skill otherwise. "Four chapters and an outline of the rest" isn't much good either. Some people can write fine beginnings and fall flat on the middles— regardless of the exciting promise in outline or synopsis. Contracts on such incompleted ventures are rarely given to beginners. Moreover, having your "trial submission" coldly turned down can discourage you from finishing the book. Wait to query until you are established; then you'll probably work from contract with an advance, given to you on a page or two of synopsis because your ability and sales appeal is well known.

On non-fiction projects a query can only establish whether a publisher has or has not covered your subject matter. Before writing, however, you should first study his complete catalog as well as the *Subject Guide to Books in Print,* available in most libraries; no publisher will want a new book on his list which will compete with one he already has.

Regardless of his response to your query, the publisher is not obligated in any way. If he should show interest—and you do not have a finished manuscript to send him at once—he may take the first acceptable one that comes along on your subject, quite possibly because *you* put the bee in his bonnet. A good rule to follow: *Write before you talk!*

Never submit a manuscript to more than one publisher at a time regardless of the weeks and months involved in the making of an editorial decision. Multiple submissions of stories (unless covered by special editorial dispensation), and books are considered unethical, at least by publishers. Should you take a chance and do so anyway, think how embarrassing it would be for two publishers to accept your story simultaneously! You'd have some explaining to do, and certainly one of the editors, and quite possibly both, would be furious with you — permanently. Don't take that chance.

Never send a carbon of a book to an editor, because her first thought will be that you have made multiple submissions—and back will come your manuscript, probably unread. What's more, a big question mark will be added to your name in the editor's mind—and editors have long memories, refreshed by notations on file cards. Publishing is an orderly business, and once you submit to a house, records are kept of your dealings with it.

However, when you submit a manuscript to a book publisher, you may at the same time submit a clear carbon copy to a magazine—as a serial possibility—with a cover letter stating that the original is being considered by a book editor. This is ethical, because separate rights are involved and you may sell them separately. For the record, state that you wish to retain book rights, and at the top of your first page of text, above the estimated-words line, type *First Serial Rights Only* as a reminder. In this instance, it's a must procedure, because these are the *only* rights you should sell to the magazine.

Some editors will allow you to submit a clear photocopy of your manuscript—one that can be written on easily with a ball point pen—if you indicate on your first page or in a covering letter that it is *not* a simultaneous submission. Others, of course, regard photocopies with the same suspicion they reserve for carbons. Even the editors who accept photocopies may fail to return them, if they become accidentally separated from their return postage.

Never send an editor (*even your favorite*) *two manuscripts at the same time.* Editors seldom make a simultaneous purchase of two stories, so in effect you are giving your editor a choice. One story is bound to come back, while on separate submissions you might sell both.

Seasonal material must be submitted five to eight months ahead of schedule, and even ten months is none too soon. Magazine content is planned far in advance, and sometimes material is scheduled ahead several years.

Although editorial decisions often are agonizingly slow in coming, be patient. Most editors are conscientious, but they work with small staffs. The whole department may have only four people to run it—with hundreds of stories to read, besides a myriad of other editorial chores that must be done on schedule. Editor's jobs are not nine-to-five affairs. Most of them take manuscripts home to read at night and on weekends. In the bedroom of one of my editors I once saw a market basket, loaded with manuscripts, hanging from the knob of her night table! This sight strengthened my patience with editors considerably.

Stay away from editors' offices unless you're invited to visit. Don't bother an editor with needless correspondence. If she is interested in your material, she'll call you.

Magazine Payment Methods

Short story payment is made on acceptance or on publication. First class magazines should pay on acceptance. However, there is a group (with individual magazine circulations of over 200,000) that I formerly considered in the top echelon, which now pay on publication. Since the author is not even told, at the time of acceptance, *when* that publication may come, the arrangement seems to me grossly unfair to the author. Of course no one forces authors to submit to these houses, but I say again: *writers should know their markets* and the consequences of having their work accepted by some of them. The markets which pay the most and *on acceptance*, should go on the preferred list for your submissions. It is only sensible and business-like.

When promise is made to "pay on acceptance" it means that you will get your check as soon as the accounting department can process it. Before you endorse the check, remember that the "rights" you're selling are sometimes printed on the back of the check, above the place intended for your signature.

Some magazines send a short contract form for you to sign. Read it carefully and don't be afraid to question anything you don't understand. Other magazines make the purchase without stating either in letter or contract that they are buying *all* rights to a work, including the right to copyright. If they *do* make such a statement, don't panic. Their reason is that many copyright experts believe a valid copyright cannot be secured for magazine material unless all rights are purchased. If you don't know what rights are being bought, *ask before you cash the check*.

Vanity Publishers

The *Bookman's Glossary* (R. R. Bowker) defines a "vanity publisher" in this way:

> A trade designation for publishing concerns that specialize in publishing books at the author's risk and expense. They sign publishing contracts with inexperienced authors by appealing to their vanity or natural desire to see their writings in print at whatsoever the cost. They seldom have a sales staff.

Success of a bona fide publishing venture depends (for both the publisher and the author) on how many copies of a book are sold. The publisher who has invested his hard cash in a financial advance to the author, in the considerable expense of preparing a manuscript for publication, and in distributing it by means of a large staff of salesmen, is interested in getting his money back— and in making a profit. The vanity publisher, who has not invested anything, has no such interests at stake and therefore no incentive to sell the books he publishes. His expenses and profit are included in the sums paid by the author.

Sometimes such publishers offer a fantastic royalty return (in the contract) to the gullible author—something like 40%. Some go all out and make it a straight 100%. In other words, they are *printers;* the author owns the books and can do with them—all 500 or 2,000 copies—what he pleases. It isn't long before the author discovers some hard and painful facts about *distribution.*

If your writing has commercial merit (and it must have to be accepted by a commercial publishing firm), *you* will be paid for the privilege given that firm to publish your book. You do not have to pay *them* to publish it. The reputable publishing house assumes all the expense and the risks and responsibility for distributing your book while you sit at home working on your next project.

Don't be discouraged by those first rejections. Keep submitting your book; and if at last you feel that you cannot sell it, then retire it in the hope that you'll have better luck with your next venture. But don't sink into fuzzy thinking on the subject. If commercial houses, with well-organized sales staffs felt they could not market your book, how can a vanity press do any better for you? *Do not invest your own money for the publication of your book. Your chances of financial success in such a venture are about 300 to 1—against you.*

The only exception to getting involved in such a project might be if you can easily afford the expense of a private printing (which is what it amounts to, you know). Seeing your book in print may salve your bruised feelings. Or it might be you have written a family or personal history that would not interest thousands of readers, but will interest your family and friends. If you can afford to have it printed (at about $35 per page), fine. Engage a printer and have it done, and present copies to your family and friends.

In any case, know what you are about and what is involved. The general feeling (well-founded on fact) is that vanity press books are badly written; if illustrated, the illustrations are of poor quality. No one wants to review them. As a reviewer I've had pathetic letters from authors who discovered they were stuck with the selling end of their publications. There was nothing I could do for them. There is no point in wasting review space on such printings because the book stores will not stock them (except possibly on a local level) and the libraries will not buy them. The author's money has been wasted, and such publication hasn't done a thing for his reputation. Everyone in the trade knows which houses require "cooperative" subsidization for publication, so if anything, the writer's reputation will suffer.

Sell your books the hard way. It pays!

The Business Side of Writing

If writing is your business and not a sometime hobby, and you can prove it, your business expenses are deductible on your income tax returns—just as your income from writing (a self-employed occupation), is taxable. Here's where those rejection slips may come in handy, so don't throw them away! They're your proof that what you've been writing has been done with the sincere *intention* of selling your material. The fact that you have not sold anything *yet* does not alter the situation. Many a new business starts off in the red before any profits are shown.

What You Can Deduct

Your typewriter, desk, chair, filing cabinet—these are deductible items, provided you have some record of their purchase. Such items cannot be deducted in one lump sum, but must be prorated on a depreciation scale based on their useful "life" to you. (Ten years is usually considered fair, so you may deduct one tenth of the cost each tax year.)

Your work area is deductible on a proportionate basis, whether you own a house or rent an apartment. (Be sure to consult a professional tax expert or someone at your local IRS office, before arriving at any figures.) If you build a study onto your house, that is prorated on something like a forty-year depreciation scale—but every little bit helps.

Pencils, pens, typewriter ribbons, paper, paperclips, Scotch tape, file cards, file folders, printed business stationery, postal cards, wrapping materials, postage—everything normally used in the business of being a writer is legitimately deductible, provided you have some record of purchase. If you deal with a stationer you can save all his bills, but you should also buy a Day Book (deductible) and write down in it, in ink, every single item you buy for your work.

The kind I keep comes from the dimestore; on the left I enter *Income* and on the right, *Expenses,* using one page for each month of the year. Every item has a date of purchase and whatever is necessary to identify it. This record I transfer into an itemized ledger and at the end of the year an accountant (fee deductible) makes up my tax form.

Reference books, trade journals, magazines, and newspapers are deductible, although those which continue to be useful after one year (as an unabridged dictionary) should be depreciated over their estimated useful life.

Memberships in professional organizations are deductible, as well as fees paid to typists and literary consultants. Writing courses and seminars you attend may be deducted, although they might cause some question if you are not a full-time writer.

Travel expenses for business meetings (consultations with editors over contract terms!), for talks and lectures, or for publicity in connection with your published work are deductible. Travel for research may be deductible, depending on where you go and what your project entails. Even a vacation can be combined with research, and the portion of expenses connected with the business of writing deducted. *A diary to support your claims is a must.* If you use your car, distances between travel points must be recorded for mileage deductions. If taxis are used in the city, keep track of your destinations and purpose of the trip to authenticate your claims.

Fiction writers sometimes meet raised eyebrows when they claim travel-research expenses. The general idea seems to be that everything we need for our stories comes straight out of our heads. If you're ever challenged on such deductions, produce whatever records you can and explain how *you* work. Very probably a portion of your expenses will be allowed.

A writer who makes a profit must pay the proper proportion for Social Security credit (on the self-employed basis). Tax laws change from year to year, so unless you have a professional accountant in charge of your affairs, be sure to keep abreast of all the new developments.

Looking Ahead—You and Posterity

More and more universities and libraries, as well as local historical societies, are showing an interest in collecting memorabilia from writers. It might behoove *you*, as a serious writer, to start saving the work drafts of your books and stories and any outlines, summaries, research notes, sketches, dummies, diaries, journals, as well as letters, and book talks—in fact, anything of interest related to you and your work that might be of value to such collections.

If anyone in your family has had the foresight to save your childhood writing efforts, you might take steps to recover such items. These and work drafts of early books are especially hard to come by, what with the general shortage of storage space and the natural urge to clean house periodically. Next time such an urge comes over you, consider twice what you throw away—it may be your claim to immortality *and a deductible tax item*, for such gifts to institutions are tax deductible, under whatever current tax regulations are in effect. Better check that wastebasket right now.

Chapter 21

When You Sell a Book
—Contracts and Other Matters

Most books are bought on a royalty basis, by contract.

The mass-market cheap editions (low in price, not necessarily in the quality of the writing) are usually bought outright, with one lump sum paid for *all* rights. Payment for full-length books ranges from $500 to $1500, while the popular little full-color books bring from $125 to $500, unless the author has a "name" and can dicker for better terms. Publishers claim that these low-priced items are very expensive to produce (especially those in color) and to distribute, and therefore they cannot do any better for the authors. But these little books often sell for years, so it might be to your advantage to try to place that kind of manuscript with a royalty-paying house before submitting it to the mass-market publishers.

The fly in that honey is that *picture book royalties are split on a fifty–fifty basis with the artist;* and sometimes, when the pictures are considered more important than the text, the division may be on a seventy-five–twenty-five basis in favor of the artist. Still, you do retain an interest in your literary property rights (you and the artist, jointly), and those just might pay off handsomely.

Your Literary Rights and Your Book Contract

Rights to a booklength literary property include the following items: prepublication serial (first serial rights); book publication, including book club rights; magazine, second serial rights; newspaper second serial; book reprint; dramatization; motion picture; television; radio; mechanical reproduction; condensation and abridgement; anthology; quotation; translation; syndication; commercial, etc.

When a book publisher offers you a contract, these are the rights he wants you to turn over to him in whole or in part. You are not expected to sign the contract on the spot. It is a long document, full of awesome-sounding clauses—some based on contingencies never likely to arise in the juvenile trade market. The contract is usually mailed to you for study—and study it you must so that none of the clauses will come as a nasty surprise to you later.

For his own part, the publisher agrees to have your manuscript printed and manufactured as a book; to put the book on sale throughout the United States and Canada, and to distribute it through bookstores *entirely at his expense*. The publisher also agrees to pay you a sum of money as an advance against future royalties. And for the various rights mentioned, he agrees to pay you a percentage of the money collected. Some of these rights and percentages can be negotiated.

First serial rights, sold *before* the material appears in book form, belong to the author. You can have that specified in your contract. (Some contracts state that they must be sold before the contract is signed.)

If your material is resold for magazine or newspaper publication *after* the book appears (second serial rights), then your earnings must be divided fifty—fifty with the publisher of your book. Incidentally, "serial" refers to the appearance of your material in a periodical—a magazine or newspaper—in one or more parts.

Book Clubs

There are more than two dozen juvenile book clubs featuring hard cover trade books as well as paperback editions. The Junior Literary Guild is the oldest; Scholastic Book Services is the biggest, and their paperback distributions often reach astronomical figures. The clubs handle books for all ages, and it is possible to have one book distributed by several clubs, if non-exclusive rights were sold by your publisher. In that case, each club, or paperback distributor, leases the distribution rights for a specified length of time. Authors, as a rule, are delighted by this plus sale —but they can do little to promote it. The whole transaction is handled through the publisher and all money received is usually divided on a fifty—fifty basis. (If yours is a heavily illustrated book, you may have to divide your share with the artist.)

Paperback Books and Reprints

The tremendous demand for paperbacks has given authors another outlet to tap. (Originals may be submitted directly to interested publishers; follow your market listings on these.) Reprint rights, however, are handled through the publishers. Always.

Movie Rights

I'm sorry to say that as a rule juvenile stories do not sell to movies. Hollywood script editors won't even read them, and along with a lot of other people in the trade, I feel they miss a great deal of good material that could be adapted to the screen. Miracles do happen occasionally, so it's something to dream about. However, educational companies do make films, records and tapes of unpublished material, so that is an attainable developing market.

Television Rights

The tremendous appetite of television for material has improved our chances for sales in that line. Animal and family stories have been filmed successfully, but submissions usually must be made by the special agents of the publisher, or an author's agent. Although *published books* will sometimes be read, *manuscripts* submitted by hopeful authors are invariably returned unopened, to avoid nuisance suits for plagiarism and piracy.

Foreign Sales

On books for juniors, this market is better for the ego than the pocketbook. After commissions paid to the publisher's foreign representative or agent, there isn't much cash left to divide between the publisher and the author. There is, however, an immense sense of satisfaction in having your work considered good enough to merit translation or republishing in a country other than your own.

Commercial Rights

These protect your (and your publisher's) interests in any commercial enterprises that make use of your story characters—dolls, toys, gadgets. Nice—but rare.

Royalties

Royalties on junior books are usually 10% of the retail price, which means that on a $3 book, the author would get 30¢ per copy. This is by no means standard. Different percentages are offered, and sometimes these are based on the *net* price, which is the retail price minus all the trade discounts. In effect, this can mean a return of only 6% per copy, based on the list price.

But even with a so-called "straight 10%" there are numerous "whittle" clauses in your contract which may reduce your royalty by as much as 50%. There isn't much you can do about them (the Authors' League is working to improve the situation), but at least you should know these clauses are *there* and what they mean.

There might be a stipulation to reduce royalties after a book has been in print a certain length of time and the sales begin to taper off. Or if a small printing (of one or two thousand copies) is made after the book has been out two years. Small printings are expensive, but it's better to take the reduction than to see your book go out of print.

When the unbound sheets of your book are sold (for reinforced bindings needed for libraries), there is a substantial reduction in your royalty rate.

An expense to watch for concerns galley proof corrections. Most contracts have a clause that reads something like this: *"The cost of alterations in the galley proof or page proof required by the author, other than corrections of printer's errors, in excess of ten per cent (10%) of the original cost of composition shall be charged against the author's royalties . . ."*

This should effectively discourage you from starting to rewrite your book after it is set in galleys, because even the change of one short word for a long one or the addition of a phrase may require the resetting of a whole paragraph. At that rate your 10% leeway will be used up in no time and you'll receive a horrendous bill.

You are, of course, responsible for everything that is in the book, whether it's fact or fiction. Should you quote directly any material written by another person, you are expected to procure (at your own expense) written permission to reprint such passages, and present this to your publisher along with the manuscript.

Options

Option clauses are included in most contracts. Usually you must agree to submit your next book to the same publisher. Sometimes this clause will read: "the next two books"—but then, the refusal of the first (of these two) negates the obligation on the second. *Make certain that this is clearly stated.* If it is not, you may discover that you have agreed to give that publisher a straight option on the next two books. That is, even if he refuses the one, you still must submit another for consideration, with no assurance that it will be taken. Meanwhile, the one refused becomes a kind of albatross. If you submit it to another publisher and that publisher decides to take it, he'll want an option—one that you can't give! As someone has said so aptly: A contract is a legal and binding document—and it can bite the hand that signs it. *Yours* if you don't read what you are signing.

Once a decision is made to accept your book for publication, you may be sure that all its pros and cons have been thoroughly considered. They *want* it! If you have any questions about the contract terms, ask to have them explained. The most beautifully printed contracts can be altered.

You must learn to protect your interests. Your editor will only respect you the more for managing your affairs in a calm, sensible manner. "Authors will accept anything instead of trying to negotiate better terms," an editor once told me. Your editor may not be able to agree to everything you want changed, but it will be a step in the right direction. As you learn to write better, become better known, and as your sales figures improve, *you* will become a more valuable property, and you'll be able to negotiate more favorable contract terms.

The Advance

On signing the contract, you will usually get an advance payment. If the manuscript is complete and ready for final editing, a full advance of $500, $1,000 or more may be paid to you. The sum depends on many factors—your reputation as a writer or an authority on the subject, the projected sales on your book, the house policy on advances, and so on.

Some companies pay as little as $150 as an advance, with a like amount on publication. I understand there are others which pay no advance at all. I'm happy to say none of them are among the ones I write for. *Writer's Market* makes every effort to find out such details and print them. Be sure to check these listings when making up your manuscript itinerary. You don't want to be unpleasantly surprised on acceptance.

If extensive changes need to be made on a book, or it still needs to be completed, the author may get only half the advance on signing, with the rest paid on delivery of an acceptable manuscript. That certainly is fair. Whatever sums you do get, remember they are made against future royalties. If you take a big advance, it may take quite a while to make it up in copies sold and start collecting royalties after publication. But since you keep the advance even if your book never sells enough copies to pay it off against royalties, a large advance can be to your advantage, too!

Most houses make royalty settlements twice a year—which is a long time between paychecks. But if you're a real producer, you'll have a few advances on new works in between; and perhaps you'll turn out a few short stories. Being a free-lance writer is not the easiest of occupations, and most writers have another job while they're building up a royalty-paying backlog of books. It's a long haul to become self-supporting at writing—so don't give up a steady job the moment you get your first short story check or sign that first contract!

When Your Book Is Accepted

With the prospect of actual publication, every author wants his manuscript to reflect his best writing. So does his editor. He may make a great many suggestions for revision or just a few, depending on the quality of the manuscript and his critical ability. Whatever the constructive suggestions, the author should accept them with good grace and consider them in a creative frame of mind—and get on with the job promptly. Your book is already tentatively scheduled on the production timetable.

Your editor has the right—and the duty—to *edit* your book. Some of your sentences may be shortened; some words simplified; some cut out altogether. Spelling, punctuation, and grammar may be altered to conform with the publisher's house style.

Among other things, your book title may be changed, if the editor feels it lacks appeal or clarity. A good title should give a clue to what the book is about, without revealing too much. It should not be a label, but a lure.

When questioned about titles, young readers make such comments as the following (and librarians agree with them): "We like the title to tell us what the book is going to be about." "I like a name in the title, so I'll know if it's about a boy or a girl." "It should show if it's an adventure and where . . . or if it's a mystery . . ."

Your book will require a jacket, and perhaps illustrations, if the story is for younger readers. The artist will be chosen by your editor, although as a courtesy she may ask if you have someone in mind. The final choice belongs to the editor, but *if you are a professional illustrator, and your style is appropriate,* you may get the happy job of doing your own book.

Besides art, the jacket needs flap copy. The part that tucks into the front of the book will tell briefly what the story is about. Your editor will take care of that. *Your* job is to provide copy for the back flap—a brief biographical sketch and a few words on how you came to write *this* book. Read some jacket copy on new books and pattern yours accordingly.

Include a good, clear photograph of yourself, on glossy paper, with the biographical sketch. It may be a studio portrait or an informal snapshot (as long as your face stands out clearly). Any expenses connected with this publicity picture are tax deductible.

All this, along with working on your new project, should keep you busy. And then, one day, the *galleys* will arrive! Your original, copy-edited manuscript will come with these long galleys.

The same rules apply to the proofreading of galleys as to your typescript: a few pages at a sitting; a sheet of blank paper or a blotter slid under the lines to help spot errors. Even the most careful printer can make an occasional mistake, so read carefully. "P.E.'s"—Printer's Errors—are no-charge items. Several other people will check the galleys, but you're the most interested party, and you'll hate yourself if mistakes you might have caught slip into the final printing.

Use the standard proofreaders' marks as shown in the sample on the opposite page.

Page proofs may or may not be sent to you. Here changes should not be made except under the most pressing circumstances. Again, proofread carefully and return promptly.

And then at long last comes the day of triumph. The Book arrives! All six, ten, or twelve free copies promised to you in your contract. *Any others you want you'll have to pay for,* but because you're the author, your publisher will give you a 40% discount. Do remember these basic economics, even in your initial wild excitement over Your Book's Birthday, and don't rush around giving away copies.

PROOFREADER'S MARKS

MARGINAL MARKS	MARK IN LINE OF PROOF	MEANING
ℐ	Ask not̲e̲ what your country can	Delete
⑤	uɐɔ ʎɹʇunoɔ ɹnoʎ ʇɐɥʍ ʇou ʞs∀	Reverse
⌒	Ask not what your countȓy can	Close up
#	Ask not what̆your country can	Insert space
¶	for today. Ask not what your	Begin new paragraph
☐	Ask not what your country	Indent one em
⊏	⊏ Ask not what your country	Move to left
⊐	Ask not what your country can ⊐	Move to right
qu?	Ask not why your country can	Query to author
tr	Ask not waht your country can	Transpose
country	Ask not what your can do for	Insert
x	Ask not what your country can	Broken letter
no ¶	Ask not what your country can	Run in same paragraph
w.f.	Ask not what your country can	Wrong font
ℐ/stet	Ask not what your country can	Let it stand
⋀	"Why your country cannot	Insert comma
⋎	Ask not what your countrys	Insert apostrophe
⁶⁶// ⁹⁹	Ask not he said	Insert quotes
=	Your fellow countrymen	Insert hyphen
em	What your country today	Em dash
;	What your country does why	Insert semi-colon
⊙	The country is like this	Insert colon
⊙	This is your country	Insert period
?	Is this your country	Insert interrogation point
l.c.	Ask not What your country	Lower case
rom	Ask not what your country can	Set in roman type
ital.	Ask not what your country can	Set in italic type
caps	Ask not what your country can	Set in capitals
s.c.	Ask not what your country can	Set in small capitals
ld.	Ask not what your country can do for you but what you can	Insert lead between lines

To make several corrections in one line, give marginal symbols in order, separated by slash marks:

cap/ℐ/tr   Ask not not what your country can

A *Clipping Service*

Most authors want to see the notices and reviews of their work. Publishers do supply copies of press clippings, but I have not found them to be very conscientious or quick about it. You may arrange to go to your publisher's office to see your "press" if you live within a reasonable distance. But most authors like to *have* their clippings—to gloat over, moan over, or gnash their teeth at, and certainly not in plain sight of the editor and staff.

For a stipulated fee a clipping service will send you all mentions of your work, and this, too, is a deductible expense. My own choice for many years has been the Literary Clipping Service, Inc., in New York City. Here you pay in advance for 8, 50, or 100 clippings *with no time limit*. This last is of particular importance to the writer for young people, because unlike grownups' books, ours go on being reviewed for months after publication. Services with monthly rates are not practical for us.

How to read your clippings: *Calmly*, of course! That, however, is easier said than done. No matter what you write, the reaction is likely to be mixed. Still, no single critic wields absolute influence over your book's success or failure. If any specific faults are pointed out, make note of them and don't repeat them in your next book—if you agree that they are faults. Above all, don't go into a decline because somebody didn't like your book. The degree of equanimity with which you can take criticism is an indication of your maturity both as a person and as a writer.

If bad reviews or rejections depress you excessively, try the Voodoo recipe I've evolved. Name a potato after your reviewer (or editor), put it in boiling water, and boil it to a pulp. It can cheer you no end! (Me, too.)

Whatever your opinion of the review and the reviewer, *never under any circumstances write him an angry letter*. It would neither change his opinion nor his review. If it will make you feel any better, pour out your hurt feelings into your typewriter, onto your cheapest second sheets. But having said it all, be sure to tear it up!

If you get a particularly pleasing and perceptive review, you may write that reviewer a thank-you note. For some reason such messages are rare, and reviewers find sincere appreciation of their efforts quite touching.

Agents—To Have? or To Have Not?

But suppose your manuscript does not follow the happy rainbow course. Suppose it is turned down time and again. Would submitting it through an agent make a difference? No. *An agent cannot sell an unsalable manuscript.*

If you have publishable material for young readers, you do not need an agent to place it for you. I have signed more than fifty book contracts, and I have never had an agent. What's more, I can name dozens of other authors who do not have agents. Anyway, most agents will save you the agony of decision by refusing to handle your work until you've made a name for yourself on your own.

In certain instances an agent can be of considerable value. If you live far from New York, an agent can expedite book submissions, saving you both time and postage. If the agent is also a good critic, you are doubly lucky.

However, in some agencies, the juvenile department is a kind of step-child, and your book will be sent around without being screened by an expert at the agency. Editors quickly learn which agents actually *know* the quality of the material they are submitting. Thus, some agents' folders sit atop the pile of incoming manuscripts, and some wait their turn at the bottom of the heap. My briefing as a reader for several top publishing houses always included instructions not to be unduly impressed by the fact that a manuscript came in through an agent.

Agents and friends can open doors and sometimes expedite a reading, but they do not influence editorial decisions. Sometimes they prompt a sterner look at material to offset any effects of influence! Publishing a book requires a sizeable investment of cash, time, and highly specialized skills. It can easily cost $5,000 to produce an unillustrated book. When pictures in color are involved, the cost of the plates alone may go higher than $10,000. It is the editor's job to exercise wise stewardship over her employer's money and trust in her judgment.

Very short books, picture books, short stories, and poetry are almost never handled by agents in the juvenile field.

How to Find a Good Literary Agent

1. Through the recommendation of an established author who has read your work and found it good.

2. Through The Author's Guild, Inc., 234 West 44th Street, New York, N. Y. 10036.

3. Through some book publishers.

4. The Society of Authors' Representatives, 101 Park Avenue, New York, N. Y. 10017, has a printed list of its members. These agents are also listed in *Writer's Market* and in *LMP*.

To Do and Not to Do

Do not call on an agent (or publisher) to discuss your work when it has not been read. This will mark you as a nuisance.

If you send an unsolicited manuscript to an agent, he may charge for reading it. But if he finds the material marketable, or asks to see more of your work, he will refund the money.

Agents do not have formal contracts with the writers they represent. It's more of a gentleman's agreement, and may be dissolved by word or letter if either or both parties become dissatisfied. Incidentally, all expenses connected with your agent's fees are tax deductible.

It is not an agent's job to teach you how to write; nor to rewrite for you. He can direct you to reputable people who do this work, however, when he thinks the material warrants it.

The agent's business is to sell the finished product on a professional basis—at a ten per cent commission of whatever your work earns. Until you reach a professional level in your writing, he cannot afford to handle you on this basis, and you might as well resign yourself to the fact that marketing your material will be a do-it-yourself project. Follow the suggestions in this text and you will not be sailing your little ship on uncharted seas.

Chapter 22

When You Do Not Sell
—How to Read Rejections

Having read the previous chapters, you must surely realize that when your manuscript is returned by a publisher, it's not because you don't have an agent; it's not because you are an "unknown"; and most assuredly it's not because it was not read.

Everything that comes into a publishing office is *read*. Editors are always on the lookout for new writers. Words may live for centuries, but authors are not so durable. A new crop must be developed, and your chances of being "discovered" are as good as anybody's *if* you can write.

Along with natural attrition, writers have an annoying way (from the losing editor's point of view) of going off to another publisher for one reason or another. This is especially true among those who start in the denominational presses, where editors are more apt to take the time and trouble to train a new author, for just this reason. But because the pay scale in this market is usually low, a writer who begins to sell leaves for greener pastures. Someone must take his place—or the magazine must cease publication.

The only advantage the established writer has over you is professional skill, which can be depended upon to produce publishable material. But even professional writers sometimes lose their touch. What the editor hopes for, each time she picks a manuscript from the stack on her desk, is the enthusiasm and vitality of an up-and-coming author—and so no manuscript is summarily passed up.

"Well then," you might say, "if that's the case, why aren't editors nicer to new writers? They could at least tell us *why* they won't accept a story, instead of just sending a printed rejection slip." But that is just what they *cannot* do, at least not often. Not with the hundreds and even thousands of manuscripts coming into an office run by a small staff. Primarily an editor is paid to edit books or get out a magazine—not to conduct correspondence writing courses at her employer's expense.

Specific criticism is not offered on a book or story unless the editor feels it will make the material publishable. Should you get a personal letter, or even a note suggesting definite changes in a manuscript, it mans that the editor is *interested*, even though she does not always add, "Let me see this material again." This last could raise a writer's hopes too much, for he might think it a definite promise of acceptance, which it is not.

The thing to do *at once* is follow the suggested revision and resubmit the material, with a covering letter. Even if a sale does not result, you will have made a friend. That editor will read your next effort all the more eagerly and make even more specific suggestions, because you have proved yourself receptive and *professional* in your attitude. With any luck at all, you'll *sell* to that market before too long.

Even the briefest message scrawled on the rejection form is a definite sign of encouragement. It means that your material is better than average. Submit to that market again and again to show that you are a producer. They'll notice.

Rejections must not be allowed to send you into the doldrums. Each one is an expression of opinion by an individual publisher, and some other house might be delighted with the story. Look again at my folder record on "Binkie and the Ostrich"!

If your manuscript comes back from four publishers, read it over carefully. It may be that you'll now see what is wrong with it. Check it against the lists of "musts" in this text and be sure they're *there* in your piece. Then send it out again on a continuing itinerary, or return it to the editors who have rejected it, with a note saying that you have revised the story and perhaps it now will fill their needs. Editors will respect you for the effort.

Some of the publishing houses (magazines) have a printed rejection form that does list reasons for returning a story. While a penciled checkmark is not very communicative, still it is better than nothing. Here are some of the form statements and what they mean:

We are overstocked. Magazines often are. You can try them again in a few months.

We seldom use this type of material. That you might have found out if you'd read a few issues of the magazine.

It is too adult. You should have gauged the age bracket of the publication before submitting.

It doesn't fit our editorial needs. You can't beat that one—it can mean anything, like your writing isn't good enough. Yet.

It is out of season for us. You've submitted too late or too early.

Too long. Limit approximately 900 words. You should have known about that, too.

Subject matter appears very frequently. Some subjects are regular magnets to authors. When you study markets, make a list of the subjects of the stories published and then try to come up with something unusual. (That's how I came to write about an affectionate whale; a pet ostrich; a camel; a family that lived on a wrecked paddlewheeler.)

We do not publish serials or continued stories. / We do not publish plays and playettes. / We avoid stories suggesting crime and violence. / We prefer stories appealing to boys as well as girls. If any of these are checked, the editor *knows* you didn't study her magazine or bother to get a contributor's guide.

We prefer a story with a strong plot and great suspense. Everybody wants those!

We dislike negative suggestions. Something to watch in writing for young people. Keep your own neuroses out of your stories.

The Editors Speak—

. . . I hope you develop some good writers in your classes

because we are not getting many good stories. It seems to me that the younger the children, the harder it is to get good writers for them . . . there must be a plot with some interest and excitement to it. At the same time, the story must be written in simple language and must not be beyond the experience and comprehension of the small child. We like stories to be imaginative but not utterly ridiculous. The writing should have good style so that the story will be rhythmic and pleasing to the ear when it is read aloud. Stories should help children to understand their world and to meet their problems better but at the same time they should not sound moralistic and obviously "this will teach you a lesson."

I would say that the commonest reason for turning down stories for this age group is that the stories are too trivial—there is just no point to them.

—Aurelia Reigner, Former Editor
Stories, Trailblazer, Venture

What makes a submission unacceptable: An obvious answer—it is not well-written. The mother who tells stories to her children and is besieged to tell more, should not take this claque too seriously . . .

There are submissions which are well-written, and yet not publishable in a particular house. Picture books are frequently sent to publishers who do not do picture books; non-fiction material or textbooks sent to houses whose policy is to do fiction only.

Fiction work well-written, well-plotted, but either so long or so brief that there is no way to make a satisfactory revision to conform to the publisher's requirements. Or else, good material sent to a house with no regard of the age group for which the publisher creates a list, or the interest level.

While we don't observe the Thorndyke formula, nevertheless, we frequently find that the language used is not suitable for a particular age level.

Non-fiction: there is a demand for non-fiction, but that does not mean that anything goes. Undertaking what is euphemistically termed "research"—reading a few books, encyclopedias and magazine articles—does not always qualify a reasonably facile journalist to deal with books on science, archeology, the arts, etc.

We publish about 50 books for children each year. We receive about 100 manuscripts each week. That gives you an idea of the number that are turned down . . .
—Frances Schwartz, Editor
Abelard-Schuman Limited

What They Don't Tell You

Readers' reports must be frank to the point of bluntness—that's what they're paid for. These excerpts should give all writers something to think about:

. . . None of these characters seems to be a real person. Ellen and Dick are abnormally eager to absorb information, and all their relatives only too glib at giving them full length lectures on the history of the city and its landmarks . . . fictional and factual matter unsuccessfully integrated . . . Not recommended.

. . . *Hero is an observer, not a participant* . . . / . . . too cute . . . / could easily resist this one! / . . . Impossible to read aloud . . . rhythm awkward. Meter and rhyme make no sense . . . Sounds silly. / Transparent plot. All too predictable . . . / Short story, *not* a book. / Protagonist grown-up. / Stuffy characters . . . / SOMEONE SHOULD TELL THIS AUTHOR THAT THE DIFFERENCE BETWEEN WRITING FOR CHILDREN AND GROWN-UPS IS THAT WRITERS FOR CHILDREN DO NOT SNEER AT THEIR AUDIENCE . . . / . . . seems like an unusual amount of activity for one summer. Solution incredible. / Good nonfiction material . . . well put together, research valid . . . alas, too many on similar subject. Competition fierce. Regretfully, not recommended for publication.

Here's the fire some teen novels draw:

Paper doll characters . . . no dimension . . . / . . . Slapstick, hysterical comedy . . . / . . . Characters don't feel strongly about anything but the winning of the school team. *In today's world young people should be shown involved in the life around them* . . . / . . . don't think this could be rightly called a novel . . . no central theme, no motivating conflict, no real drama. It is just talk, talk, talk, and the talk is often stilted and unreal enough to be funny (unintentionally on the author's part). These characters never carry on a conversation. They lecture to each other in long, long paragraphs . . . people are no more than sticks, mouthpieces for the author who knows a great deal about her subject and would have done better to put her knowledge into nonfiction . . .

. . . Would like to send revision suggestions to this author, but on the last two MSS what came back was an entirely different book each time! complete with brand new flaws.

How are decisions arrived at? In some of the larger publishing houses the editors meet at regular intervals to discuss readers' reports on the promising manuscripts—with the manuscripts stacked two and a half feet high at times. Final decisions may be arrived at by committee vote. In other houses, the editor is an autocrat: the responsibility for the department is hers, and so are all the final decisions. That's the way I prefer it; but what with all the mergers and less experienced editors taking over after retiring heads, more and more decisions are made in committee.

Chapter 23

How Editors Help Writers

Here are some extracts from my file folders, dating back to my earliest writing days. This is the kind of helpful criticism you begin to get when your work shows signs of promise.

> . . . you have sufficient material here for a good one, but I feel you could improve it. The middle of the article is much more interesting than the beginning, which sounds as though one looked up "ostrich" in a reference book. Couldn't you put the middle part first, and also think of 14-year-olds and try to tell it as you would to them—a little more human-interest approach?

> When you sent us the story "Lighthouse Adventure" you may have forgotten that we still had "A Fish for Jill" which you wrote at our suggestion last year. We considered both stories and finally decided in favor of Jill . . .

And I was hoist on mine own petard! Remember what I said earlier about sending in two stories to the same editor and giving her a choice? It took me several such experiences to learn that lesson. But "Lighthouse" did sell eventually. Another editor wrote:

> . . . I like the story in general and the level at which it is written. But I feel it is lacking in suspense. The story just unfolds, without rising to any climax—or situation which must be overcome. To give you an idea of what I mean: Cap'n Perry and Pete must go out of their way to deliver the vegetables. About halfway to the lighthouse they notice a storm building up in the north. They know it will arrive quickly

and they haven't time to make land. So they decide to head for the light.

As they approach they notice the light isn't working—and the afternoon steamer is due by *in ten minutes.* The beginning of the storm hits them, first a lull and inky blackness, then a terrific blow. By dint of fine seamanship, they reach the passage to the light, and make fast . . . get in, discover keeper unconscious, turn on the light—just as steamer nears a danger point. With relief they see it change course ·to safety.

With less space devoted to getting the story under way, and more to the storm and handling of the boat, I think you'd have a real hair-raiser. However, it's your story and you know best what you'd like to do with it.

This is the attitude of every good editor: to try to bring out what the author has in mind in the most effective way possible. The story must remain *his* and not become an echo of the editor's thinking.

> . . . This story has character, appeal, and reader satisfaction, but we believe that all of these attributes could be further realized by the introduction of a little more dramatic conflict. As the story now stands, the pattern is perfectly clear from the outset.
>
> We have discussed this matter editorially and a few suggestions were made . . . but of course the ultimate invention would be your own . . .

You should have seen the list of suggestions! My anguished cries must have been heard clear over to Philadelphia, because subsequently another letter came:

> . . . For heaven's sake don't get discouraged about revisions and think you're the only one who has to do them. Many published authors are reluctant to talk about the painstaking revisions they must do under an editor's guidance, but just the same, they do them. Everyone has a blind spot to some aspects of his own writing . . .

And a few weeks later, after I'd calmed down, digested the editorial suggestions, and revised the book, I had this communication:

> It gives me a great deal of pleasure to offer you a contract
> for *Silver Yankee* . . .

When You Are Told to Cut

> I have just finished *Showboat Holiday* and I think it's
> fine. The only objection I have to it for serial use is that the
> action is too slow. That of course can be easily taken care of
> in the cutting . . . *We could use it in ten chapters, but each
> chapter shouldn't be over 1,800 words in length* . . .

The book manuscript ran to 55,000 words. That meant a cutting
of 37,000 words! But each time you offer a full-length manuscript
for serial use, you have to face as drastic a cut. The magazine
editors will not, as a rule, do the job for you.

Faced with such a monumental task, many authors—even
established ones—go into a state of shock. Some give up the idea
of selling first serial rights altogether. They shouldn't. Cutting
provides invaluable experience—and a look at your own work,
almost through a stranger's eyes. But how do you do it? Where
do you begin? My magazine editor had helpfully suggested:

> . . . *you can combine two chapters into one all through the
> story and by cutting out detail and shortening conversation,
> the action will snap along* the way I like it to in a serial . . .

True enough about the action—but what about the really big
word cuts?

Fortunately for me, I had already been doing drastic condensation of best-selling novels for newspaper syndication. Each
novel of 100,000 words or so had to be cut into fifteen installments
of about 1,500 words each, and the whole was not to exceed
36,000 words. It was splendid practice for condensing my own
gems! And you may benefit from my experience.

The Technique of Cutting for Serialization

First of all, be sure you know the story thoroughly. Even though
this one is your own, skim through it. As you do so, check off in

the margin any ideas you get for cuts. Do not stop to mark off anything at this point.

Consider all the minor characters and sub-plots you can do without. In the serial version you must concentrate on the main characters.

Descriptions must be cut to a bare minimum—and in a drastic cut you almost never refresh the reader's memory through repetition. The story must zip along. Paragraphs of descriptions can often be cut to single sentences or eliminated altogether.

All paragraphs can be trimmed down, but since the cut is so tremendous, it would be foolish to go through the whole book doing that. You have to do away with whole *pages* of stuff!

So, the next step is to divide the book into the number of parts your serial is to have. Ten is generous. Often the serial version is in five or six parts. The important thing is to *be sure each part ends on a note of suspense, and the more gripping, the better*. Keep that in mind as you mark off the segments.

The beginning chapters must be cut with extra care because the character and his situation is introduced there, along with the necessary plants and pointers. But anything that makes for a "slow beginning" must be lopped off. Here is a clear object lesson on how *you* write—and you'll probably write brisker beginnings forever after. You may have to put in brief transition bridges between pages of cutting to carry the reader over smoothly.

To see your cut story clearly, use lightly penciled brackets around the material you want to leave in. When you are sure of your cuts, box in the material with a solid black non-smudge pencil.

Do not bother to count words, *count only the lines*. A serial chapter that must be 1,800 words long would have 180 lines of 10 words each. (Remember the suggested typing format?) Even a fraction of a line must be counted as a full line for printing purposes. However, if you can cross out a word or phrase here and there, *all in the same paragraph*, count these up; each time they add up to 10 (or the number of words in the last line of the paragraph), you can deduct one line from that page.

This kind of operation requires intense concentration, so even if you belong to the interruptible sex, make it clear you must not be disturbed on any account. You can accomplish a great deal in two unharried hours, but do not work any longer without at least a half-hour break.

When it's all done and published, you will certainly miss all the lovely passages you've cut, but even *you* will be surprised at how smoothly the serial reads. And somewhere in your subconscious will be planted the idea that *anything* can be cut. The result: tighter, crisper, *better* writing.

Success Stories

To paraphrase Marcus Aurelius: *Flinch not, nor despair—and don't give up too soon on submitting your material,* as long as *you* have faith in a particular manuscript. It may well be that all the "experts" are wrong—except you and the publisher who finally accepts your manuscript.

Time and again I get ecstatic phone calls and letters from clients and former students that sound like this:

> Just a note to let you know that my mystery is finally going to be published! After holding it nearly a year, the Big Decision was made—and my editor tells me the book will be out this fall.
>
> It may cheer your class to know that my book was rejected about 30 times and has been going the rounds for over 5 years. . . . I never would have been so persistent, of course, if you hadn't assured me the book had a chance . . .

> Sold an article . . . and if you ever need an example of perseverance in marketing for your writing classes, I have it! This article went the rounds off and on *for 4 years.* I was astounded not only to sell it at all, but to receive a glowing letter about it from the Editor-in-Chief. Have saved same and other correspondence about it, because the letters showed how editors differ . . .

Of course they do. Editors are people! In checking my own submissions in my 3-by-5 card file, which handily duplicates my folder records, I find that some of my short pieces went out as many as fifteen times!

An even more spectacular record is held by two fairy tales of which I was especially fond. On and off—over a period of ten years in the one case, and fifteen in the other—I sent them out as the market climate changed. Then both were enthusiastically bought by a top-paying new quality market, for a fee three times more than I could have hoped for when they were written.

As for differing opinions among editors, here is a letter that I prize:

> . . . This rather stern criticism comes from me most re-
> luctantly. However, I owe it to you to report honestly and
> so I have done so. You may or may not decide to revise your
> manuscript in the light of it. *In either case I feel sure you
> will have little difficulty in finding another publisher who will
> want to bring out the book for you* . . .

The italics are mine. Downcast as I was by the rejection, the last sentence really brought me up short. It reminded me of another helpful editor I'd heard about, a kindly Methodist who wrote on a rejection slip: *The moral tone of this isn't high enough for us. Try the Presbyterians.*

But the rejection letter that delights me most (now!) is this one:

> I read *A Dance for Susie* with a great deal of interest
> and believe it has much that is good in it. I wish we could
> be more optimistic about our chance of publishing it success-
> fully for you.
>
> Unfortunately, we're afraid that we simply couldn't find
> a wide enough market for it to make publication profitable
> for either you or us. We may be quite wrong about this and
> for your sake I hope we are . . .

Well, they were. *Susie* was accepted on the thirteenth sub-mission, published by Dodd, Mead in 1953—and grew into a series of five books, with the original six-year-old heroine growing a little older in each one. The first four books were serialized in *Children's Activities;* by the time the fifth was ready, the maga-zine had merged with *Highlights,* which did not use serials.

As for finding a wide enough market—"the littlest Susie" sold well over 10,000 hardcover copies, and was listed among the Best

Books of the Year by the *New York Times, Chicago Tribune,* and the *Saturday Review of Literature. Susie and the Ballet Family* and *On Your Toes, Susie!* are Scholastic Arrow-TAB Club selections and respectively have sold over 250,000 and over 500,000 copies. Which means that three-quarters of a *million* little girls have purchased these two books of the series alone! And my editor, Dorothy Bryan, originally had to persuade her editorial and sales board that *Susie* would be a good investment.

When the fifth book, *Susie and the Ballet Horse,* was published, it was dedicated to Susie's godmother, Dorothy M. Bryan, and this is what she wrote me:

> Your ten copies have gone off to you. Everyone who sees the book is very pleased with the appearance and I know that the girls are going to love the story with its many popular ingredients. Of course, I am particularly proud of that "godmother" dedication. Thank you so much for that. No one realizes more than I do how much patience authors must have to put up with editors, so I value this dedication extra-specially.
>
> My love and my appreciation goes to you.

And my love and appreciation go to all the valiant editors who have put up with *me* all these years!

As for you, surely these examples have been spirit lifters. If you have any manuscripts tucked away in your files, get them out now. Read them over. Revise again and polish, if that's indicated. If the stories seem good to you, retype and send them out again on brand new itineraries based on your study of the *current* markets. Your very next submission may bring you a check instead of a rejection.

THE HARDEST STORIES TO SELL ARE THE ONES YOU KEEP STASHED AWAY IN THE BOTTOM DRAWER OF YOUR DESK. All the others have a chance to be published!

PART II

SPECIAL WRITING PROBLEMS
AND PROJECTS

Chapter 24

Research—Ideas Unlimited

Probably the most frequently quoted rule a writer hears is *Write what you know*. Sensible advice! But *what you know* need not be confined to the scope of your personal experience. You can easily widen that experience, and *you can learn about* anything if you're willing to spend time on concentrated research. Besides being fun, finding out about things you don't know is like tapping an ever-bubbling spring of ideas.

The primary requisite for writing from research is an intense interest in the particular subject. Secondly, you must know how to go about collecting the necessary information on it. Thirdly, you must know how to *organize* the mass of material you collect. You cannot rely on your memory, and a stack of notes a foot high is useless unless you can find what you need *at once*.

Two Kinds of Research

There are two kinds of research: *historical* (period) and *contemporary* (present day).

There is scarcely a time in history that has not been covered in one or more books. In conducting research on a period in history, you should read both fact and fiction. Consult at least three authorities before you accept anything as fact. Fiction should be read not only for additional information (which you can corroborate through the factual sources), but for a sense of place and time. These are universal procedures for writers of period fiction.

A classic example of a perfect period reproduction is *A Tale of Two Cities,* by Charles Dickens. If the reader didn't know better, he'd feel certain that Dickens actually *lived* through the French Revolution, so real is every minute detail of people, places, and events. Yet Charles Dickens was born in 1812 and died in 1870, while the Bastille was stormed on July 14th, 1789. In preparing to write his book, Dickens read some 300 books on the subject!

Your Starting Point

Regardless of the object of research, the library is to the writer what the secret cave was to Ali Baba: an inexhaustible storehouse of riches. And the reference librarian is his "open sesame" to all its professionally filed secrets.

Lose no time in getting acquainted with your local library, its reference sources, and its staff. Librarians are interested in authors' projects, and you need never hesitate to ask for help. But because they must serve many others in your community, you should learn to help yourself as much as possible.

Also remember that your local library, no matter how small, has borrowing facilities from larger libraries, and once the material you need is tracked down, it can be borrowed for you (unless it is extremely valuable or irreplaceable). However, long-distance borrowing takes time. Weeks and sometimes months may elapse before the material is in your hands, so plan your writing projects with this possibility in mind.

Things You'll Need to Know

What you should look for, in preparation for your "period" story, is material that will make you familiar with the days and ways of a time and place: everyday homely details, the speech idiom, the "thinking" of the time, what people knew, what they strove for: the world as it was *then.*

If you plan to use an actual place, focus your research on the particular country for background detail; then narrow it down to the particular city, even to the streets where the action will

take place. Fine detail maps may be available to help you reconstruct the setting accurately. In the United States, local historical
societies often prove most cooperative.

You must be able to visualize the homes and the rooms of the
period: their furnishings and even the view from the windows.
You must know what children and grownups wore in that day,
their manners, the books they read, how they talked, the foods
they ate, the toys the children played with. What was the mode
of transportation? *What historic events and people were contemporary with the time of your story action?* Make a chronological listing of these. Weave actual happenings into your tale
if you can do so without distorting history.

All these facts must seep into your mind as you make notes—
until *you* can feel yourself *there.* Then you will be able to give
your reader the proper sense of time and place and identity
with an era.

You'll use only a fraction of the information you collect, because your aim is not to teach history but to entertain your reader
with a *story.* What you have learned you must use only for the
purpose of creating convincing, authentic atmosphere and background for your characters. You are not to take the reader on a
sight-seeing tour and point out the historic landmarks. Use only
such facts as will forward the action of your plot. Never succumb
to the temptation of showing off how much you know.

Source Books

Whatever your project, the first step is background reading. Start
in the encyclopedias, adult as well as junior editions. Along with
the brief over-all information, the articles will also give you a
bibliography of other sources. Copy each of these references
onto a separate 3-by-5 "bib" (bibliography) card, listing the title,
author, and any other pertinent data that may be helpful in
locating the item.

Periodical Sources

Magazine and newspaper articles are also a fertile field for information. The *Reader's Guide to Periodical Literature* indexes articles, by subject and author, that have been published in more than 100 general magazines. Bound volumes go back to 1900. Since the *Guide* comes out monthly throughout the year, it is only a matter of a few weeks before the latest articles are listed for reference.

This is only a listing of *where* the articles can be found. Make a separate listing for each article on 3-by-5 file cards. Now comes the leg-work. Since your library may not have the magazines in its files, you may have to go to a larger library, or to a backdate magazine source. Consult the librarians on this.

Poole's Index to Periodical Literature lists the contents of thousands of volumes of American and British magazines published between 1802 and 1906. The scope of coverage is breathtaking, with authentic sources for 18th and 19th century social customs; articles written on the War of 1812, the California Gold Rush, the Civil War, etc., by people who lived through these events. Mr. Poole was an American librarian and bibliographer, and the magazines he indexed may be found in the collections of older libraries throughout the country.

The *National Geographic Magazine* is a treasure trove of people, places, customs, and curious facts. Its *cumulative indexes* run from 1899 to 1946 in Volume I, and from 1947-1963 in Volume II, with annual supplements published thereafter. Most libraries have an ample stock of back issues.

The *New York Times Index* is published throughout the year. Bound volumes and the micro-film index go back to 1851. The *Index* entries often give a brief synopsis of the story, which can sometimes answer your questions. Microfilm editions of the paper are also available, and if your library has them, locating the information you need is simple. However, if this service is not available, and if what you're looking for is a story of universal interest, chances are it was printed on nearly the same day all over the country. Thus your hometown paper, on file in your library (as part of local history), would probably have it. All you need to do then is find the issue and the page—with the help of your reference librarian.

Incidentally, the *London Times Index* (*Palmer's Index to the Times Newspaper*) goes back to 1790!—and what a key that is to the life of past eras, not only in the stories, but in the advertisements and the announcements on the microfilmed pages. It can be found in the specialized newspaper collections of the Library of Congress, the New York Public Library, the libraries of other large cities, and in some universities.

Person-to-Person Research

If the time you are interested in is not too remote, you may be able to find old documents, diaries, letters, and even "old timers" whom you can interview. Living witnesses are not always reliable, however. Their memories may be unclear or their feelings strongly prejudiced. For that matter, they may have lively imaginations and lead you off the track altogether! Better check their "memories" against authoritative published material, whether you're working on a fiction or non-fiction project.

More Aids to Research

In your search for books on your subject area, consult the other sources in the reference room of your community library, again making individualized listings of titles and authors on 3-by-5 cards. The *Subject Guide to Books in Print* is a hefty annual. Under the alphabetically arranged subject headings are listed the authors and the titles of their works, the year of publication, the publisher—and the price, should you be inclined to buy the book. This *Guide* deals mostly with non-fiction.

Books in Print, also an impressive annual publication, begins with the author index and has the title index in the second half. Obviously, you have to know one or the other to have any success in finding anything. This lists both fiction and non-fiction, currently available for purchase.

The *Cumulative Book Index*, which the librarians call the *CBI*, is usually kept in the librarians' work room. It has been published since 1898. The listings are under author, subject, and editor (or compiler of material). Here you will find listed many books which may be out of print (o.p.), that is, no longer available for purchase through regular trade channels, but probably on library shelves—somewhere. The card catalog in the reading room will tell you if the titles you want are there; if not, it may be possible to get them through the inter-library loan system. The *CBI* listing includes books published in English all over the world.

These are but a few reference room aids to your research. The best way to find out how your library can help you is to spend a day or two there and see for yourself just what is available. There are biography indexes; current biography volumes; short story indexes; folklore encyclopedias, reference books on the arts, the sciences, technology, the various *Who's Who's;* lists of specialists in *who knows what*—and it is always heartwarming to discover how graciously the experts agree to help even a budding writer with information. We'll deal with this phase of live research in the next chapter.

Make backgrounds authentic by studying pictures, photographs, and paintings of that period. In order to furnish your period properly and to dress your characters in keeping with their era, begin with books on period furniture and costumes and continue your studies at museums. The Metropolitan Museum of Art in New York City has a splendid Costume Institute, with period costume displays and a library. Other large cities have similar facilities, but if you can't manage to see the real thing, don't despair. With your writer's imagination you can reconstruct what you need to know from books.

You and Your Research

Your research must be exhaustive and *accurate* not only to uphold your own integrity as a writer, but also to foil those carping critics who crouch ready to spring on the mere suspicion of error on your part.

In period stories, beware of anachronisms—using people, places, words, and things out of their proper time. Don't have your characters tugging at zippers before these were invented, or waltzing when they should be dancing the minuet. An *Oxford Dictionary* is practically indispensable for period story writing, since it indicates when a word first came into use. Running an "Oxford check" on the vocabulary of your story characters will also keep their dialogue consistent with their time.

How to Keep Track of Your Research

Of course you will want to take notes on all your reading. You may want to jot things quickly on a stenographer's pad and then copy or type them into your loose-leaf research notebook, reserved solely for this purpose. This is my method. On the other hand, if you can read your own writing after a lapse of time, you may want to make the notes directly in your research notebook.

In any event, use a comfortably-sized book, not too small and not too large. Put in identifying tabs or dividers for each project to make it easier to store and sort your findings. After the project title, for example, you might have tabs for clothing, food, furnishings, nicknames, or settings. *Use brief notes.* Learn some standard short forms or abbreviations and use them consistently. You might even evolve your own form of shorthand—just be sure you can read it back.

As you do research on a certain historical period, possible characters will flock into your mind to people the setting and to provide action and reaction for you. This approach is better than starting with a complete character already formed in your mind, because the initial research will help you create a character in keeping with his era. He will not then be wearing period-correct clothes and thinking present-day thoughts. *In writing period stories you must keep the characters completely in the mood and under the influence of their time.*

Invariably, as you read—fact, fiction, in the adult and juvenile areas—plot situations will begin to take shape. These you should jot down in your work book, and as you write in its various sections, the story will grow and develop—until you are really inside your period characters and at home in their era. It is then that you will be ready to write the first draft of your tale.

Your Bibliography

Be sure to keep a list of all the sources you consult—for several reasons. If your project is non-fiction, your editor will expect a bibliography to back up the authenticity of your work (which may or may not be printed at the back of the published book). If any fact is questioned in your work—whether it be in fiction or non-fiction—you can produce your research authority to prove your point. In preparing to write my very short book *Thanksgiving*, I read more than 30 books on the subject, plus articles and pamphlets, and listed every one of them to present to my editors with the final draft.

Don't worry about "knowing too much" about your subject. You'll never put in even half of what you have learned, but it will be there: a solid background of facts to give you confidence in your ability to carry this project off with colors flying.

Chapter 25

Contemporary Research—
Open Sesame to the Here and Now

Into this category fall all the present-day things you don't know but would like to write about: people, places, professions, the arts, sciences and even "how-to" procedures it might be necessary for your characters to know. Research begins in general with the steps outlined for historical study and then branches out according to the information you require.

Stories where occupations are used either as background or as career-information romances require a thorough grounding in accurate, up-to-date occupational facts.

How to Get the Facts

First read everything you can obtain on the particular field you wish to cover. After you have read both fact and fiction, *in the adult and juvenile fields,* the nebulous main character you've had in your mind will start to materialize into a flesh-and-blood person. However, even if you have given him a name and a home background, you still do not know enough about the occupation to begin the actual writing. Instead, your next step is to contact someone actually in that occupation and at least one school where its skills are taught. Perhaps a friend—or a friend-of-a-friend— can introduce you to an architect, doctor, model, nurse, engineer, designer, banker, or whatever you need.

Lacking a personal introduction, you can write brief letters to professional people and/or the schools you wish to consult, telling them what you are planning to do. (Someone at the school may send you on to an expert.) List your writing credits, if any. Be honest. Should this effort be your "first," don't worry unduly about getting an interview. If your letter is concise and sensible, the interview will probably be granted.

In order to make the most of such interviews, you must come prepared with leading questions. If you possibly can, find out something about the person you're going to see. *Who's Who* or a professional listing may be helpful. In any case, never sail in with a blithe, "Do tell all about your fascinating work." You are not ready to interview until your reading has put into your mind specific questions that you want to ask.

When your authority discovers that you do know something about his work, you'll get full cooperation and possibly other leads to fill in your background details.

Keep a list of the names and addresses of the people you interview on a page next to the bibliography record in your research book. You'll be able to contact them again, if necessary, and (since they are not paid in cash for the time and information they give you) you can thank them graciously with an inscribed copy of your published book.

That Special Trade Talk

Each profession, craft, or occupational skill carries with it a special vocabulary characteristic of itself. This is often the hardest thing to worm out of the authority you are interviewing. His special vocabulary is a part of his daily life and he no longer recognizes it as such. But a little persistence and gentle prodding will elicit a few catch phrases to add authenticity to your story and make your reader feel "in the know."

Never neglect to get this private trade talk into your research. Even if you're not working in a given field, jot down whatever "backstage terminology" you encounter in conversation, in reading, or in a movie, and file it under the proper heading, such as: medical talk; theater jargon; astronauts; musicians. It may save you lots of time in the future. What's more, some word or phrase may even spark a story idea or catchy title.

Occupations—the Same—but Different

Some occupations, though basically the same, have important differences in different countries. For example, to refer to something I know well: ballet in America and ballet in England are approached in an entirely different way, and in France there are differences not common to either one. If I had used British or French sources exclusively in the beginning of my writing, I would have given an entirely wrong slant on the subject to my American readers.

Circuses vary the same way, even to their trade talk, as Celeste Edell discovered when she researched her book, *Here Come the Clowns.* English circuses are very different from ours, and I suppose Spanish or Rumanian or German ones are even more so.

In consulting published material on your subject, note the date of publication. Things change with the passage of years. Also note the country or origin, especially in the case of books. We import a great many translations, so be sure the locale or occupation you're reading about is really the one you need for your story.

Always check the acknowledgment and the bibliography in each book you use for reference. These may be time-saving leads to other sources.

In writing the career or occupation story, make your hero a novice to the business so that as he learns about it, the reader also learns, in a natural course of story events. Readers of fiction do not want to be jolted out of the story by a block of exposition or barrage of statistics. They just want to be *there*, where the story people are, and to live their life with them.

How to Make and Do

If your story people need to build a boat, tie fisherman's flies, make a telescope, climb a mountain, conduct scientific experiments, do magic tricks or get themselves involved in any of a zillion projects *you* don't know a thing about, what do you do? Look it up, of course. There's probably a fine clear book on how to do it, and all you'll need to do is follow instructions. It's as simple as that—and fun!

The Open Road—Using Travel Backgrounds

Should you be planning a trip in this country or abroad, consider utilizing some place that you'll be visiting in a story or a book. But don't expect the plot to come to you on location, without prior preparation on your part. Prepare a channel for ideas to flow toward you by reading about the area you plan to visit. The nucleus of the story may begin to form right then. Whatever ideas you get jot down for future consideration.

When you reach your destination, you will see it with the knowing, selective eye of the writer in search of definite story material. You'll recognize characters as they walk past you, and background and atmosphere will soak into you. You'll be able to accumulate enough of both in a few days to make your story come alive, because of your preparation to be receptive and responsive. *Take lots of photographs*—of people, streets, alleys, houses, particular objects—to stimulate your memories and bring your notes to life when you get back to your workroom. Make notes of the strange sights, sounds, colors, foods, smells, even the climate and how it affects the scene around you.

And don't overlook a visit to the local library or school! The librarians or teachers will probably be delighted to meet you, for writers are considered rather special people by them. If you do not speak the language, someone in the community is sure to know at least a little English. Through the good offices of your new-found friends you may be able to get much more than the tourist's view of the area, and learn of local customs and legends which you can later utilize.

Here, too, advance preparation will pay off. The leading questions you ask will show that you already know something of the area and its people—a compliment to them.

Many places have historic sites carefully preserved or reconstructed. If your story is to be a period piece, be sure to visit these and let your imagination and your prior reading take you back to the time you'll be writing about.

If you want to see examples of location visits that paid off, read *Skye Cameron*—set in New Orleans, around 1870; *Secret of the Samurai Sword*—modern Japan; *The Fire and the Gold*—San Francisco during the 1906 earthquake and fire. All these are by Phyllis Whitney, who is especially adept at this kind of writing.

The secret of success in utilizing brief travel research is to write from a non-native viewpoint. Do not select a native boy or girl as your viewpoint character. You cannot know enough to write from inside such a character with any depth. A magazine feature, a picture story, or a book for very young readers may come off successfully from a short jaunt to Italy or India, Africa or Thailand, but for older readers you need to know the thinking and ethnic culture of these people much more intimately. Plan to use an American hero, and view the foreign scene through his eyes. In that way your story can be plausible and convincing.

In planning regional stories of our own country based on a short visit, use a main character with whose viewpoint you're familiar, and transport him to the area which will be strange to him. His reaction to everything that is new and different will be natural, and the reader will see the area and learn about it through his eyes. As examples of how this can be worked out, read my *Silver Yankee*, set on a South Carolina plantation in the present day, with bits of history woven in; and *Buttons and Beaux*, where the heroine comes from California to New York City and the world of high fashion.

Story Take-Off from the Home Pad

If you cannot pay an actual visit to the site of your story, there are other ways of getting a look at it. If you should be writing about North American deserts, as I did in *Sizzling Pan Ranch* and *Camel Bird Ranch*, then visit a natural history museum. The one in New York City was a tremendous help to me in visualizing my setting, complete with flora and fauna. As to how it "felt"—

imagination, stimulated by my reading, took care of that. The zoo helped too with its camels and ostriches and other creatures, for whose habits and appearance I was already prepared. A writer must not go out into the field for "live" research until his head is crammed full of facts and details through his reading. Then he will see much more and absorb particulars that might otherwise be missed.

State and local chambers of commerce will send you packets of valuable material. Tourist maps range from the general to the particular, with fine layouts of towns and cities and streets. Local historical societies can also provide interesting details. Getting to know an area can be greatly helped through a subscription to a local newspaper. A few weeks or months of faithful reading will make you feel like a native. That's a tip I got from one of my colleagues in Vermont, at the Cooper Hill Writers' Conference. It works!

With such concentrated study you can be *there* in no time, and take the reader with you. When I was writing the California stories, even the weather reports for the Imperial Valley were of the utmost concern to me—at my desk in New Jersey. After all these years I still feel a kinship with that area and remember with delight a review on one of those books. The critic said that I wrote of the desert "with the affection and enthusiasm of a native"!

Launching Foreign Settings from the Home Pad

If you plan to use a foreign setting, basing all you know about it on research, there is one other source open to you besides those already described: the foreign embassies. Do not write to U. N. Missions, for most of them are understaffed and have no facilities for answering your questions. Instead, write to the cultural attache in Washington, D.C. of whatever foreign embassy you want to contact. State your queries clearly and you will usually get a generous response.

As a common courtesy, include a stamped, self-addressed envelope with any requests you make by mail.

Return with Interest on Your Research Time

Extensive research can be costly time-wise, but there are ways to make it pay off. You can use the same research for several books, stories, and articles, and possibly cull it for anecdotes with which to enliven the interviews and book talks you'll be bound to give, once it becomes known in your area that you are a "real live author."

The background research for my *Sizzling Pan Ranch* was woven into a teen-age romance, *Camel Bird Ranch;* and additional research for the latter was also used in the book *Binkie's Billions.* A number of articles were based on this desert research also; and the short story "Desert Christmas," published in a *Scholastic* magazine, has been reprinted several times.

There you are: *Write what you don't know—but find out all about it first!*

You can't afford to make mistakes in geography, history—local or global—the arts, or the sciences. If you do, you and/or your publisher are certain to get caustic letters pointing out your errors. To err may be human, but to do so in print can prove disastrous. Spare no pains in checking and rechecking your notes, whether from experience or research.

Whichever way you've come by the background knowledge, your reader should feel convinced that you know it all first hand.

There's magic in "found out" material. It's all fresh and new—and tremendously exciting. The "finding out" has led me into strange and fascinating places: into a lion's cage with a frisky young 280-pound lioness in it! And into a Hawaiian party shop—where I learned how to make an orchid salad. It has taken me up a narrow cobwebbed, winding stairway into a Norman-Gothic tower, where I discovered an imaginary dragon, along with facts for *Lady Architect;* it sent me into the perfumed glamor of Mr. John's crystal-chandeliered millinery kingdom, and into the Oriental Room of the New York Public Library—where I learned about Chinese water clocks and time sticks.

"Choose backgrounds with which you are familiar . . . Write what you know . . . " Pooh! If the "rules" of writing were hard and fast, maybe the craft would be easier to practice. On the other hand, people like Jules Verne and Edgar Rice Burroughs would have been complete failures; certainly the one never travelled *20,000 Leagues Under the Sea;* and the other was never closer than 3,000 miles to Africa when he wrote *Tarzan of the Apes.*

The one thing to remember about research is that no matter what fascinating material it reveals, the human elements, the problems, the conflicts—*the story*—must be your first and foremost concern. Your research, just like your background, should make itself part of the plot. It must not at any point jerk the reader out of the story and make him realize that he is being not entertained but taught.

There are dangerous siren voices in contemporary research. Frequently, when I have been preparing to write a story with a theater background, or of ballet or television or the fashion world, it has been very difficult to call a halt to the "finding out." The research was such fun! It was easy to persuade myself that I didn't know enough, in order to keep on watching rehearsals, castings, testings, fabulous fashion shows, talking to interesting and exciting people and exploring the backstage mysteries of their professional lives.

But of course I was as ready as I ever would be, and one day I had to admit I was just procrastinating, indulging in the writer's age-old crutch for "reluctance to begin." This is where discipline must step in—and where *you* must take action and start working at organizing your book.

Chapter 26

Bringing Them Back—Alive!
The Writing of Biography*

I was about to title this chapter "Footprints on the Sands of Time" when I remembered what my husband, who is an expert on rewrites of this type material, calls this special field: "Bringing Them Back—*Alive!*" Certainly that is a much more graphic way of saying exactly what a biography should do for its subject, no matter how many years separate him from the present day. This quality of *aliveness* is especially necessary in biography for young people.

Brought up on fast-paced fiction in a rocket-fueled world, they won't sit still for an academic recital of chronological facts, or tales of white-washed heroes with as much life and reality about them as toga-draped and laurel-crowned statues.

I once came across an eloquent reader's report in a publisher's office: "This biography reads like Washington looks on the dollar bill—awesomely noble, but kind of *stuffed* . . . "

Our heroes must not appear stuffed—or stuffy. The biographer must dig for warm human-interest details—glean them from painstaking research not only into the subject's life, but also into his time. It may be necessary to read the lives of his contemporaries as well, and even fiction of the period to learn about the "things" of life in his day.

Our national and world heroes are emerging in biographies

---

*This chapter is based on a lecture delivered at the Drexel Institute in Philadelphia.

even for the very young, in truer colors than was customary some years ago. This is all to the good, although sometimes editors do have to step in with discretion and good taste, and keep an author from relating episodes which are too earthy (even if documented), but which are nothing more than incidents, with no formative values and no bearing on the subject's overall historical importance. This kind of "realism" smacks of petty mudraking. I have a strong aversion to debunking heroes. If ever our young people needed heroes to look up to, it is certainly *now*.

Biographies are not written about people who gave up in the face of what appeared to be insurmountable odds.

Beethoven wrote his greatest music after he became deaf; Milton his greatest poetry after he became blind. Louis Braille might have been just another leather worker but for the dreadful accident with the awl that cost him his sight. Elizabeth Blackwell suffered unspeakable humiliation as she struggled against male prejudice to become the first woman doctor. And George Washington Carver's achievements should put to shame anyone of any race or color who bemoans lack of opportunity for lack of success. The men and women whose lives are worth remembering stretch over the whole of history—and a good biography can bring them back vividly alive.

But how is this done? Through research, yes. But before there is any direction for the research, there must be a subject.

How Does One Choose a Subject?

The biographer is always alert to subject possibilities. Sometimes an affinity comes completely by chance, as it did for Jean Lee Latham when she happened to read the introduction to a book published by the United States Department, Hydrographic Office—*The American Navigator*. The book, written more than 150 years ago by Nathaniel Bowdith, was still considered the "sailor's Bible" all over the world. This amazing fact caused her personal "geiger counter," as she calls it, to hammer out, "Dig here for treasure!" She did, and her book, *Carry on, Mr. Bowditch,* won the Newbery Medal in 1965.

You can also prospect on your own in the curriculum guides

used in our schools. Large cities have curriculum libraries; smaller ones have reference copies you can pore over. If you know the age of the child for whom you wish to write, you can then consult the proper grade curriculum and see what is covered in those courses. In history, geography, social studies, science, the arts and political history you can find men and women to write about who met conflict, challenge, adversity, and prejudice because they believed in what they were doing and were selfless in doing it. Our young pople need to be made aware of the fact that it takes courage and determination to pursue a dream. The bravest sight in all the world is still that of a man or woman fighting against great odds—and it makes good reading, too!

Subjects for the Very Young

The biographer must know the interests of his reader at his particular age, stage of development, and range of experience. The very young child will be most interested in *doers*—men and women of action; the people he hears about in school, and the ones in whose honor holidays are celebrated. Good subjects are explorers, adventurers, Indians, presidents—any of the makers and shakers of the world who can be told about simply and colorfully.*

There is a great deal of duplication of subjects in biography, but teachers and librarians are always on the lookout for fresh, lively treatment.

Biographies for Pre-adolescents

The eight to twelve age readers demand lots of action in everything they read, biography included. They're apt to be dreamers

---

*For good examples of biography for the very young, read the books by Ingri and Edgar Parin D'Aulaire: *George Washington, Abraham Lincoln, Benjamin Franklin; Columbus,* by Helen Diehl Olds; *Daniel Boone,* by Esther Averill; *Juliette Low,* by Ruby Radford; *Dan Beard,* by Miriam E. Mason; *Sacagawea: Bird Girl,* by Flora W. Seymour; *Buffalo Bill* by Augusta Stevens; *Walt Disney's Surprise Christmas Present* by David Collins; *Abner Doubleday, First Baseball Boy,* by Montrew Dunham; *George Washington Carver,* by Sam and Beryl Epstein; *Booker T. Washington,* by Lillie G. Patterson; *Marie Curie, Woman of Genius,* by Adele deLeeuw; *The Ringling Brothers,* by Molly Cone.

and hero-worshippers who begin to think about emulating their favorites—astronauts, explorers, inventors, soldiers, sailors, baseball players—even writers! Their dreams are Big, and consciously or subconsciously they think: if *they* did it, maybe someday I can, too. In the meantime their thoughts are reflected in their play.*

Biographies for the Teens

There is no need to mince words when writing for these young adults. The good and the bad that make the whole man or woman should be there for the reader to see. Issues are faced, whatever they may be: racial bigotry, religious prejudice, social mores—but they must be related to the period and time of the subject, to give the reader an understanding of that world at that time. And it all should be done without editorializing—without giving the author's opinion. The message must come through the story being told.

This is adult thinking and writing, yet tempered to the understanding of the teen-ager. At Julian Messner, where biographies are a specialty of the house, they are neither squeamish nor prudish about facts, as long as these bear a motivating influence on the character. As their editor and publisher put it:

> How could you write about Leonardo da Vinci without mentioning his illegitimacy—when he had to bear that cross all his life? But the point is not belabored, nor the fact that so many of the kings had mistresses or the queens took lovers. Taste and tact point the way to the handling of such matters. You might read *Leonardo da Vinci,* by Elma Levinger; *The Doctor Who Dared, William Osler,* by Iris Noble; *Cancer, Cocaine and Courage, Dr. Wm. Halsted,* by Arthur Beckhard. These are outstanding biographies in *narrative form.*
>
> Then turn to *Champion of World Peace: Dag Hammerskjold,* by I. E. Levine; *Louis Pasteur,* by Laura Wood; and

---

*Good books to study for this age group: *Mark Twain on the River,* by Sterling North; *Clara Barton,* by Mildred M. Pace; *Jenny Lind Sang Here,* by Bernadine Kielty; *Drake: The Man They Called a Pirate,* by Jean Lee Latham; *Louisa May Alcott, Her Life,* by Catherine Owens Peare; *Patrick Henry, Patriot,* by Teri Martini; *I'm Nobody! Who Are You?,* by Edna Barth; *Martin Luther King,* by Edward Preston.

Franklin D. Roosevelt, by David Weingast—and here you find what is called *reportorial handling.* Following along in chronology, the author tells his story straight, with more reliance on quotes from source material to highlight a situation, a characteristic or a dramatic event.*

The teen-age reader is also interested in *doers,* but his ideas and ideals have been developing and he can now appreciate the worth of men and women who have given their lives—in one way or another—for ideals, dreams, to research, for the healing of mankind, for human rights—for all the freedoms man holds dear. Young people can be swung on an idea as if it were a cord. That is why we have a voluntary enlistment of thousands of teen-age girls as Candy Stripers—junior nurse's aides; and a newer movement among the boys as Junior Corps Men; and hundreds of young people going into slums to coach disadvantaged children. The idea that swings them can be good—or bad—so there are also hundreds who take part in senseless riots and destructive "parties."

How can we, writers, make the good ideas more available and inspiring? Well, the first step is to help the teachers and librarians create readers, for words are the greatest idea makers on earth. The next step is to give them the right things to read. Good fiction?—Yes. But they can always say, no matter how realistic the writing, "It's just a story. It didn't really happen." They cannot say that about biography. It *happened*—and our fact-oriented children are reading more and more biography, which in recent years has been made into more attractive reading matter. *How?* Through the use of certain fiction techniques.

Ah! But biography is like history—and therefore sacred. It must be based on documented facts. No liberties may be taken with the facts; no flights of fancy are permissible.

————

*Other biographies you might read and study: *Amos Fortune: Free Man,* by Elizabeth Yates; *Pablo Picasso,* by Howard Greenfield; *Aaron Copeland,* by Arnold Dobrin; also, *Voices of Joy, Voices of Freedom,* by the same author, a collection of brief biographies of contemporary show business greats; *Grace Kelly,* by Marjorie Katz; *The World of Mary Cassatt,* by Robin McKnown; *Friend, the Story of George Fox and the Quakers,* by the versatile Jane Yolen; *More than a Queen, the Story of Josephine Bonaparte,* by Frances Mossiker; *Henry David Thoreau, Writer and Rebel,* by Philip Van Doren Stern.

True. But no young person—and few grownups, for that matter—will dig into a biography that bristles with the footnotes of scholarly research. Acknowledgement of sources and bibliography can be made neatly at the back of the book for readers who wish to verify authenticity. With or without a published bibliography, editors are quite fussy about such matters, and first of all depend on the reputation of the author; and secondly, they double-check by having several experts read the manuscript before it goes to the printer.

How to Present the Facts and the People

So then, what is the most acceptable style for a juvenile biography—acceptable to the reader, that is? *The narrative form—* called by some bound to be technical—*fictionalized biography,* because the author utilizes his research for dramatic effects. He uses dialogue when it helps bring a character to life or enrich a situation. Often he translates quotes from letters and other writings into dialogue or probable thought for his characters. Having "lived with" his subject for months, perhaps even years, through meticulous research, he *knows* his man or woman. He has stepped into and out of his subject's skin many times—and if under such circumstances he "invents" a scene or creates some dialogue or puts thoughts into his subject's mind, it is something that might very well have taken place. Certainly this does not detract from the authenticity of the work.

Before he begins the actual writing, a biographer should know his subject well enough not to be over-awed by his public image, the mask and the legend that inevitably grows around any famous person, fencing him off from ordinary mortals, or tagging him one-dimensionally as: Truthful George; Thrifty Ben; Honest Abe; Saintly Florence Nightingale.

Of course they were all these—but much more besides—and far from perfect in every thought and act; subject to all the universal needs and emotions, frustrations, joys and griefs. *How they coped with it all—and won—that's the story!* This is where the homely or amusing or endearing anecdote comes in and transforms figureheads into warm-blooded, understandable people whom one can know and love. The biographer may love his subject, but he must not worship him.

F. N. and I

When I first began to think of a biography of the Lady with the Lamp, I didn't dare call her anything but *Miss* Nightingale, accompanied by a mental genuflection that threw all sensible perspective out of focus. She seemed to float above the ground in a luminescent halo. If I had started to write then, F. N. would have emerged as a disembodied ghost with about as much substance.

I collected and read avidly everything I could on F. N. here, then wrote for material available only in England. Soon letters were flying between my sister-in-law, who undertook to do the leg work there, and my home. Before long, we had discovered and embroiled in our project "Flo's" nephew, Sir Harry Verney. He was eighty-four at the time—and twenty-nine when his famous aunt died. He had known her well. Now Sir Harry did everything to help locate necessary material and data. Oddly enough, on this side of the ocean, I had found out something *he* didn't know! and our friendship deepened as we started to track down a mystery—a small notebook that had been pilfered from an exhibit. That may yet have a happy ending!

One clue led to another, chipping away at the plaster cast of sainthood I had built around my subject, until the real extraordinary and warmly human person began to emerge. But it wasn't until she comfortably became "Flo" to me, as she was to her friends and family in her lifetime, that I felt I knew her well enough to write about her.

Biographies should never be written in haste. To bring them back *alive* takes time.

The story should usually be told in strict chronology, taking the subject up from childhood through youth to adulthood, showing his character development and motivation toward what he ultimately became.

The achievement of the hero is the reason for the biography. Some famous men and women have accomplished several remarkable things in the course of their lives, but for purposes of a juvenile biography, you must select the one of greatest importance in the largest sense. This, then, becomes the main theme of your biography, and your whole story must be focused on it. *Only the facts and events that contribute to this main theme must be used and all other sidelights firmly excluded.* You can't tell *all*—and it is much better to have the reader want to know more than to surfeit him with information. The fact that a fact is a fact is no excuse for including it in your biography—unless it contributes to your main theme.

How to Block Out a Plan of Procedure

Read several definitive adult biographies for an over-all picture of your subject, jotting down the most important events of his life, along with any anecdotes that may be connected with them. Out of these you can block out your chapters. The work book plan, suggested in Chapter 13 for organizing fiction projects, can be utilized for biography too.

Title the chapters so they engage the reader's interest, suggesting the important episode covered. If there is a threat, a danger, an opportunity, some triumph or failure—suggest it in the title.

A short summary of each chapter will help you see your material more clearly—and will keep you from wandering off at tangents.

With your book roughed out, you can now set out on further research. It may be you can travel to the place of your subject's birth, or where he spent the greatest part of his life, or where he made his greatest achievement. Perhaps there is a museum where his memorabilia are kept. Essays, articles, newspaper items, diaries, letters, photographs, paintings, all these will put you into more intimate contact with him.

Your beginning is most important; if you don't catch your reader there, you may not catch him at all! Since flashbacks are seldom a good idea with young readers, you should find an exciting incident as early as possible in your subject's life. If the day of his birth was marked in some special way, begin there, taking him on to the next stage of his life quickly. But if he was born uneventfully, then look for the first dramatic incident that would make a good opener, slipping in his birth date as soon after as possible—and proceed chronologically, according to your outline.

After an interest-gripping beginning, the middle, as in a novel, should have challenges and conflicts and crucial decisions. Even though the younger reader may know some of the story, he still should be made to wonder: how will the hero manage to survive—physically or spiritually—in the face of this or that adversity? And all the while the subject must be *shown in action*, and as much as possible through the single viewpoint—*his*. From time to time, however, someone else's point of view will be needed to round out the hero or explain some situation—and this will require skilled writing.

The end may be treated variously, but a summation is usually called for. What was the result of your subject's achievement? How did it affect him, those around him, his nation, or the world—and how is his life evaluated now?

Anyone who tells a biographer that his form of writing is easier than writing a novel takes a grave risk of incurring bodily harm. True, the biographer has his "story" in the life record of his subject. But he can use only a fraction of it, and therein lies the art of writing biography: *selection*—the sifting of a mass of notes, references, and cross-references, even though the ultimate "product" may be only a slim volume destined for the very young. The agony of selection and organization and the final soul-searing decision of *what must be left out* can be truly appreciated only by another biographer.

Biography and Why People Read It

How he did it is always intriguing. What was the magic formula? The good answer is "through hard work, perseverance, and dedication." Our young people must realize that nothing worthy is ever accomplished without supreme effort.

Why was he impelled to reach those heights? How was the hero prepared for his job in the world? This, too, is important.

Opportunity does not come to him who only sits and waits, but to those who are prepared to recognize and bag it as it flies by.

Writing about Living Persons

And now we come to the life stories librarians and teachers would like to see on the shelves:

> Full length biographies of modern scientists (in the news yesterday), spacemen, and other national heroes such as sports champions, Olympic winners (who made their mark a week or so ago), musicians, outstanding performers of stage, screen, or whatever, modern authors, composers, statesmen, politicians, the current President (the day after election), and other men and women worthily prominent in the world.

Instant biographies would be nice to have. The moment some great historical feat is made public, teachers in all grades send the children swarming to the library with biography assignments on the hero of the latest deed!

Sometimes the publishers have been watchbirds, and such timely biographies have been in preparation—in fact are ready, all but the final date of the accomplishment, whatever it may be. Away zoom the final pages to press and soon the book is on the bookstands. But there exists an important item to consider: new legalities applying to the biography of *living* persons. These are enough to give an author nervous prostration.

Time was when a person in public life was, in effect, in public domain, as far as the writer was concerned. Not so at the moment. *Unless you have his written permission to write an authorized biography you may wind up in court!* The fact that you consider it a "laudatory" biography is open to question and to anybody's interpretation of what is "laudatory" and what constitutes "invasion of privacy."

You cannot put any words in the subject's mouth or any thoughts into his head, even though you have read them in newspaper or magazine articles—the subject may claim he was misquoted. And you can surmise absolutely *nothing*.

How then is current biography to be written? You might try to get written permission from your subject. But he may refuse you, even though your book is to be written for young people, because of the possible devaluation of an "exclusive" in the adult field. In some instances, for a fee, such permission may be granted along with several personal interviews—and the signing of a "consent" clause, which means that the subject is to read the finished manuscript and agree—or disagree—to allow to have it published in the form in which it stands.

Anyone who comes into my classes with the idea of writing a biography of a living person is told of this state of affairs and advised to let established authors *and their publishers* wrestle with the legalities of the current scene. As for their own project, I say: Pick out a safely distant historical figure and bring him back *alive!*

Chapter 27

Mystery Stories—
Whodunits for All Ages

Along with all the other elements that go into a well-crafted story, *a mystery must be mysterious.* It must have some important secret that cannot be easily discovered nor readily explained. The enigma, riddle, puzzle, or special problem must involve the story actors to such a degree that they immediately set off to track down one clue after another, despite all obstacles. So much suspense should be generated that even reluctant readers are compelled to skim over the printed words at a pace never before achieved "to find out what happens next." Most boys and girls like mysteries regardless of their reading skill, and that is why librarians are always on the lookout for bafflers for all ages.

The writing of junior whodunits can be rewarding on many counts, but you should not attempt them unless you enjoy that type of story yourself. A lively, inventive imagination is a must, as well as a mastery of the craft of writing. You cannot plunge in at the first glimmer of an idea, for the course of a mystery story must be charted every step of the way.

Before you try this kind of writing, get the *feel* of good, currently published mysteries. Your community librarian will tell you which are the most popular with the young crowd. Take an armful home and familiarize yourself with the plots and suspense devices used for each particular age group.

What Isn't Done

It won't take you long to discover that there is a vast difference between juvenile and adult mysteries. For one thing, no bleeding corpses are strewn about. Any murders in stories for eight- to fourteen-year-olds are apt to be ancient history used as creepy catalysts for present action (see *Cutlass Island,* by Scott Corbett). There is a bit more leeway when the main characters are in their late teens or early twenties. Then their sleuthing may lead them into adult cloak-and-dagger situations with unsavory grownups, but even so, violence and gore are not welcomed by the editors.

Amelia Walden has a string of smoothly written spine-tinglers: *A Spycase Built for Two* has a CIA girl-agent heroine who is sent on a perilous mission to Portugal. *What Happened to Candy Carmichael* has a detective and his girl assistant careening to Trinidad, Paris and Italy on the trail of an international conspiracy. *Valrie Valentine Is Missing,* throbs with suspense against a colorful international background.

As a rule it is safer, with quality houses, not to have story youngsters tangling with adult criminals, on the theory, I suppose, that this might encourage risky heroics in real-life situations. However, some editors feel that young readers can enter into the spirit of the tale without rushing out to do likewise, as evidenced in stories in *Young Miss* magazine, and in books like *The Affair of the Rockerbye Baby,* by Antonia Barber, where three youngsters foil a Manhattan kidnapping.

What You Can Write About

Mystery stories should be written primarily for entertainment, although worthy philosophies can be slipped in unobtrusively.

In one of her articles, Phyllis Whitney said:

> "In my books I've dealt not only with everyday human problems. I've written about racial prejudice. I've given young people a picture of Hiroshima as it is today. I've written about apartheid in South Africa. Not to bog down the story . . . never to preach. But to give substance and meaning and value, so that the book can't be dismissed as 'just another

mystery.' And, of course, to satisfy my own need to write about precepts I believe in. Sometimes they are world-shaking matters, sometimes not—but they always are of importance to *me* . . . "

So you see, the few sensible taboos mentioned should not cramp anybody's search for subject matter or cause him to repress his own convictions.

Anything that will be of interest to boys and girls in the age bracket you've selected can be used for a mystery story. Crosby Bonsall must have had fun when she wrote and illustrated *The Case of the Hungry Stranger* for beginning readers. All the ingredients are there: the clubhouse, the fellows—Tubby, Snitch, Skinny, and Wizard, who decides that he's a private eye. His services are needed almost at once when Mrs. Meech descends on them to demand, "Who ate my blueberry pie?" And then the methodically hilarious sleuthing begins until the culprit is found —wearing a deep blueberry smile.

Ah See and the Spooky House, by Vivian L. Thompson, is written on a slightly older level. The empty house at the top of the hill suddenly isn't empty anymore, and there's something very strange to be seen through a hole in the fence. Two big eyes! A big hungry mouth! A long green head! It's all pleasantly shivery, and completely logically Chinese when the secret is revealed. Read it.

Teri Martini's *Mystery of Hard Luck House* is just spooky enough to titillate young fans without scaring the wits out of them, which is as it should be for the eight to twelve age group. One reviewer referred to this book as "mystery-cum-family," for everybody was involved before the strange diary and the peculiar noises were explained. The discovery of an old quilt, ugly and strangely frightening, provides a look into a secret past locked for years in the mind of Jerry's grandmother, in *The Secret of the Crazy Quilt,* by Florence Hightower. A marrow-freezer for the ten to fourteen's.

Mysteries might involve animals and birds—wild or domestic. Keith Robertson combines mystery and humor in his *Three Stuffed Owls,* in which two boys uncover a diamond-smuggling plot, learn a thing or three about taxidermy, and acquire a clever pet pig named Mildred, for good measure. Flora Gill Jacobs'

The Haunted Birdhouse, is a huge Victorian birdhouse (!) and the goings on there provide fun and suspense for mystery fans as young as seven or eight. *Dead Man's Cat,* by Carol York, is a hair-raiser, involving a spiritualist who can call back the dead. There's a missing stamp collection, a greedy family, an elusive, all-knowing cat—and a race against time, a surefire pace-setter. Jean Nielsen weaves a mystery around a *Phantom Palomino,* supposedly ridden by a legendary ghost, and at the same time alleviates the loneliness of a girl who has moved to a new town in California.

Have you an interest in archeology? Ancient history? How it can be exploited is illustrated in *Mystery at Long Barrow House,* by Nancy Faulkner, where three youngsters search for a burial mound. In *Secret of the Unknown Fifteen,* by Margaret Crary, four science-minded teen-agers collect artifacts and old records to recreate the strange story of some early midwestern settlers. The prolific Jean Bothwell makes the summer of 1775 memorable for Pliny Barstow in *The Mystery Candlestick.* Danger and excitement are centered around the Revolutionary spy underground.

Detectives in Togas, by Henry Winterfield, has seven lively boys romping around in ancient Roman times. *Shadow Hawk,* by Andre Norton, is set in Egypt, in the days of the Pharaohs, and the story zips along as fast as any present-day adventure. The historical tale must catch and hold the attention of the reader through a sense of immediacy, of importance *now* (while he's reading), regardless of the time when the story takes place.

Many science-fiction stories are really mysteries. Science-fiction fans are experts, so you must know your subject before you attempt to enter this field. (See the section on "Modern Fantasy" in Chapter 2.)

A mystery element might be injected into a sports situation. Almost any aspect of camping involving boys and/or girls affords excellent background for mysteries.

Underwater exploration, salvage operations, marine biology, natural history, and scuba diving furnish mystery material with a liberal dash of dangerous adventuring. Frank Crisp is a master of this sort of tale. One of my young neighbors used to haunt me daily to see if a review copy of *anything* by this author had come in. When it did, he would cart it away triumphantly—and wake up an hour earlier to read it before going off to school on the 7:30 A.M. bus!

Mystery Titles

What you call your story is very important. The title should definitely promise adventure and mysterious goings on. It's much better not to be arty or terribly clever and original. Just be sure to have the word *mystery, secret, ghost, phantom, haunted, treasure, the case of* or *detective* in it.

Background Settings

Consider using the places you visit as background settings for your mysteries. Scott Corbett's *Cave Above Delphi* was the result of a trip to Greece. The picturesque modern setting of that country is woven into a mystery surrounding a missing ancient gold ring. *Mystery of the Talking Totem Pole* grew out of a visit to Alaska, and Gladys Hall Murray won the Dodd, Mead *Calling All Girls* prize competition with it. Phyllis Whitney has repeatedly used the backgrounds of places she has visited here and abroad for her mysteries. Winner of two "Edgars" awarded by the Mystery Writers of America for the best juvenile of the year, she is a leader among writers who specialize in edge-of-the-chair suspense tales.

If you have no opportunity to travel, there's nothing to stop your working from researched background material. That's how Lane Peters wrote *Mystery at the Moscow Fair*.

Incidentally, the book titles mentioned here and elsewhere are not necessarily the "bests" of their kind in all instances. I have purposely made a cross-section selection so that your own critical faculties will be exercised.

To get the most out of this study reading, you should first skim through the book quickly. If it's a good mystery, it will pull you along in spite of yourself, so you might as well succumb. (But if the story does *not* hook you, or if you find yourself jerked to a stop at any point, analyze it at once and see what flaw in the writing did it—and don't be guilty of it yourself in the future!) On a second reading, take the story apart to see just how the author put it together. Exactly what was the "mystery"? What devices were used for suspense? How were the clues introduced? How were the characters developed? And what plus-qualities, if any, were utilized in the story theme?

Even with all the analysis, however, you may feel stymied in trying to write your own mystery. For one thing, you will realize that this specialized form of writing demands a great deal of you both as a storyteller and a craftsman. Tight plotting is a must, and the story should build to the inevitable, suspenseful, *terrific* climax. The following suggestions will give you a working plan that should start you in the right direction.

Planning Method for the Mystery-Plus

A quality mystery must have sound values apart from the mystery element. The characters, background, and situation should have all the makings of a good story; the addition of the baffling enigma can then fuse the whole into first-rate reading fare, the kind that sets up long reserve lists in the libraries. If you write one such book, you'd better get busy on the next and the next, because you'll have an eager audience of faithful fans waiting.

But how do you think up a mysterious mystery? Rarely, if ever, does it spring into your mind full-blown. Straining over the mystery elements *before* you have a basic story to work with is putting the cart very much before the horse.

Instead, proceed in precisely the same way as for any other kind of book. If you want to use a certain setting, then characters that will fit into it (or act like square pegs and provide instant conflict) will be the next thing to think about, *pencil in hand*. As characters emerge, consider some human situation in which they might be involved—something that will pose a problem, provide opposition, engage the reader's sympathy for the hero and antagonism toward the villain.

Because you'll want boys and girls to read your story, have both taking active part in everything that happens. Read over the chapters in this text that deal with conflict, opposition, suspense, and the basic needs that motivate people of all ages. Check over the chapter on characters, and see to it that yours have contrasting personalities.

All the time you're evolving your basic framework, keep in the back of your mind the idea of injecting some mysterious adventure into the lives of your characters—a puzzle so important that it becomes the focal point of the story, complicating and aggravating the lives of the people in it. What can it be?

When you really know your characters and setting, let your imagination go. Suppose something strange happens: a brick comes loose in the fireplace revealing an old letter—some family secret—instructions on how to find a treasure. Does this sound too familiar? It needn't be, if you think further and harder, and give it a fresh twist of some kind. The treasure, for example, might turn out to be something completely unexpected, more puzzling even than the original puzzle. (The trouble with treasure hunts is that very often the reader outguesses the characters.)

Suppose your main character moves into an old house (or comes to visit there) and finds a strange locked room; a hidden alcove behind a fireplace leading to a tunnel; a secret staircase that seems to lead nowhere; some strange bones in the garden. Suppose he overhears a peculiar conversation—in the middle of the night. *What if* some message falls out of a book or a plea for help is written on one of the pages? *What if* the main character starts to unravel the mystery and someone—equally mysterious— tries to foil him at every turn? Why? What is at stake?

Be sure to involve your main character personally, so that the solving of the mystery is of utmost importance to him and he actively takes part in everything that happens. He might even *cause* some of the happenings. At no time must your lead be a mere narrator, watching and reporting what others do. The hero-sleuth must be a *doer*, and even though he blunders about now and then, he must be an interesting, likeable person who carries the reader with him to the end.

The degree of mystery, opposition, and complications must all be governed by the age of your intended reader. (The younger your prospective reader, the "gentler" your mystery should be.)

Mystery buffs become experts in this medium in no time, and

while often they'll be willing to go along with the author for the fun of it, they can also be very critical of the devices used to mystify them. Boys especially will complain if a mystery is "silly" or if they guessed "whodunit" right away. "Kid stuff" is not for them. Older teens will demand well-written adventure yarns, plotted every bit as carefully as adult fare.

Something has to be happening all the time. Red herrings must be interlaced with real leads to clues. There should be one main, basic mystery which will be solved at the very end after a hair-raising "life-or-death" climax. But there should also be minor happenings which send the main character off in the wrong direction, or have him jump to the wrong conclusion. Smaller mysteries can be explained along the way, while the big one still eludes solution.

Mystery suspense can be introduced quite easily with advance planning. Foreshadow something here, withhold information there—for a while. Strategically withheld information will whet the reader's curiosity. A message of some kind might be received, read, and put away without revealing the contents to the reader. Or the character might glance at it and be shocked or dismayed, but make no explanation until the next chapter. A character might say too much and stop. Or he might suggest he knows more than he is telling. If you use any of these devices, the true information must come out in due course.

Never use false clues, or place undue emphasis on anything that is not eventually revealed or used. There's an old writing rule that says, "If you point out the gun on the wall, eventually it must go off." Just so, if you point to a spot of blood on the floor (which will be pleasantly titillating to normally bloodthirsty youngsters), you must account for it. And if you have a ghost walking, or any "haunts" haunting, *they* must be logically explained in the end. The unexplained supernatural has no place in junior fiction.

Mysteries are not easy to write, but nothing about good writing—or any accomplishment—is easy. Whether this field is for you or not you'll never find out until you try it. You may discover you've a real flair for mysteries and capture a row of "Edgars" for your study to prove it!

Chapter 28

Writing for the Look 'n' Listen Age
—the Three-to-Sevens

At one time or another everyone tries to write a picture book. But though many are called, few get published. Why? Because the writing of picture books is a specialized art in a highly specialized field.

Know thy reader. This motto should be on the desk of· every would-be picture-book writer. Not knowing one's reader is probably rejection cause number one for those aspiring to write for the three to seven age group. It is responsible for stories which are much too long, too involved, full of grown-up ideas children "ought to like," and sugar-coated sermons written dotingly to some imaginary "perfect" child or to an equally nebulous "naughty" one.

The first step in producing a suitable story for this age is to get to know little children as intimately as possible. If you don't have youngsters, or the ones you do have are not the right age for this kind of study, become an honorary aunt or uncle to some near-by small fry, and observe the tricycle set from the closest range possible. Tell them stories, read to them.

When did you last read with a child? Or better still, with two or more children on either side of you and the picture book in your lap? When they are not passive listeners but participants encouraged to interrupt, exclaim, comment and discuss, children can be led to tell you what kind of stories they like and don't like and why. Gradually they can be trained to comment even on your own efforts without being overly polite.

Visits to a nursery school, a kindergarten, a first grade—where you can observe the infinite variety of small, uninhibited personalities asserting themselves, displaying their interests and their skills, and sounding off on their own big ideas may also prove valuable—if the youngsters forget you're there and act naturally. Be sure to forestall the grownup in charge from introducing you as that "nice writer who is going to do a story all about us!" This will ruin everything and you might as well go home. *No* introduction is much better. Be in the room before the children arrive, and sit out of the way pretending to occupy yourself with something that looks like an uninteresting report or check list. Soon the children will forget you're there and you can tune in on them.

Playgrounds are another fertile field for observation—and story ideas. Listen to the children talk, watch how they play, note their favorite games, their favorite "pretend" characters, the causes for their laughter and their tears.

If, back in your study, you still have difficulty in visualizing a child of the age you need—either as a story actor or story listener, here is a trick that has helped my students. Clip from magazines pictures of likely-looking young children and use them as prototypes and as "audience" for your tales. Look straight at them as you write and later read your material. If these pictured youngsters become real to you, you will not condescend to them from your superior adult world. You will not sermonize, you will not dash off adult whimsey under the impression that you are writing for children. *You will write directly to the child of his own world, in his own language.*

Know Thy Product

Collect an armful of picture books from your community library and study them thoroughly. You will find that stories for children from three to five average 500 to 1,000 words, but sometimes run much shorter. For those of four to six, a simple plot begins to enter in, with three or four exciting little incidents brought to a satisfactory conclusion. The books usually run thirty-two to forty-eight pages, including those allotted to front matter: title pages, copyright, etc. The five- to seven-year-old requires a bit more plot—and possibly a sixty-four page book, with not quite so many illustrations.

Your best method for getting the *feel* of a picture book may be to select several you especially like and type out the texts, word for word. Seeing the books in typescript will give you a clearer impression of the amount of text that is acceptable, and also of how text and pictures are balanced.

For submission, however, editors advise writers to type their stories straight through, triple-spaced or double-spaced twice between the lines. Do not type a line or two to a page.

Editors also suggest that in the planning stage you dummy up your story. That is, imagine the picture and place the text with it, so that you will not run over the usual length of such a book, or underestimate it. When your first draft is ready, mark off the possible pictures, drawing a pencil lightly between the lines of text. Then count up the number of *different* pictures you have. Variety of scenes or character groupings and action is a must.

A fairly equal amount of text for each page is preferred, rather than a line or two on one page and a solid block of type on the next. And remember, *in a picture book the pictures must carry about half of the text; descriptions are cut to a minimum, if not altogether.* The final layout and picture-text matching will be done in your editor's office. Do not send detailed notes on what the pictures are to be. However, where clarification is definitely required, brief notes, single-spaced between lines of text, may be made in parentheses. Don't overdo the suggestions; editors come equipped with lively and well-trained imaginations.

Speaking of Illustrations

Unless you are a professional artist, do not attempt to illustrate your story. Editors have their own very definite ideas of how their books are to be illustrated, and the responsibility of illustrating your story is entirely theirs. Even if you are a good artist, do not present a complete array of finished sketches in full color! Some publishing houses never use color, while others use it sparingly, because color raises the costs of production. Do not prejudice the editors by letting them think you expect your work produced on the grand scale.

Have a Story to Tell

And now, knowing the boundaries of your product, you must have a story to tell. This means a story with a pattern, with growth and a climax. Too many beginners get a character in mind and sail off in a welter of cute sentences, some rhymes, and possibly an initial cunning situation. Without a carefully thought-out plan, they soon dissolve into no-story or an inconclusive little incident. I am not referring here to the plotless text or the concept story—what rain is, what heat is, what day or night or whatever is; or to the journey story, where a character sets off on a quest and goes skipping from one place to another, asking a question and hopping on again until the right answer is reached. Stories of that type are legion—and very hard to sell. Occasionally they do get a benign nod, but only because some novel twist caught the editor's attention, or she knows just the artist to bring this particular little piece to life.

In general, even the simplest picture book must have a story, in the sense of a beginning, a middle, and an end. Events must occur in a logical sequence that leads to a logical—or perhaps to a surprising—*happy* conclusion.

The child from three to seven is *read to*. You need not confine yourself to the "easy reading" vocabulary of some 200 to 500 words.* Nevertheless, you still want to choose simple, rhythmic, expressive words a child can understand. A pattern of repetition can be a successful attention-keeper for the very young, who cannot follow a wandering plot. The repeated words become a pleasing, familiar landmark.

------

*Some educational researchers claim that four's and five's understand from 1,500 to 2,300 words, use only about of third of them. Their attention span is short—fifteen to twenty minutes. The six-, seven-, and eight-year-olds have a listening vocabulary of about 24,000 words, a speaking vocabulary of some 2,500, and a reading vocabulary of only a few hundred.

For this age, plot should be the simplest plan of cause and effect: because of this, that happened. See Roger Duvoisin's popular *Petunia* stories, the silly adventures of a foolish but lovable goose; Wanda Gag's classic *Millions of Cats;* Lois Lenski's *Cowboy Small;* and that rhythmic delight, *The Sugar Mouse Cake,* by Gene Zion, illustrated perfectly by the author's wife, Margaret Bloy Graham. And then there's Rosemary Wells' *Unfortunately Harriet*—and what happens when she spills varnish on a new rug!

Plot Material

There is ample plot material for the picture story. Everyday happenings in play activities, family fun, home adventures make good subjects when given a fresh, unhackneyed treatment. Pets, toys, all sorts of possessions can furnish springboards for lilliputian adventures.

The child's inner world can be delved into also. Although his fears must be treated carefully, they offer fine story material. Fear of the dark, swimming, playmates, or animals can be dealt with *and resolved.* And the universal needs: to be secure—home, mother; to be loved; to achieve; to belong; to know—all these are also good material.

FANTASY—The World that IS but Never WAS

Fantasy has its place in plot material for the very young—and more of it is published now than a few years back. But making the unreal seem real, the impossible plausible, and writing straight-faced, endearing nonsense requires not only a bumper gift of special talent, but also the ability to make of it a polished art. Such polished writing is not usually within the scope of the newcomer to the field.

Still, you may be a "natural" at the fantastic, able to write it with a precious kernel of truth—like Dr. Seuss. Only you must not write *like* Dr. Seuss, or Sendak, or Godden, or Brunhoff, or Cleary, Duvoisin, White, Milne, or Titus. You must write like *you,* revealing the uniqueness of your imagination through your own individual conceptions and style. Neither imitation nor rehashed old favorites are wanted by the editors—unless they are retold, translated, or adapted folk tales. Here we shall deal only with original creative efforts.

You may have a flair for bare-faced tall tales, like the comic stories of Bill Peet. In his *Ant and the Elephant,* seven tons of helpless pachyderm gets wedged in a deep ravine—and what happens? Help comes from the least likely source—an ant! Now who'd think of an ant to help an elephant? That's imagination, and a good surprise twist.

Wendy and Harry Devlin created *The Old Black Witch,* who lives in an old New England house—and will not leave, even though Nicky and his mother have bought the place for a tea room. This fancy has been retitled rather soberly as *Winter of the Witch,* and made into a full color 16mm film, starring Hermione Gingold, who warms up that cold title.

Virginia Kahl began her writing career with a medieval lady in *The Duchess Bakes a Cake.* The noble cook adds yeast to her cake mix, "six times for good measure" and cake and she rise to the sky. There seems to be no way to rescue her, until she sensibly calls down to her family and friends, "I'll start eating down; you start eating up." In a follow-up book, *The Baron's Booty,* a Robber Baron kidnaps her thirteen daughters—and wishes he hadn't! Walter Dean Myers has pioneered in the right direction. In his *The Dragon Takes a Wife,* lonesome Harry the dragon wins a wife with the help of a swinging black chick of a fairy named Mabel Mae. No, this is *not* adult whimsey and it is genuinely charming and funny.

Of course everyone in the world knows about the wild imagery of Dr. Seuss. And speaking of wild (and original), there is a book that must be mentioned, because it comes up so often in discussions: *Where the Wild Things Are,* by Maurice Sendak. The text has very few words, and these are sometimes referred to as "lyrical." It deals with young Max, who is so bad that he is sent to his room and to bed supperless, because he has behaved "like a wild thing." Anger unleashes Max's creative genius, and he imagines himself going off with a crowd of wild-looking creatures, and even ruling over them, which is very good for his bruised ego. There is considerable excitement among the horrendous monsters Max has imagined for himself. And there was consternation among some of the grownups when the book won the Caldecott Award, given annually "to the most distinguished picture book of the year."

The dissenters with the award called the drawings grotesque, too frightening for little children. But the children instantly took the book for their very own! Max and his wild escape from grownup rules and power was a vicarious leap for freedom for them. They recognized it as such and revelled in it. But it took Harper's intrepid editor, Ursula Nordstrom, never content to trip along the safe paths of sweetness and light, to publish the book, as an uninhibited forerunner (as she has published so many others, for all ages, long before it became the thing to deal with controversial "shocking" subjects—which, nevertheless, are the very subjects young people think about).

Of course the "wild" aspect of this book is entirely dependent on the skill and imagination of the artist, who in this case is also the author. Such unity of achievement is not always possible where author and artist do not even meet.

Stories which will get serious consideration from editors must be well conceived and competently presented. Stories of personified animals, like the little badgers in Lillian and Russell Hoban's *Frances* concoctions: *Bedtime for Frances, A Birthday Party . . . A Baby Sister . . . Best Friend for Frances,* and so on. Each one is amusingly tender, child-like, and "real"—and each has a smidgen of universal wisdom to impart painlessly to the reader. The rules of good plotting and planning are always observed in stories that really endure.

Imagined experiences—as long as they are not dreams—like trips into space, or backward or forward in time, or into the ocean depths as in Mark Taylor's, *The Bold Fisherman,* are good subjects. John Jonah Jones, who has for years told fantastic fish stories is spiritedly called to account for his exaggerations by the denizens of the deep. Junior grade science fiction, imaginatively laced with a background of facts will get an eager reading, if its entertainment value is high. There is no dearth of subjects!

So, although fantasy is far from easy to bring off acceptably in today's competitive market, it can be done. I am not going to discourage you from attempting it—just warn you again of the rocky road ahead. Editors are swamped with bad fantasy (and awful picture books), but a gem will always shine through—and I assure you, every manuscript that comes in is sampled by the hopeful First Reader. A Discovery is such a triumph!

Maybe the triumph will be yours.

Stories in Verse

These are troublesome. Over and over editors have told me:

" . . . we have found children's books written in verse extremely difficult to sell. This is true, amazingly enough, even with poetry of well-known authors. As a result, we have to be extremely wary about undertaking this type of project unless we are thoroughly convinced that it has a very special spark and charm which gives it lasting appeal—and a sound, sure sales potential."

But stories in verse *do* get published, and if you're one of those whom nothing will discourage, you will continue to tell your stories in rhyme. There are people who have a natural flair for this; the words seem to bubble over in them spontaneously. But like writers in prose, they too have blind spots and on occasion, tin ears. One reason why verse stories fail to come off is that lines are forced, contrived to rhyme. The reader stumbles over them and the whole effect falls flat.

Look 'n' Listen material, especially verse, must always be tested by reading aloud. Try each line, couplet, rhyme. Substitute a word or phrase. Sometimes juggling the lines will do the trick; sometimes altering the position of the stanzas. It's painstaking labor. You must read—change—read again, *listen*.

Years ago, my husband had the rare privilege of observing Jasha Heifetz select a violin for his concert work. The artist played classic Guarnari, Stradivari, Amati, and finally made his choice. When someone in the group around him asked why he chose that particular instrument, he replied simply: "It sings to me."

Your verse should sing to you. Until it does, don't send it to an editor.

First Aid for Unsuccessful Stories in Verse

Many a story in verse seems to have two strikes against it at the outset. If you have trouble selling your book, *consider recasting it in rhythmic prose.** Or try sending it to the magazines which publish that type of material. The economics of magazine publication is entirely different from that of book publishers, and so the criteria used are not the same. Material for each edition is chosen to appeal to a wide variety of tastes and ages, and stories in rhyme get a very nice treatment. You might build up a regular market for your writing and, in the end, that might lead to book publication.

Most editors take a jaundiced view of personified inanimate objects. I once had a student submit a story about a gasoline pump that fell in love with a red convertible! Elves and fairies and cuteness get a cold reception. Animals which talk to people are anathema to some publishers, though not all. Hackneyed plots are not welcome: the ugly duckling, the story which happens in a dream, the little old bus, tugboat, truck, train or whatever that goes out and proves itself as good as new. Editors want authors to think up fresh new things to write about.

What the Writer Needs

The writer for this age group needs eyes and ears to see and hear all the small sights and sounds of the child's world, as well as the great big obvious ones. Get down to the child's eye-level—physically—squat, kneel, sit, lie down flat on your back or your stomach, and see as he does: objects, towering grown-ups, pets, toys, grass, bugs. Remember how high ceilings were when you were very small? How big all the rooms? How deep the shadows? How *tall* your Christmas trees? A heart that feels, or perhaps remembers, the terrific impact of infant joy, tragedy, and triumph is essential too.

The greatest need of a story for very young children is *sim-*

---

*Wilma Yeo's *Oliver Twister and His Big Little Sister* started out in verse, but emerged triumphant—and published—in rhythmic prose.

plicity. But it must be an artful, colorful simplicity evolved from the choice of words and the images they bring to the young listener's mind. It does not mean what editor Dorothy Haas calls "subject-predicate-object monotony" kind of old-fashioned schoolbook sentences. So, *"Out,* Dick! *Out,* Jane! And take Spot with you!" Today's kindergarten is a launching pad, and today's youngsters demand much more of those who write for them.

Writing for the very young is not for everyone. It's not something that can be taught or learned without that extra gift which lets the writer be a child again—in spirit.

What the Editors Look For

Ask an editor, "What do you want in a story for the three to seven age? What do you look for in a manuscript?" and you will probably plunge her into a thoughtful silence.

When I pressed an editor friend for an answer, she said, "Well—the story must be short. *But the idea must be big enough to justify making it into a book.* It should have universal appeal. It should reflect needs and experiences common to us all—*but with freshness."* Freshness, then, is a key word.

The young child wants the story in his book to reflect his everyday world because, familiar though it may be to us, to him it is still a thing of wonder—each moment a new discovery. That sense of discovery must be put into your writing.

What the Reader-Listener Wants

For the youngest, the world is beautifully expressed in Charlotte Zolotow's *One Step, Two,* where every inch of a walk from the tot's house to the end of the block is a voyage of discovery, happily experienced and set down by the child's mother—who suddenly sees it all for the first time herself. Zolotow's, *William's Doll,* is entirely different—and about as much today as you can get in a picture book. This strong-minded little boy wants a doll, but his family won't hear of it. How would you solve it in a story? Now check Zolotow's conclusion.

"Cats and dogs are more likely to appeal to small children than less familiar animals"—but that is one of those editorial statements with a veritable hedge of exceptions. Hippo stories send children into gales of laughter: *How Hippo!* by Marcia Brown; James Marshall's *George and Martha* (hippos) explore the delicacies of friendship and find its fullest joys. This pair may well be on the way to rival *Babar*. Louise Fatio's *Happy Lion* is a perennial favorite. Jean Horton Berg, unequivocally states: *NOBODY Scares a Porcupine*—and there's a nice heartening message with this one. As for *mice*, their charms seem endless in picture books, but if you have a mouse story in you, make sure to give it a sparkling new treatment. A mouse is a mouse—but not when you're writing a picture book about one. On a more sophisticated level, there's Eve Titus' success with her French mouse, *Anatole*. He's an enterprising fellow who becomes a taster in a cheese factory. Naturally one such good story leads to another, so this is a series, but each book stands on its own merits.

Tigers can be funny, stupid, dangerous or glorious. In Constantine Georgiou's *Rani, Queen of the Jungle,* there is a lyrical sense of peace and beauty, kindness and love. Newborn Rani is brought to the Gentle House and is reared there, in the comfort of a spacious estate in India. She grows into magnificent adulthood and is released into her natural jungle habitat by a great flood that lifts her over the wall. There is a sense of rightness in Georgiou's poetic prose, with every word carefully considered. And yet, if you will read it softly, slowly, it comes through as if the words were only just thought of. This kind of writing lifts craftsmanship into an art.

For the very young child, the story must be short and must come to a satisfying conclusion at one sitting. Nor must it bore the adult reading it, or embarrass him with its preciousness or cute phrasing. The reader of picture books is two people—and you must work to please both.

The humor in young children's stories has to be direct and obvious. And it must hinge on situations which are within the child's range of understanding. It must not involve experiences and situations with which a child in normal circumstances is not likely to be familiar. This is the area in which "adult whimsey" goes astray most frequently, with a story that is completely over the child's head.

Right out of universal experience comes *The Growing Story*, by Ruth Kraus, (so long in print now, it must be considered a classic). A little boy finds that he, like his puppy and his chickens, has grown with the changing seasons. How does he discover this? When he puts on last year's clothes!—not through pages of explanation.

No roses for Harry, by Gene Zion, will appeal to every child who has resisted being made to wear something he did not like. Harry is a very masculine little dog, but he is given a sissy-looking sweater *with roses* on it! How he gets rid of it will tickle every funny bone the reader-listener has.

One of the most touching picture books to cross my reviewing desk is *Alexander's Animals* by Barbara Hobbs. The hero is a lonely little boy who invents imaginary animal playmates: a porcupine, a penguin, a crocodile, a giraffe, an elephant. His mother appears to be totally unsympathetic until the day she "understands" and presents him with a real live puppy playmate. Whereupon all the imaginary creatures silently steal away, "For somebody else, somewhere, is surely looking for a porcupine, a penguin, a crocodile, a giraffe, and an elephant." The book is eloquent with simplicity and understatement.

My own, *The Lost Birthday Present*, strikes a note of drama with the title, and goes on to tell about the twins, Ginny and Peter, whose loving grandparents try to find "an exactly right super special birthday present" for them. They find it on a ranch in Arizona—Tiny Timmie, a miniature burro—and have him shipped east. Almost at his destination, the tiny creature escapes. About half the book is devoted to Timmie's adventures before he is happily found, just in time for the birthday celebration. The animals involved, incidentally, *seem* to talk to each other. They *never* talk to people, so this is a "real" story.

In this book I have utilized a "grownup" touch—chapters, only three to five hundred words long, but enough to break the book up into interesting sections. This appeals especially to the six- and seven-year-olds.

The Five Senses

Remember, children love the texture of things, the smells, the tastes, the color, the sounds of things; plan to use as much sensory detail as possible in your stories. But it has to be an integral part of the story, not just words thrown in at measured intervals. As a writer for the young, train yourself to gather these impressions not only in grownup words, *but in words a small child might use.* Listen to the living sources of a vitally expressive vocabulary running about your house or neighborhood, or chattering in the seat behind you on the bus. Your eyes and ears must always be open, and the impressions you collect should be kept at the tips of your wits to garnish whatever tale you concoct.

> " . . . not even Anderson . . . can match the inventiveness of the small child, who hears the grapefruit juice going *dupple, dupple* from the can, the waves making a *suchsush* against the ship, the rain coming down in *dlocks* . . .
>
> (The child) listens to those who speak his language. It is a language of action, of sensory images, a language telling of the touch of things, and their colors, odors, sounds. It has movement, pace, rhythm. For the child is not a static creature. Out of his reservoir of sensory responsiveness come rushing up words that move with the rhythm of this thought; galloping, bumping, coasting, swinging words . . ."

This is from Dr. Claudia Lewis' book, *Writing for Young Children,* in which she has made a scientific as well as an artistic study of children's language, showing how it reveals what is going on inside of them.

And the Finished Product

Whatever a beginner's blithe ideas may be about writing "those cute little books," they soon undergo a change if he sincerely tries to carry such a project through. The picture book is one of the hardest things to write. It requires brevity and therefore the sternest discipline and testing of writing skill—not a word wasted, rewriting time and again—four, five, ten times, for the desired effect.

Dr. Seuss estimates that he writes and draws more than 1,000 pages for each sixty-four-page book *he* completes. Whenever you grow weary and permissive on rewriting, think of that.

Walter de la Mare said: "Only the rarest kind of best in anything can be good enough for the young." So the picture book writer must be a perfectionist, for the production of a children's book of lasting value is a highly demanding art. And once beloved, a book will be read and reread to thousands of children, possibly for generations!

Chapter 29

Further Reading . . .
Reference Sources at Your Elbow . . .
Other Annotated Aids

For further reading and study here is a selection of annotated material from my own shelves. To a truly good textbook you can return again and again for inspiration, stimulation and additional knowhow. Such a book grows in value, and helps you grow as a writer.

Whatever texts you choose to read, do so a little at a time, not in great indigestible gulps. And remember, *all* the advice is not for you. Accept it if the ideas fit your own thinking on writing. Some material you may not appreciate now, but will recognize as pure gold later on. Other material may never be of use to you, even though I have found it helpful.

These are the books (listed in order of importance under each category) I recommend to my classes and to you:

Reference Items on My Bookshelves

Reader's Digest Great Encyclopedic Dictionary. 150,000 entries, plus 18 supplements, especially helpful to the writer. Literally at my elbow. (Reader's Digest.)

Roget's Thesaurus of Words and Phrases. A *must* for every writer. Published in several editions, hardcover and paperback.

Webster's Elementary Dictionary. For children from the 4th through the 6th grade, including some words for 7th graders. Some editors advise: "If it's not in the Elementary Dictionary—don't use it!" (Merriam.)

Webster's International Dictionary—Unabridged. When you really need to know *all* about a word. (Merriam.)

Oxford Universal Dictionary of Historical Principles. A one-volume indispensable aid for historical and period writing. Indicates when a word was first used. ((Oxford.)

Columbia-Viking Desk Encyclopedia. For quick fact checks. (Viking.)

Bartlett's Familiar Quotations. John Bartlett. A springboard for ideas, titles, suitable quotes. A *must.* (Little, Brown.)

Webster's Biographical Dictionary. Concise. International in scope. (Merriam.)

Book of Proverbs. I assume you have a Bible. However, various small books of proverbs, epigrams and folk wisdom are handy when searching for themes and titles.

Shakespeare. A one-volume collection. Preferably with the famous quotations printed in red for easy reference. Source of titles, themes and thoughts.

Poetry Anthology. Especially valuable for study of figurative language; also for title ideas and theme phrasing.

Dictionary of Folklore, Mythology and Legend. Two volumes. Maria Leach, editor. Subject matter frequently ample in details, also suggests other reference sources. (Funk & Wagnalls.)

Atlas. A must.

Chronology of the Modern World. Neville Williams. 1763 to the present time. The events of two centuries, year by year, include history, politics, science and technology, the arts, economics, literature, music, law, theater and film, religion, sports, education, discovery, statistics. The book is updated periodically. (McKay.)

American Facts and Dates. Gorton Carruth, editor. Interesting events, arranged in chronological and concurrent order. Valuable for relating actual historic happenings to period fiction plots. (Crowell.)

Encyclopedia. A good set can save many trips to the library!

What Shall We Name the Baby? Subject covered in many volumes, in all sizes and price ranges. A real time saver when name-hunting for your story people.

Dictionary of Literary Terms. Sylvan Barnet, Morton Berman, William Burto. Terminology for the writer. (Little, Brown.)

Bookman's Glossary. Mary Turner, editor. The terminology of the book trade. (Bowker.)

Books About Children's Books

Your Child's Reading Today. Josette Frank. Wise, helpful and practical, by the consultant on children's books for the Child Study Association. (Doubleday.)

A Parent's Guide to Children's Reading. Nancy Larrick. By an educator, an editor, a project consultant and writer. (Doubleday.) Also in paper. (Pocket Books.)

Children and Books. May Hill Arbuthnot. Your community library should have this. There are excerpts from books, examples of illustrations and helpful information. Used as a text in library schools. (Scott, Foresman.)

Children and Their Literature. Constantine Georgiou. Presents a perceptive survey of the many facets of the children's books field, with hundreds of comments, examples and book lists. (Prentice-Hall.)

Margin for Surprise. Ruth Hill Viguers. Warm, enthusiastic, by a librarian and former editor of *The Horn Book Magazine.* (Little, Brown.)

Books, Children and Men. Paul Hazard. Available in a quality paperback edition. *Must* reading for all writers, editors, librarians and parents. (The Horn Book.)

Juniorplots. John T. Gillespie and Diana L. Lembo. Two professional librarians and educators analyze the plots of eighty selected books. Principal and secondary themes are also mentioned. Because the titles represent various reading levels and interests as well as quality and style of writing, this is of value to aspiring writers as well as librarians and teachers. (Bowker.)

Introducing Books. John T. Gillespie and Diana L. Lembo. A guide for the middle grades. A selection of eighty-eight books for children nine to fourteen, with emphasis on the reading of fourth and fifth graders (ages nine to eleven). Selections under such helpful headings as Getting Along in the Family, Making Friends, Developing Values, Understanding Physical Problems, Respecting Living Creatures, Evaluating Contemporary Problems, Reading for Fun, etc. Especially helpful for the writer: each book's plot analysis, the theme, and additional reading suggestions. (Bowker.)

Best Books for Children. Nearly 4,000 titles, currently available, annotated and arranged by grade and subject, with author, title and illustrator index. (Bowker.)

To Help You Understand Children and Grownups

Psychiatry Made Simple. Abraham P. Sperling. A difficult subject presented in lucid, concise terms. Available in paperback. (Doubleday.)

The First Five Years of Life, The Child From Five to Ten, The Child From Ten to Sixteen. Arnold Gesell and Frances Ilg. Use to bone up on specific areas as related to your writing problems. (Harper.)

Between Parent and Child, Between Parent and Teen-Ager, Between Teacher and Child. Dr. Haim G. Ginott. Warm your wits by the glow of this man's wisdom and gentle humor. Characters, motivation, plots—all there for developing through your own creative insights. (Macmillan.) Also in paper (Avon.)

Your Personality And You. Sarah Splaver. Aimed at the high school boy and girl. Chapters cover home environment, family relationships; school and social setting; emotions; facing up to fears, grief, jealousy; coping with popularity and its problems—positive and negative. Material which can help you work up *your* teen-age characters. (Messner.)

Schoolchildren: Growing Up in the Slums. Mary Frances Greene and Orletta Ryan. Do you want to write for the disadvantaged child? You'll really have to know whereof you speak. This profoundly moving book, reconstructed entirely from classroom conversations of Negro and Puerto Rican children is blazingly illuminating—and heart-rendingly candid. As you must be when writing for this group. (Pantheon.)

Government Pamphlets. Don't overlook these valuable and inexpensive writer's aids. Send for a list of up-to-date publications dealing with children and children's problems. Address: Department of Health, Education and Welfare, 4th and Independence, Washington, D.C.

More Springboards for Ideas

Your Career If You're Not Going To College. Sarah Splaver. Not everyone *can* go; not everyone *should* go—and in your writing you can show that the world can be bright for those who don't. (Messner.)

Job and Career Guide. A sturdy pamphlet with ideas galore. Prepared by *American Girl Magazine.*

A *Treasury of Success Unlimited*. Og Mandino, editor. Ideas unlimited, too. Be sure to note possible leads to other sources in the list of acknowledgements. (Hawthorn.)

Some Textbooks from My Shelves

Writing, Illustrating and Editing Children's Books. Jean P. Colby. An overall view of the field by an editor-writer who knows first-hand all the aspects of our trade. (Hastings.)

Writing For Young Children. Claudia Lewis. The *only* book I know of specifically on this subject. There should be more. Alas, out of print, but your library may have a copy. (Simon & Schuster.)

Writing Juvenile Fiction. Phyllis A. Whitney. A foremost authority who practices what she preaches. Enormously successful in both the juvenile and adult fields. (Writer.)

Writing For Christian Publications. Edith Tiller Osteyee. Excellent, especially for this special field. (Judson Press.)

Writing Advice and Devices. W. S. Campbell. Read and study! (Doubleday.)

The Art of Dramatic Writing. Lajos Egri. Definitely!

Modern Fiction Techniques. F. A. Rockwell. Don't miss her chapter on titles. Best I've ever read. (Writer.)

A Guide to Creative Writing. Roger Garrison. Excellent—especially on sensory details. Alas, out of print, but your library may have a copy. (Holt.)

Techniques of the Selling Writer. Dwight V. Swain. You'll probably have to grow up to this one — as a writer — but keep it in mind. Indexed. (University of Oklahoma Press.)

Writing and Selling Non-Fiction. Hayes B. Jacobs. Be sure to glean this for its wealth of practical tips on all phases of the writing profession. Thoroughly indexed! (Writer's Digest.)

For That Stamp of Professionalism

Elements of Style. William Strunk and E. B. White. A classic in guides to good writing. Seventy-one pages of text—a must! Available in paperback. (Macmillan.)

ABC of Style. Rudolf Flesch. A splendid guide to plain, *effective* English. In dictionary form. Never out of my reach. (Harper.)

The Art of Readable Writing. Rudolf Flesch. Will help to rid you of a lot of cluttery, fluttery words. Also available in paperback. (Harper.)

A Manual of Style. More trade talk and sound advice. At every book editor's elbow. (University of Chicago Press.)

A Practical Style Guide for Authors and Editors. Margaret Nicholson. Outlines the author's and editor's individual responsibilities and the technical how-to's of preparing a manuscript for the printer. Sections on abbreviations, capitalization, numbers, punctuation, *indexing*, copyright, fair use, getting permission to quote, proofreading. (Holt.)

Magazines for Writers

Writer's Digest, 9933 Alliance Rd., Cincinnati, Ohio 45242.

The Writer, 8 Arlington Street, Boston, Massachusetts 02116.

The Horn Book (book reviews and articles on children's literature), 585 Boylston Street, Boston Massachusetts 02116.

School Library Journal (book reviews and articles), R. R. Bowker Co., 1180 Avenue of the Americas, New York, New York 10036.

Writer's Yearbook (an annual published by Writer's Digest.)

Market Lists

Writer's Market. Complete, annotated market coverage. Listings include agents, publishers, editors, specific manuscript requirements, contracts, rates paid—everything the working writer needs at his fingertips when he is ready to market his material. (Writer's Digest.)

Literary Market Place. Suited more to professionals than to newcomers in the field. (Bowker.)

Chapter 30

Bon Voyage!

To learn *about* writing you must read. Yet no book can *make* a writer of you. I have done my best to point you in the right direction, but the journey you must make yourself.

Writing is never easy. "I was amazed to learn that there was so much *to* it," an earnest student told me once. There is, indeed. I cannot promise you that after the joyous miracle of the first sale—or the tenth, or twentieth—it will be easier.

But writing is a vocation so compelling that even after you know all the hard work involved, there is still nothing else you'd rather do. You cannot give it up—at least not for long. There's heady stuff in being a maker and shaker of worlds of your own creation. You can *be* anything and anyone in any time or place or occupation. And, when you are writing for the young, you are doubly blessed because you form the habit of viewing everything around you with the fresh eyes of youth. Yours is always a big, wide, shining world—regardless of the headlines.

What *you* think and say in your books and stories is far from inconsequential, for everything a child reads becomes a part of him, and quite possibly an influence upon his future life and thought.

Emerson said: "The crowning fortune of a man is to be born to some pursuit which finds him employment and happiness, whether it be to make baskets or broadswords, or canals, or statues, or songs."

I hope you too will find in your writing *employment and happiness*, for to the committed writer, profit is only the by-product of his work. Happiness is the chief product.

TEN COMMANDMENTS FOR WRITERS

 1 Love thy Subject.

 2 Love thy Reader.

 3 Thou shalt not Begin without Prior Meditation.

 4 Thou shalt Know thy Characters as well as thou knowest thyself — even better!

 5 Thou shalt not Begin until thou Knowest Whither Thou Goest, and have a well-thought-out Plan for the Journey.

 6 Thou shalt STOP when thy story is finished.

 7 Thou shalt not Worship thy Words as Images Graven in Precious Marble.

 8 Thou shalt make a Clear, Dark-ribbon copy of thy Work.

 9 Thou shalt Study thy Markets diligently, and ONLY THEN send thy Manuscript into the world.

 10 Thou shalt not brood upon its fate, but set about the Workings of thy Next Project, with good will and a high heart.

Index

Books of Interest From Writer's Digest

The Beginning Writer's Answer Book, edited by Kirk Polking, Jean Chimsky, and Rose Adkins. "What is a query letter?" "If I use a pen name, how can I cash the check?" These are among 567 questions most frequently asked by beginning writers — and expertly answered in this down-to-earth handbook. Cross-indexed. 270 pp. $8.95.

Bylines & Babies, by Elaine Fantle Shimberg. The art of being a successful housewife/writer. 256 pp. $10.95.

The Cartoonist's and Gag Writer's Handbook, by Jack Markow. Longtime cartoonist with thousands of sales, reveals the secrets of successful cartooning — step by step. Richly illustrated. 157 pp. $9.95.

A Complete Guide to Marketing Magazine Articles, by Duane Newcomb. "Anyone who can write a clear sentence can learn to write and sell articles on a consistent basis," says Newcomb (who has published well over 3,000 articles). Here's how. 248 pp. $7.95.

The Confession Writer's Handbook, by Florence K. Palmer. A stylish and informative guide to getting started and getting ahead in the confessions. How to start a confession and carry it through. How to take an insignificant event and make it significant. 171 pp. $7.95.

The Craft of Interviewing, by John Brady. Everything you always wanted to know about asking questions, but were afraid to ask — from an experienced interviewer and editor of *Writer's Digest*. The most comprehensive guide to interviewing on the market. 244 pp. $9.95.

The Creative Writer, edited by Aron Mathieu. This book opens the door to the real world of publishing. Inspiration, techniques, and ideas, plus inside tips from Maugham, Caldwell, Purdy, others. 416 pp. $8.95.

The Greeting Card Writer's Handbook, by H. Joseph Chadwick. A former greeting card editor tells you what editors look for in inspirational verse . . . how to write humor . . . what to write about for conventional, studio and juvenile cards. Extra: a renewable list of greeting card markets. Will be greeted by any freelancer. 268 pp. $8.95.

A Guide to Writing History, by Doris Ricker Marston. How to track down Big Foot — or your family Civil War letters, or your hometown's last century — for publication and profit. A timely handbook for history buffs and writers. 258 pp. $8.50.

Handbook of Short Story Writing, edited by Frank A. Dickson and Sandra Smythe. You provide the pencil, paper, and sweat — and this book will provide the expert guidance. Features include James Hilton on creating a lovable character: R. V. Cassill on plotting a short story. 238 pp. $8.95.

Law and the Writer, edited by Kirk Polking and Leonard S. Meranus. Don't let legal hassles slow down your progress as a writer. Now you can find good counsel on libel, invasion of privacy, fair use, plagiarism, taxes, contracts, social security, and more — all in one volume. 249 pp. $9.95.

Magazine Writing: The Inside Angle, by Art Spikol. Successful editor and writer reveals inside secrets of getting your mss. published. 288 pp. $10.95.

Magazine Writing Today, by Jerome E. Kelley. If you sometimes feel like a mouse in a maze of magazines, with a fat manuscript check at the end of the line, don't fret. Kelley tells you how to get a piece of the action. Covers ideas, research, interviewing, organization, the writing process, and ways to get photos. Plus advice on getting started. 220 pp. $9.95.

Mystery Writer's Handbook, by the Mystery Writers of America. A howtheydunit to the whodunit, newly written and revised by members of the Mystery Writers of America. Includes the four elements essential to the classic mystery. A comprehensive handbook that takes the mystery out of mystery writing. 273 pp. $8.95.

1001 Article Ideas, by Frank A. Dickson. A compendium of ideas plus formulas to generate more of your own! 256 pp. $10.95.

Writing for Regional Publications, by Brian Vachon. How to write for this growing market. 256 pp. $10.95.

One Way to Write Your Novel, by Dick Perry. For Perry, a novel is 200 pages. Or, two pages a day for 100 days. You can start and finish your novel, with the help of this step-by-step guide taking you from blank sheet to polished page. 138 pp. $8.95.

Photographer's Market, edited by Melissa Milar. Contains what you need to know to be a successful freelance photographer. Names, addresses, photo requirements, and payment rates for 3,000 markets. 672 pp. $12.95.

The Poet and the Poem, by Judson Jerome. A rare journey into the night of the poem — the mechanics, the mystery, the craft and sullen art. Written by the most widely read authority on poetry in America, and a major contemporary poet in his own right. 400 pp. $9.95.

Sell Copy, by Webster Kuswa. Tells the secrets of successful business writing. How to write it. How to sell it. How to buy it. 288 pp. $10.95.

Songwriter's Market, edited by William Brohaugh. Lists 1,500 places where you can sell your songs. Included are the people and companies who work daily with songwriters and musicians. Features names and addresses, pay rates and other valuable information you need to sell your work. 480 pp. $10.95.

Stalking the Feature Story, by William Ruehlmann. Besides a nose for news, the newspaper feature writer needs an ear for dialog and an eye for detail. He must also be adept at handling off-the-record remarks, organization, grammar, and the investigative story. Here's the "scoop" on newspaper feature writing. 314 pp. $9.95.

Successful Outdoor Writing, by Jack Samson. Longtime editor of *Field & Stream* covers this market in depth. Illustrated. 288 pp. $11.95.

A Treasury of Tips for Writers, edited by Marvin Weisbord. Everything from Vance Packard's system of organizing notes to tips on how to get research done free, by 86 magazine writers. 174 pp. $7.95.

Writer's Digest. The world's leading magazine for writers. Monthly issues include timely interviews, columns, tips to keep writers informed on where and how to sell their work. One year subscription, $15.

The Writer's Digest Diary. Plan your year in it, note appointments, log manuscript sales, be prepared for the IRS. With advice such as the reminder on March 21 to "plan your Christmas story today." It will become a permanent annual record of writing activity. Durable cloth cover. 144 pp. $8.95.

Writer's Market, edited by William Brohaugh. The freelancer's bible, containing 4,500 places to sell what you write. Includes the name, address and phone number of the buyer, a description of material wanted and rates of payment. 960 pp. $14.95.

The Writer's Resource Guide, edited by William Brohaugh. Over 2,000 research sources for information on anything you write about. 488 pp. $11.95.

Writer's Yearbook, edited by John Brady. This large annual magazine contains how-to articles, interviews and special features, along with analyses of 500 major markets for writers. 128 pp. $2.50.

Writing and Selling Non-Fiction, by Hayes B. Jacobs. Explores with style and know-how the book market, organization and research, finding new markets, interviewing, humor, agents, writer's fatigue and more. 317 pp. $9.95.

Writing and Selling Science Fiction, compiled by the Science Fiction Writers of America. A comprehensive handbook to an exciting but oft-misunderstood genre. Eleven articles by top-flight sf writers on markets, characters, dialog, "crazy" ideas, world-building, alien-building, money and more. 197 pp. $8.95.

Writing for Children and Teen-agers, by Lee Wyndham. Author of over 50 children's books shares her secrets for selling to this large, lucrative market. Features: the 12-point recipe for plotting, and the Ten Commandments for Writers. 253 pp. $9.95.

Writing Popular Fiction, by Dean R. Koontz. How to write mysteries, suspense, thrillers, science fiction, Gothic romances, adult fantasy, Westerns and erotica. Here's an inside guide to lively fiction, by a lively novelist. 232 pp. $8.95.

Writing the Novel: From Plot to Print, by Lawrence Block. Practical advice on how to write any kind of novel. 256 pp. $10.95.